THE MAGIC OF
BELIEVING

THE MAGIC OF BELIEVING

WITH STUDY GUIDE
BY THERESA PUSKAR

CLAUDE M. BRISTOL

Includes Bonus Book

T.N.T.: It Rocks the Earth

Published 2018 by Gildan Media LLC
aka G&D Media
www.GandDmedia.com

FIRST EDITION 2018

Front Cover design by David Rheinhardt of Pyrographx

Interior design by Meghan Day Healey of Story Horse, LLC

Library of Congress Cataloging-in-Publication Data is available upon request

ISBN: 978-1-7225-0009-2

10   9   8   7   6   5   4   3   2   1

To
Dr. R. C. W.
who gave me the first clue

To
L. B. N.
who persuaded me to use it

To
E. L. B.
who is a part of it

To
V. P. C. and W. C. B.
without whose urgings this book
would have never been written

To
Merton S. Yewdale
whose friendly advice and enthusiasm
was a constant inspiration

And To
the memories of great independent
thinkers of all times this book
is affectionately dedicated.

*"If thou canst believe,
all things are possible to him that believeth."*
MARK 9:23

Contents

Book 2
T.N.T.: It Rocks the Earth   353

Introduction

Generally speaking, people are more interested in themselves and their success than anything else. For this reason Claude M. Bristol's book, The Magic of Believing, ought to enjoy widest readership. In simple straightforward language, Mr. Bristol has set forth some basic principles of the fuller use of the mind in achieving practical objectives. He has illumined these potential uses with a wealth of descriptive instances, many of them based on his own personal experiences and observations embracing many years as a newspaper man and a successful business executive. He has traveled extensively over the world and has long investigated and studied what he calls "Mind Stuff." Claude Bristol has been helping people to help themselves for twenty years and I have been conversant with what the author has done with his theme during the period. I am also conversant with persons mentioned in this interesting book and with various successes they have achieved. Mr. Bristol believes deeply that any person can achieve any given aim if he believes strongly enough and he presents a well-documented case to prove his point. He makes no claim to being a "mental healer," but his observations on the relationship of mind to health are of more than passing interest. The Magic of Believing does not delve into the occult. At the same time it does not limit the possibilities that telepathy and the use of the subconscious present. The Magic of Believing should be an inspiration to any one who reads it carefully because, in its development and its documentation, it is a clear picture of how the great potential possibilities of the mind may be utilized to achieve the ambitions of anyone interested. Having served in World War I as well as having had a part in the war effort where I came in close contact with service people of World War II, and being aware of potential postwar problems, I should like to see a copy of this book in the hands of every ex-service man and woman as well as all others sincerely interested in making a place for themselves in the years to come.

—Palmer Hoyt Editor and Publisher

The Denver Post, Denver, Colorado

Notes on the Study Guide

Welcome to the world where magic is made manifest! You have just committed to shifting your life in ways that you may never have dreamed possible. By reading and re-reading this book, along with following through on the exercises mapped out for you in the *Study Guide*, you will instill new, more positive and innovative messages into your mind. This, coupled with taking action steps, will assist you in gaining a greater sense of hope and well-being in your life as your desires come to fruition.

Claude M. Bristol wrote *The Magic of Believing* in 1948. At that time, he was revolutionary in bringing the ancient tenets of manifesting to the masses. The world had just survived two massive wars that brought destruction, depression and discouragement to so many. The time was ripe for shifting mass consciousness by bringing messages of positive change to all who were willing to listen.

The time is now ripe for you to shift into high gear and forward motion as you commit to your greatest and highest purpose. While you may at times find doing so daunting, know that you are not alone in your trepidation. In response to our deepest fears, renowned author Marianne

Williamson so aptly stated, *"Our deepest fear is not that we are inadequate. Our deepest fear is that we are powerful beyond measure. It is our light, not our darkness that most frightens us. We ask ourselves, 'Who am I to be brilliant, gorgeous, talented, fabulous?' Actually, who are you not to be?"* To feel fear is natural, however, to act despite your fear is what makes the difference. You have already taken the first step. That wise inner voice within you spoke, and you listened. You followed its lead and purchased this book and accompanying study guide. Thus, the time for you to blossom and live your deepest dreams is now.

After several years of working in the motivational world, and having heard the tenets outlined in this book for decades, I find myself reflecting. I am amazed at all of the new insights I gained and messages I received, some as if for the very first time. Despite years of studying and writing in the self-help world, I am amazed at the negativity that I still allow into my consciousness as I work towards living my deepest dreams. To help move us out of the negative, the author shares many stories that help to inspire and shift us into better feeling places. The more we focus on them, the closer we get to seeing ourselves as the central character in our own delightful success stories.

Read through Bristol's text several times, allowing it to infiltrate both your conscious and subconscious mind. Be sure to take the time to also thoroughly respond to the questions posed in the *Study Guide* as well. At times, you may be tempted to say to yourself, *"I'll get back to that response"*, and then rush through. I encourage you not to do so. Stop and take the time to do each exercise. Taking the suggested action steps listed in this guide will turn basic learning tools into transformative action-based applications. Following through on them, sets into motion your dedication, discipline and commitment to manifesting your goals. In the end, as you build on these exercises, your desires will start to manifest in the world. You will not be disappointed!

You will find a great deal of repetitiveness throughout *The Magic of Believing* book and accompanying study guide. This repetition is a conscious and deliberate choice made by the authors. Emphasizing and re-emphasizing philosophies and practices, so that you will both consciously and subconsciously integrate their wisdom into every cell of your being, is integral to the success of this process. You will note that as you follow the instructions suggested throughout Bristol's book and this accompanying manual, the specifics of your dreams, the contents of your visions, and the insights you gain may shift and change. As you grow, so will your desires. I encourage you to see each exercise as a new opportunity to redefine your dreams and reactivate your energy. Enjoy this journey of rejuvenation and self-discovery as you fully embrace the *magic* of believing!

Theresa Puskar
Study Guide Author

STUDY GUIDE

Introduction

1. The title of this book is THE MAGIC OF BELIEVING. What are your thoughts about the title? Do you believe that there is magic in the act of believing? Please explain.

2. Claude Bristol opens the book with the following quote from William Shakespeare, *"The fault, dear Brutus, is not in our start, but in ourselves, that we are underlings."* This quote suggests that fault does not lie in fate or *"in our stars"* but in ourselves. Do you believe that you are 100% accountable for what happens in your life? Please explain.

3. The editor, Palmer Hoyt opens the introduction stating that *"Generally speaking, people are more interested in themselves and their success than anything else. For this reason Claude M. Bristol's book,* The Magic of Believing, *ought to enjoy widest readership."* Do you believe this statement to be true? Why or why not?

4. Is self-interest something that you believe should be shamed upon? Why or why not?

5. The renowned leader, Gandhi stated that, *"The best way to find yourself is to lose yourself in the service of others."* What are your thoughts on this quote? Do you believe that you are better focusing on others, rather than yourself? Explain.

6. Perhaps focusing on others works only if you do so, not from a place of shame and "I should", but from a place of really wanting to do so. If we force ourselves into caring because we "should," then our intentions are not coming from a pure sense of altruism. Do you think you can culti-

vate caring for others? Do you think that perhaps you first need to focus on self-care? Then once you have mastered that, you can truly, and honestly focus your attention on others? Write about your thoughts on this.

7. Hoyt states that Mr. Bristol outlines basics for the *"fuller use of the mind in achieving practical objectives"*. Is your interest in this book to expand the use of your mind? Why have you chosen to read this book?

8. The editor mentions that Mr. Bristol has traveled extensively all over the world, gaining insights and experiences. How important do you believe world travel is in the evolution of your personal development?

9. To what destinations have you traveled?

10. Write a list of the insights and experiences you have gained in your travels.

11. Write a list of destinations that you would eventually like to visit and why you would like to do so.

12. Claude Bristol has extensively studied "Mind stuff". On a scale from one to ten (one being "very little" and ten being "a great deal"), rate the extent to which you have studied "mind stuff".

1——2——3——4——5——6——7——8——9——10

13. The editor states that *"Mr. Bristol believes deeply that any person can achieve any given aim if he believes strongly enough and he presents a well documented case to prove his point."* Do you believe this to be true? Explain.

14. Hoyt states that the author *"helps people to help themselves."* On a scale from one to ten (one being "very little" and ten being "a great deal"), rate how effective you are at being focused and disciplined in helping yourself.

1——2——3——4——5——6——7——8——9——10

15. While the editor asserts that the book does not delve into the occult, he states, *"it does not limit the possibilities that telepathy and the use of the subconscious present."* Do you believe in telepathy? Explain.

16. Have you ever witnessed examples of effective use of telepathy? If so, please describe them.

17. The editor ends his introduction stating that he believes that after reading this book, ex-service men and women who have suffered post war problems could really make a place for themselves in the years to come. Have you suffered any traumas in your life that you believe are holding you back from greater success? Please list them, along with the ways in which you believe they have inhibited your success.

Book 1

The Magic of Believing

Chapter 1

How I Came to Tap
the Power of Belief

Is there a something, a force, a factor, a power, a science—call it what you will—which a few people understand and use to overcome their difficulties and achieve outstanding success? I firmly believe that there is, and it is my purpose in this, first complete exposition of the subject, to attempt to explain it so that you may use it if you desire.

About fifteen years ago the financial editor of a great Los Angeles newspaper, after attending lectures I had given to financial men in that city and after having read my brochure, *T.N.T.: It Rocks the Earth*, wrote:

"You have caught from the ether something that has a mystical quality—a something that explains the magic of coincidence, the mystery of what makes men lucky."

I realized that I had run across something that was workable, but I didn't consider it then, neither do I now, as anything mystical, except in the sense that it is unknown to the majority of people. It is something that has always been known to a fortunate few down the centuries, but, for some unknown reason, is little understood by the average person.

When I started out years ago to teach this science through the medium of lectures and my brochure, I wasn't certain that it could be or would be grasped by the ordinary individual; but now that I have seen those who have used it double and triple their incomes, build their own successful businesses, acquire homes in the country, and create sizable fortunes, I am convinced that any intelligent person who is sincere with himself can reach any heights he desires. I had no intention of writing a second book, although many urged me to do so, until a few months ago, when a woman in the book business, who had sold many copies of my first little book, literally "read the riot act" to me, declaring:

"You have a duty to perform to the ex-service men and women, and all others who seek places for themselves in a postwar world, to give them in easily understood form not only what you contained in your *T.N.T.: It Rocks the Earth* but the new material that you have given in your lectures. Everyone of ambition wants to get ahead and you have amply demonstrated you have something that will help anyone, and it's up to you to pass it along."

It took time to sell myself on the idea, but having served as a soldier in World War I, mostly in France and Germany, and having been an active official for many years in ex-service men's organizations as well as a member of a state commission to aid in the rehabilitation of ex-service men and women, I realized that it would be no easy task for many individuals to make outstanding places for themselves in a practical world from which they had long been separated. It is with them in mind, as well as all ambitious men and women, and with a sincere desire to help, that I write this full and detailed exposition of the power of belief.

I am cognizant of the fact that there are powerful forces at work in this country that would dominate us, substituting a kind of regimentation for the competitive system which has made America great among nations. They would attempt to destroy individual thinking and initiative, cherished ever since our Pilgrim Fathers established this country in defiance of Old World tyranny. I believe that we must continue to retain the wealth of spirit of our forefathers, for if we don't we shall find ourselves dominated in everything we do by a mighty few and shall become serfs in fact if not in name. Thus this work is written also to help develop individual thinking and doing.

Since I am aware that this book may fall into the hands of some who may call me a "crackpot" or a "screwball," let me say that I am past the half-century mark and have had many years of hard practical business experience, as well as a goodly number of years as a newspaper man. I started as a police reporter, and police reporters are trained to get facts and "accept nothing for granted." For a two-year period I was church editor of a large metropolitan newspaper, during which I came in close contact with clergymen and leaders of all sects and denominations, mind-healers, divine healers, Spiritualists, Christian Scientists, New Thoughters, Unity leaders, sun and idol worshipers, and, yes, even a few infidels and pagans.

Gypsy Smith, well-known English evangelist, was making an early tour of America at that time, and as I used to sit night after night on his platform, watching people stumble down the aisles, some sobbing, others shouting hysterically, I wondered.

Again I wondered as I accompanied the police in answering a riot call when some Holy Rollers in a moment of hysteria knocked over a stove and set fire to their meeting hall. When I attended my first and only meeting of Shakers, I wondered as I did while attending various spiritualistic meetings. I wondered as I heard the testimonials at the Wednesday night meetings of Christian Scientists. I wondered when I witnessed a group of white people being immersed in the icy waters of a mountain stream and coming up shouting "Hallelujah," even though their teeth were chattering. I wondered at the ceremonial dances of the Indians and their rain-calling programs. Billy Sunday also caused me to wonder, as in later years did Aimee Semple McPherson.

In France during the first war I marveled at the simple faith of the peasants and the powers of their village padres. The stories of the so-called miracles at Lourdes, as well as of somewhat similar miracles at other shrines, also held great interest. When I saw elderly men and women in a famous old Roman church climb literally on their knees up a long flight of stairs to gaze upon a holy urn—a climb that is no simple task for an athletically trained young person—I wondered again.

Business brought me into contact with the Mormons, and when I heard of the belief in the story of Joseph Smith and the revelations on the plates of gold, I was again given to wonderment. The Dukhobors of western Canada, who would doff their clothes when provoked, likewise made me wonder. While in Hawaii I heard much about the powers of the kahunas who, it was claimed, could, by praying, cause people to die or live. The great powers attributed to these kahunas profoundly impressed me.

In my early days as a newspaper man I saw a famous medium try to make the "spirits" respond before a crowded courtroom of antagonistic scoffers. The judge had promised the medium he would be freed if he could get the "spirits" to speak in the courtroom. They failed to materialize and I wondered why, because the medium's followers had testified to remarkable prior séances.

Many years later I was commissioned to write a series of articles on what is known in police parlance as the "fortune-telling racket." I visited everything from gypsy phrenologists to crystal-ball gazers, from astrologers to spiritualistic mediums. I have heard what purported to be the voices of old Indian "guides" tell me the past, the present, and the future, and I heard from relatives I never knew existed.

Several times I have been in a hospital room in which people around me died, while others with seemingly no worse ailments were up and apparently fully recovered within a short time. I have known partially paralyzed people who claim they have cured their rheumatism or arthritis by wearing a copper band around their wrists—and have known others who claimed a cure by mental healing. From relatives and close friends I have heard stories of how warts on hands have suddenly disappeared. I am familiar with the stories of those who permit rattlesnakes to bite them and still live, and with hundreds of other tales of mysterious healings and happenings.

I have, moreover, made myself familiar with the lives of great men and women of history; I have met and interviewed many outstanding men and women in all lines of human endeavor; and I have often wondered just what it was that took them to the top while others were lost in obscurity. I have seen coaches take apparently inferior baseball and football teams and infuse them with "something" that caused them to win. In the depression days I saw sales organizations, badly whipped, do an abrupt about-face and bring in more business than ever before.

Apparently I was born with a huge bump of curiosity, for I have always had an insatiable yearning to seek explanations and answers. This yearning has taken me to many strange places, brought to light many peculiar cases, and has caused me to read every book I could get my hands on dealing with religions, cults, and both physical and mental sciences. I have read literally thousands of books on modern psychology, metaphysics, ancient magic, Voodooism, Yogism, Theosophy, Christian Science, Unity, Truth, New Thought, Couéism, and many others dealing with what I call "Mind Stuff," as well as the philosophies and teachings of the great masters of the past.

Many were nonsensical, others strange, and many very profound. Gradually I discovered that there is a golden thread that runs through all the teachings and makes them work for those who sincerely accept and apply them, and that thread can be named in the single word—belief. It is this same element or factor, belief, which causes people to be cured through mental healing, enables others to climb high the ladder of success, and gets phenomenal results for all who accept it. Why belief is a miracle worker is something that cannot be satisfactorily explained; but have no doubt about it, there's genuine magic in believing. "The magic of believing" became a phrase around which my thoughts steadily revolved.

I am convinced that in the so-called secret fraternal organizations there is a real "royal secret" which very few members ever grasp, and the conclusion must be that "no mind ever receives the truth until it is prepared to receive it." I am convinced also that some of these organizations, like many secret orders which have a knowledge and an understanding of life, use parables and misinterpretations to mislead. In one order, candidates are provided with a very profound book (to be studied in connection with the degree work), which itself would be well-nigh an open-sesame to life if these candidates would understand and follow its tenets; but few read it, complaining that "it is too deep" for them.

When *T.N.T.: It Rocks the Earth* was first published, I imagined that it would be easily understood, as I had written it simply; but as the years went by I found that some readers protested that it was too much in digest form, while others said they couldn't understand it. I had assumed that most people knew something about the power of thought. I was mistaken, and I realized that those who had an understanding of the subject were comparatively few. Later in my many years of lecturing before clubs, business and sales organizations, I discovered that while most people were vitally interested in the subject, it had to be fully explained. Finally, I undertook to write this book in words that anyone who reads can understand and with the hope that it will help many to reach their goal in life.

The science of thought is as old as man himself. The wise men of all ages have known about it and used it. The only thing the writer has done is to put the subject in modern language and bring to the reader's attention what a few of the outstanding minds of today are doing to substantiate the great truths that have come down through the centuries.

Fortunately for the world, people generally are coming to the realization that there is "something to this mind-stuff after all," and the writer believes that there are millions of people who would like to get a better understanding of it and prove that it does work.

Therefore, I start with relating a few experiences of my own life, with the hope that by hearing them, you will gain a better understanding of the entire science. Early in 1918 I landed in France as a "casual" soldier, unattached to a regular company. As a result it was several weeks before my service record, necessary for my pay, caught up with me. During that period I was without money to buy gum, candy, cigarettes, and the like, as the few dollars I had before sailing had been spent at the transport's canteen to relieve the monotony of the ship's menu. Every time I saw a man light a cigarette or chew a stick of gum, the thought came that I was without money to spend on myself. Certainly, I was eating and the army clothed me and provided me with a place on the ground to sleep, but I grew bitter because I had no spending money and no way of getting any. One night en route to the forward area on a crowded troop train when sleep was out of the question, I made up my mind that when I returned to civilian life, "I would have a lot of money." The whole pattern of my life was altered at that moment.

True, I had been something of a reader in my youth; the Bible had been a "must" in our family. As a boy I was interested in wireless telegraphy, X-ray, high-frequency apparatus, and similar manifestations of electricity, and I had read every book on these subjects I could find. But while I was familiar with such terms as radiations, frequencies, vibrations, oscillations, magnetic influences, etc., in those days they meant nothing to me outside of the strictly electrical field. Perhaps the first inkling of a connection between the mind and electrical or vibratory influences came when upon my completing law school an instructor had given me an old book, Thomson Jay Hudson's Law of Psychic Phenomena. I read it but only superficially. I either did not understand it or my mind was not ready to receive its profound truths, because, when on that fateful night in the spring of 1918 I told myself that some day I would have a lot of money, I did not realize that I was laying the ground-work for a series of causes which would unleash forces that would bring accomplishment. As a matter of fact, the idea that I could with my thinking and believing develop a fortune never entered my mind.

On my army classification card I was listed as a newspaper man. I had been attending an army training school to qualify for a commission, but the whole training-school course was discontinued just as we finished the course; thus most of us landed in France as enlisted men. However, I considered myself a qualified newspaper man and felt that there was a better place for me in the A.E.F.; yet, like many others, I found myself pushing wheelbarrows and lugging heavy shells and other ammunition. Then one night at an ammunition depot near Toul, things began to happen. I was ordered to appear before the commanding officer who asked me whom I knew at First Army Headquarters. I didn't know a soul there and didn't even know where it was located, and I told him. Then he showed me orders directing me to report immediately to that headquarters. A car and driver were provided and the next morning found me at First Army Headquarters in charge of a daily progress bulletin. There I was answerable only to a colonel.

During the months that followed I frequently thought about the commission to which I was entitled. Then the links began to form into a chain. One day entirely out of a clear sky came orders transferring me to the Stars and Stripes, the army newspaper; I had long had an ambition to be on its staff but had done nothing about it. The next day as I was preparing to leave for Paris I was called before the colonel who showed me a telegram signed by the Adjutant General's office at GHQ, asking if I was available for a commission. The colonel asked whether I would rather have a commission than report to the army newspaper. Foreseeing that the war would soon end and I would be happier among other newspaper men, I said I would prefer the transfer to the Stars and Stripes. I never learned who was responsible for the telegram, but obviously something was working in my behalf.

Following the armistice, my desire to get out of the army became insistent. I wanted to begin building that fortune, but the Stars and Stripes did not suspend publication until the summer of 1919, and it was August before I got home. However, the forces I had unconsciously set in motion were already setting the stage for me and that fortune. It was about nine-thirty the next morning after my arrival home that I received a telephone call from the president of a well-known club in which I had been active. He told me to call a certain man prominent in the investment banking business who had read a newspaper item about my return and had expressed a wish to see me before I resumed newspaper work. I called the man and two days later embarked upon a long career as an investment banker, which later led me to the vice-presidency of a well-known Pacific Coast firm.

While my salary was small at the start, I realized that I was in a business where there were many opportunities to make money. Just how I was to make it was then not revealed, but I "just knew" that I would have that fortune I had in mind. In less than ten years not only did I have it, and it was sizable, but I was a substantial stockholder in the company and had several outside profitable interests.

During those years I had constantly before me a mental picture of wealth.

Many people in moments of abstraction or while talking on the telephone engage in what is known as "doodling"— drawing or sketching odd designs and patterns upon paper. My "doodling" was in the form of dollar signs on every paper that came across my desk. The cardboard covers of all the files placed before me daily were scrawled with these markings, so were the covers of telephone directories, scratch-pads, and even the face of important correspondence. I want my readers to have this story, because it suggests the mechanics to be used in applying this magic which will be explained in detail later.

During the past years, I have found that by far the greatest problems bothering most people are financial ones, and in the postwar days with their intense competition, millions are facing the same kind of problems. However, it matters little to what ends this science is used, it will be effective in achieving the object of your desire—and in this connection let me tell another experience.

Shortly after the idea of T.N.T.: It Rocks the Earth came to me and before I reduced it to writing, I decided on a trip to the Orient and sailed on the Empress of Japan, noted for its excellent cuisine. In my travels through Canada and in Europe I had developed a fondness for "Trappist" cheese (made by the Trappist monks of Quebec), and when I couldn't find it on the ship's menus I complained laughingly to the chief steward that I had sailed on his ship only to get some of the famous "Trappist" cheese. He replied that he was sorry but there was none aboard. The more I thought about it, the more I hungered for some of that cheese. One night a ship's party was held and upon returning to my cabin quarters after midnight I found that a big table had been set up in one of the rooms and on it was the largest cheese I had ever seen. It was "Trappist" cheese. Later I asked the chief steward where he found it and he answered: "I was certain we had none aboard when you first mentioned it, but you seemed so set on having some I made up my mind to search through all the ship's stores. We found it in the emergency storeroom in the bottom of the hold." Something was working for me on that trip, too, for I had no claim to anything but ordinary service. However, I sat at the executive officer's table and was frequently his personal guest in his quarters as well as on inspection trips through the ship.

Naturally the treatment I received made a great impression on me and in Honolulu I often had the thought that it would be nice to receive comparable attention on my journey home on another ship. One afternoon I got the sudden impulse to leave for the mainland; it was about closing time when I appeared at the ticket agency to ascertain what reservations I could get. I was told that a ship was leaving the next day at noon and I could get the only remaining cabin ticket. I purchased it and the next day just a few minutes before noon, as I started up the gang-plank, in an offhand manner I said to myself: "They treated you as a king on the Empress of Japan. The least you can do here is to sit at the captain's table. Sure, you'll sit at the captain's table."

The ship got under way and as we steamed out of the harbor, word was received from the dining-room steward for passengers to appear in the dining room for assignment to tables. About half the assignments had been made when I came before him. He asked me for my ticket which I placed on the table. He glanced at it and then at me, saying: "Oh yes, table A, seat No. 5." It was the captain's table and I was seated directly across from him. Many things happened aboard that ship which pertain to this subject, the most prominent being a party supposed to be in honor of my birthday—just an idea of the captain's, because my birthday was months off.

Later when I found myself lecturing, I thought it would be well to get a letter from the captain substantiating the story and I wrote him. He replied: "You know sometimes as we go through life, instinctively we get the idea to do this or that. That noon I was sitting in the doorway of my cabin watching the passengers come up the gangplank, and as you came aboard, something told me to seat you at my table. Beyond that I cannot explain, any more than I can explain how I can frequently stop my ship at the right spot at the pier at the first try."

People who have heard the story—people who know nothing about the magic of believing—have declared that it was mere coincidence that the captain selected me. I am certain it wasn't, and I'm also certain that this captain who knows considerable about this science will agree with me. There were dozens of people aboard that ship far more important than I could ever be. I carried nothing to set me apart, being one of those who can pass in a crowd. So obviously it wasn't the clothes I wore or the way I looked that caused the captain to pick me out of several hundred passengers to receive personal attention.

In laying before you this very workable science, I am aware that the subject has been handled before from many angles, largely from religious and metaphysical approaches, but I am also cognizant that many people shy away from anything that smacks of religion, the occult, or the metaphysical. Accordingly, I am presenting it in the language of a business man who believes that sincere thinking, clear writing, and simple language will get any message across to the people.

You have often heard it said that if you believe you can do a thing, you can do it. An old Latin proverb says, "Believe that you have it, and you have it." Belief is the motivating force that enables you to achieve your goal. If you are ill and the thought or belief is imbedded deeply within you that you will recover, the odds that you will do so are all in your favor. It's the belief or the basic confidence within you that brings outward or material results. I speak of normal and mentally composed people. I wouldn't tell a crippled person that he could excel in baseball or football, nor would I tell a woman who was quite plain-looking that she could make herself into a great beauty overnight, since the odds are against it. Yet these things could happen, for there have been many remarkable cures; and I firmly believe that when more is learned about the powers of the mind we shall witness many cures deemed impossible today by the medical profession. Finally, I would never discourage anyone; for anything can happen in this life—and that which can help bring it to pass is Hope.

Dr. Alexander Cannon, a distinguished British scientist and physician, whose books on the general subject of thought have stirred up controversy here and abroad, declares that while today a man cannot grow a new leg (as a crab can grow a new claw), he could if the mind of man hadn't rejected the possibility. The eminent scientist claims that if the thought is changed in the innermost depths of the unconscious mind, then man will grow a new leg as easily as the crab grows a new claw. I know that such a statement may sound absurd or at least incredible, but how do we know that it will not be done some day? Frequently I lunch with a group of medical men, all specialists in various branches of medicine and surgery, and I know that if I voiced such an idea to them it would be suggested that I be examined by a lunacy commission. However, I find that some of these medical men, especially those more recently graduated from our better schools, are no longer closing their ears and minds to the part that thought plays not only in causing functional disturbances in the body, but also in curing them.

A few weeks before this was written, a neighbor came to me to explain how his warts happened to disappear. He said that while a patient at the hospital he had wandered out on the porch where another convalescent patient was conversing with a friend. The friend was saying to the second patient: "So you would like to get rid of the warts on your hand. Well, just let me count them and they'll disappear." My neighbor said he looked at the stranger for a moment, then said: "While you're about it, will you count mine, too?" He did, and my neighbor thought no more about it until he happened to look at his hands one day after he had gone home. "The mess of warts had entirely disappeared!" he told me.

I told this story to a group of doctors one day, and a personal friend, a well-known specialist, grunted, saying: "Preposterous!" However, across the table from him was another doctor who had recently been teaching in a medical school. He came to my aid, declaring that there were many authenticated cases of suggestion having been used to cure warts.

While I was tempted to ask if any of them knew that in January, 1945, the Columbia University's College of Physicians and Surgeons had set up the first psychoanalytic and psychosomatic clinic in this country for the purpose of studying the unconscious mind and the relationship between the mind and the body, I kept silent, for I felt that I was too outnumbered for an argument. I was certain, however, that none of them recalled that several years ago newspapers and medical journals had reported how Heim, a Swiss geologist, had removed warts by suggestion, and had also cited the procedure of Professor Block, another Swiss specialist, in his use of psychology and suggestion for the same purpose.

Since this conversation, considerable publicity has been given to the findings of Dr. Frederick Kalz, noted Canadian authority, who flatly states that suggestion works, in many cases, even to curing warts which are infectious and caused by a virus. In an article appearing in the Canadian Medical Association Journal in 1945, Dr. Kalz declared that, "In every country in the world some magic procedures to cure warts are known . . . It may be anything from covering the wart with spider-webs to burying toad eggs on a crossroad at new moon; all these magic procedures are effective, if the patient believes in them." In describing the treatment of patients with skin trouble, he says: "I have often prescribed the very same ointment, accompanied by some promising words, which has been tried unsuccessfully by some other medical man, and got credit for a quick cure." He also points out that especially suggestive is X-ray therapy, which works even when the technician fails to switch on the high power. Experiments with systematic fake irradiation bear out this observation. Here in Dr. Kalz's work we see examples of the magic of believing actually at work in the curing of warts and the treatment of skin trouble.

Another time my medical friends and I were discussing telepathy and I remarked that some of our greatest students and scholars believed in it, mentioning that the late Dr. Alexis Carrel, member emeritus of the Rockefeller Institute for Medical Research, was not only a thorough believer in the phenomenon but declared that there was definite scientific proof that man could project his thought even at great distances into other minds. This was a few months before the death of the famous scientist.

"Oh, he's just a senile old man," remarked another specialist at the table, a nationally known member of the American Medical Association.

I looked at him with astonishment, for when Dr. Carrel put forth his ideas in that remarkable book, Man the Unknown, published in 1935, he was regarded as one of the world's foremost medical scientists and investigators. It will be recalled that he was the holder of the Nobel Prize for his medical research.

I have no quarrel with the medical fraternity. Quite the contrary, for generally its members are sincere, able and open-minded men, and a number, whom I highly esteem, are among my closest friends. However, I have related these stories to emphasize the point that some medical specialists, especially those inclined to restrict their studies to their respective fields, refuse to accept anything that may upset their early teachings and dogmatic beliefs. This resistance is not confined to the medical profession, for there are countless specialists in other lines, including business, who know very little outside of their chosen fields, and whose minds are closed to any idea beyond their limited imagination. Frequently, I have offered to lend books to these various specialists only to be told, upon informing them of the contents, that they were not interested.

This is the paradox. Many apparently well-educated men and women in their respective fields, will, in their broad ignorance, condemn the idea of thought power and will make no endeavor to learn more about it; and yet every one of them, if successful, has unconsciously made use of it. Again, many people will believe only what they like to believe or what fits into their own scheme of things, summarily rejecting anything to the contrary. Countless men whose ideas developed the very civilization in which we five today have been hooted at, slandered, and even crucified by the ignoramuses of their times. As I write this book, I think of the words of Marie Corelli, the English novelist, who became world famous in the last century.

"The very idea that any one creature (human) should be fortunate enough to secure some particular advantage which others, through their own indolence or indifference, have missed is sufficient to excite the envy of the weak or the anger of the ignorant . . . It is impossible that an outsider should enter into a clear understanding of the mystical spiritual-nature world around him and it follows that the teachings and tenets of that spiritual-nature world must be more or less a closed book to such a one—a book, moreover, which he seldom cares or dares to try and open. For this reason the sages concealed much of their profound knowledge from the multitude, because they rightly recognized the limitations of narrow minds and prejudiced opinions . . . What the fool cannot learn he laughs at, thinking that by his laughter he shows superiority instead of latent idiocy."*

---

* From The Life Everlasting by Marie Corelli, Los Angeles: Borden Publishing Co.

However, great investigators and thinkers of the world, including many famous scientists, are in the open today, freely discussing the subject and giving the results of their experiments. The late Charles P. Steinmetz, famous engineer of the General Electric Company, shortly before his death declared: "The most important advance in the next fifty years will be in the realm of the spiritual—dealing with the spirit—thought." Dr. Robert Gault, while professor of Psychology at Northwestern University, was credited with the statement: "We are at the threshold of our knowledge of the latent psychic powers of man."

Much has been written and said about mystical powers, unknown forces, the occult, metaphysics (beyond science), mental physics, psychology (the science of mind), black and white magic, and many kindred subjects, causing most people to believe that they are in the field of the supernatural. Perhaps they are for some, but my conclusion is that the only inexplicable thing about these powers is that it is belief that makes them work.

During the years that I have appeared before luncheon clubs, business concerns, and sales organizations, as well as talking over the radio to thousands of people about this science, I have seen results that can be termed phenomenal. And, as said previously, many who have used it in their business have doubled, trebled, and quadrupled their incomes. In some cases, even greater returns have been noted. My files are filled with letters from people in all walks of life, testifying what they have accomplished by using the science. As an instance, I think of Ashley C. Dixon, whose name is known to thousands of radio listeners in the Pacific Northwest and who a number of years ago wrote me voluntarily that it had enabled him to make more than $100,000.

He said that he had studied this subject in an academic way, but had never fully believed it until he was forty-three, when with only $65 to his name, without employment, and no jobs available, he set out to prove to himself that the science would work. Mr. Dixon has given me permission to use his letter, from which I quote the following excerpts:

"Along came your book T.N.T. It put forth in workable form all that I had known before. It was like seeing Niagara Falls for the first time. One knew there was such a place; but confirmation was the actual personal contact with it. And so, T.N.T. gave me in print the facts I had known and used, but in a clear form. Here was something I could read and use day by day. Holding the thoughts till they were fully demonstrated.

"What has all this been worth to me in dollars and cents? That, of course, is the question of the average man. He wants to see something which will show up in the profit column; something material in the way of dollars and cents. Here's the answer. Since I was forty-three, broke and needing food for the family, I have made a hundred thousand dollars. Most of it is in paid-up insurance and annuities. I have sold my business which cost me $5000 (originally borrowed) for $30,000 and am now working on a contract to run for the next ten years which will net me $50,000, if I loaf; and more if I care to work. This is not a boast. It is a factual statement of what has actually happened in the past ten years . . . It cannot be done in a moment, or a day or a month, but it can be done."

In 1934, during the lowest point of the so-called depression, the head of the Better Business Bureau in one of the large Pacific Coast cities, heard of what was happening to firms and individuals who were following my teachings.

He decided to investigate my work. Later he congratulated me publicly and subsequently wrote me as follows:

"My statement that the teachings have done more to stimulate business here during the past year than any other single factor or agency is based upon statements to me by numerous executives who have been using the theme successfully in their business . . . When I first heard of the phenomenal results you were obtaining I was inclined to question the facts—they seemed too preposterous to be true—but upon investigation, talking with heads of firms using the theme and with salesmen who have doubled and trebled their incomes, as well as hearing many of your lectures and getting into the subject for myself, the terrific and dynamic force embraced by it all becomes apparent. It isn't going to be understood by everyone in a minute, but the firms and individuals that will accept what you have to give and will follow through can expect some startling and extraordinary results. You have fully demonstrated that, and therefore are to be congratulated for giving others what you caught."

This man has since risen to great heights in the business world in another city and has recently written me of having seen other practical demonstrations of the workings of this science.

As I started this book, I decided to check with some of the individuals and firms who had previously written me certifying to the phenomenal results which they had achieved by using this science. Without exception every one testified to the continuing progress he had made from the time he had first written to me. One of the most outstanding accounts is related by Mr. Dorr Quayle, whose name is well-known to the Disabled American War Veterans, and who has long been active in veterans' affairs in the Northwest. In 1937, he wrote me:

"It was no easy matter, at first, to completely accept your ideas, but my circumstances and physical condition forced me to keep at it continuously until understanding came. This, in itself, was a demonstration. You see, in February, 1924, I was stricken with partial paralysis of my lower limbs which made it necessary to use crutches to even get about at all, and at best, for only very short distances and at a snail's pace. For one who had been active in the business world [a bank executive] this forced inactivity was not easy to get used to. But it was bearable only because I received from our Government compensation—my disability being considered as due to service during the World War. However, in 1933, the Government changed its mind and dropped me from the compensation rolls and I was forced to make a living. My home and other properties were about to go from my possession. It was not a pleasant picture nor a hopeful future.

"Necessity forced me to put into practice the principles so well explained by you. Sticking to it proves them. Possibly I was favored because I could not quit the insurance and public accounting business I had started due to my inability to enter any other kind of work on account of my disability. But persistence gives confidence and continued right mental attitude followed by consistent action will bring success. I have not reached the degree of success I desire, but that does not bother me at all for now I am making a good living, have saved my properties, and know the formula that leads to the fullest success. When you have that knowing inside of you, fear has vanished and the obstruction to a continued life of all good, removed."

When I first met Mr. Quayle, it was just after he had started his business with one desk in the front of a plumbing shop. In the following years it has been a pleasure to see him move from place to place, his business growing by leaps and bounds, until today he occupies the entire ground floor of a building on one of the main thoroughfares of a great western city. Realizing that his story of achievement was a remarkable one, I asked for permission to quote his earlier letter. He replied:

"By all means, do so, if you think it will help others. By the way you might add, that I now have the whole quarters at Twentieth and Sandy and I employ twenty-two people. I have just bought the business lot between Twenty-eighth and Twenty-ninth on Sandy where I shall build my own office building. It is my sincere wish that all people would accept your teachings."

I had no idea at the time I grasped this science that I was later to put it into book form. My primary thought was to use it to save my own organization from bankruptcy; I was then vice-president of a well-known investment banking firm. We had been caught in the economic crisis and were headed for disaster. I don't know whether I was inspired or not, but I do know that I dictated the first draft of my brochure in its entirety in less than five hours, without notes or references of any kind before me. At the same time the idea for the brochure came to me, the words, "cosmic consciousness," floated before my mind; but they meant nothing then. It was only after *T.N.T.: It Rocks the Earth* had been published and had reached the hands of a woman author living in New York that I understood the significance of the words, "cosmic consciousness." She wrote me as follows:

"Seriously, it happens that I've been eating and sleeping that philosophy [the one outlined in T.N.T.] for the last ten years. It brought me to New York on no carfare; it sold my stuff to publishers when I had a lousy little job earning $30 a week . . . It took me to Europe a couple of times, and bought me silver foxes." In the same letter she urged me to read Dr. Richard Maurice Bucke's *Cosmic Consciousness*, declaring that it contained brilliant accounts of the actual experience of illumination. I did and I was astounded to discover that my experience actually paralleled the illuminations listed and explained by Dr. Bucke. In the original draft of my brochure I had described in detail my experience with "brilliant white light," but subsequently toned it down, for when I showed the manuscript to a close friend, he urged me to change the wording, declaring: "People will not know what you are talking about in referring to that 'white light'—some may think you've gone off the deep end." Consequently, I changed it; but those of you who know something about "cosmic illumination" and have read my earlier small book will catch my reference to the "light," even though I did somewhat obscure the picture in accordance with the suggestion of my friend. However, the memory of that signal experience will always remain, for in those few seconds I received more knowledge and understanding than I had ever received in my years of reading and studying.

It was in the same period that it came to me in a flash that the reason my firm was going on the rocks was not because of the threatening outside happenings and events, but because of the mental attitude of its members and employees. We were all succumbing to mass fear thoughts; we feared that the depression was weakening our spirit and sweeping everything downhill to financial disaster, and with our own thoughts of ruin we were attracting the disaster to ourselves. It occurred to me that all I needed to do to save the firm and to begin fighting the depression itself was to reverse the thinking of every person connected with our organization. I set about doing that very thing; and, as Frank W. Camp who wrote the introduction to my brochure declared, it was followed "by the most remarkable transformation of individuals and organization as well."

I am aware that some of my statements may be ridiculed by classroom psychologists, but nevertheless in America today there are thousands of people daily demonstrating for themselves that the science works. As for you, the reader, the main point to consider is whether or not it will work for you, and the only way you can demonstrate it is to *try it yourself.*

In using this science, which is given you with confident knowledge that no matter how you use it you will get results, I wish to repeat a warning given in my brochure: *Never use it for harmful or evil purposes.*

Since the beginning of man there have been two great subtle forces in the world—good and evil. Both are terrifically powerful in their respective scopes and cycles. The basic principle operating both is mind power—massed mind power. Sometimes evil appears to have the upper hand, and at other times good is at the controls. It is mind power that has built empires, and now we have seen how it can be used to destroy them—history is recording the facts.

If you read this book reflectively, you will understand how the science can be used with terribly destructive force, as well as for good and constructive results. It is like many natural forces, e.g., water and fire, which are among men's greatest benefactors. Yet both can be hideously catastrophic, depending upon whether they are used for constructive or destructive purposes.

Therefore, take great care that you do not misuse the science of "Mind Stuff." I cannot emphasize this too strongly, for if you employ it for harmful or evil purposes, it will boomerang and destroy you just as it has others down through the centuries. These are not idle words, but solemn words of warning.

STUDY GUIDE

Chapter 1

In this chapter Claude Bristol introduces you to the beginnings of how this book came into being. He shares powerful anecdotes in which he and others practiced the magic of believing to manifest their desires. You are given a profile of the author, and how he was able to transform his life and the lives of many who were open enough to heed his advice. He ends this chapter with a warning that the mind is a powerful thing and that this science should only be used to bring goodness into the world.

1. The author opens the book with a question as to whether or not there is *"a something, a force, a factor, a power, a science . . . which a few people understand and use to overcome their difficulties and achieve outstanding success"*. Do you believe that there is something you have yet to comprehend that could help you achieve your goals? Please explain.

2. After attending one of Claude Bristol's lectures, the financial editor of a Los Angeles newspaper wrote *"You have caught from the ether something that has a mystical quality—a something that explains the magic of coincidence, the mystery of what makes men lucky."* Do you believe in *"the magic of coincidence"*? Please explain.

3. Bristol claims that such understanding has been around throughout the centuries, but has not been known by many. Why do you believe this to be so?

4. The author states that he is convinced that any intelligent person who is sincere with himself can reach any heights he desires. Do you believe this to be so?

5. Do you believe you have achieved your goals or that you are yet to achieve them?

6. Write a list of the goals you have successfully achieved in your life.

7. Write a list of the goals that you would still like to achieve in your life.

8. Bristol explains that he wrote this book because he was urged to further help others by communicating the new information he had been discussing in his lectures. Do you believe that you have tasks to fulfil that would further enrich the lives of others? Please explain.

9. Reflect on your life. Have you ever taken action based on a totally altruistic desire to help others, having no focus, care or concern about yourself? If so, what was the outcome?

10. Bristol shares that he also wrote this book *"to help individual thinking and doing."* Have you taken any such initiatives to further such a cause in your life? If so, what was the outcome?

11. In response to others potentially calling him a "crackpot" or "screwball," Bristol lists his accomplishments and the breadth of his firsthand experience, knowledge and curiosity. He came to the understanding that there was a *"golden thread that runs through all the teachings that makes them work for those who sincerely accept and apply them."* That element is "belief." Do you think this is true? Explain.

12. How much power do you think that belief has in the evolution of your life?

13. Do you wish you had more "belief"? If so, why do you think that you do not?

14. Bristol references the "royal secret" among fraternal organizations as being that *"no mind ever receives the truth until it is prepared to receive it."* Do you believe this to be true? Explain.

15. If you believe this tenet to be true, please provide examples of times in your life when you did receive something because you believed you were prepared to do so.

16. Bristol claims that he believed some organizations actually created misleading interpretations in their publications in order to purposefully confuse followers. Why do you think such organizations might have had such a motive?

17. The author claims that he misunderstood the masses, thinking that they would have a greater understanding of the power of thought. On a scale from one to ten (one being "very little" and ten being "a great deal"), rate how knowledgeable you believe yourself to be on the power of thought.

1——2——3——4——5——6——7——8——9——10

18. Bristol claims that *"the science of thought is as old as man himself."* Do you believe this to be true? If so, list evidence of this throughout history.

19. The author shares an experience he had in 1918 when he first went into the service and had no spending money. One night he made the decision that when he returned to civilian life, he would have a lot of money. He said that the whole pattern of his life was altered at that moment. Have you ever made a firm decision like this, and noted how it altered your life? If so, please describe the decision and the circumstances that followed.

20. While Bristol was fascinated by electricity and had read up on it, terms like radiations, frequencies, vibrations, oscillations, magnetic influences, etc. meant nothing to him. Do you have an interest or knowledge in the mind and its relation to vibratory influences? On a scale from one to ten (one being "very little" and ten being "a great deal"), rate how much knowledge you have on the subject.

1——2——3——4——5——6——7——8——9——10

21. Are you familiar with Thomson Jay Hudson's book, *Law of Psychic Phenomena*? If not, take some time to research it, and write about your findings.

22. When Bristol asserted that he would amass a fortune, he was not aware of the power of his thoughts. How powerful do you currently believe your thoughts to be? Explain.

23. Bristol magically received a telegram that communicated an opportunity to write for the *Stars and Stripes.* He speaks of the power the forces that he unconsciously set in motion. Take some time to review your current life situation. Write a list of conditions or situations you are currently experiencing that you believe may have been created by forces that you set in motion.

24. Based on the experiences you listed in the past question, write about the forces or messages that you believe you are sending out that are affecting your life.

25. Bristol asserts that he "just knew" that he would have that fortune that he had in mind. Write a list of those events or experiences that you "just know" are going to transpire in your life.

26. It took Bristol less than ten years to amass his fortune. Do you have timelines for when you project your desires will manifest? Please explain.

27. The author states that he had a mental picture of wealth constantly before him. Think about the desires you have that you wish to fulfill. Do you see a constant picture of yourself successfully achieving those goals before you? Please explain.

28. How often do you envision your imminent success? More than once a day? Once a week? Occasionally?

29. Could you make a commitment to envisioning your successful future twice a day, for at least 2 minutes each time? If so, keep a journal of your progress. Note: When you envision your success, experience it as if it were already happening. Also, the more you can use all of your

senses to experience it, the better. So focus on what you can see, hear, taste, smell and feel. The more senses you use, the more powerful your envisioning will be.

30. Bristol mentions that he doodled $$$ on everything while he focused on his goal of great wealth. Do you doodle? Experiment with doodling about that which you desire to manifest. Write about your experience in doing so.

31. Have you read Claude Bristol's book, *T.N.T.: It Rocks the Earth?* If not, you can find it at the end of this e-book. Write a summary of your findings.

32. The author describes his experience aboard the Empress of Japan cruise ship. He really wanted Trappist cheese and made that desire known. Much to his surprise and satisfaction, the chief steward found some and brought it to his room. Why do you believe Claude Bristol was able to "manifest" the cheese?

33. Bristol shares the story of how he ended up sitting at the captain's table on the ship and attended a birthday party that was in his honor. He was a manifesting magnet. Have you ever had an experience where you were a manifesting magnet, where things just seemed to fall into place for you? Take some time to reflect on some of the things you have manifested in your life, and write about at least one such experience. If you cannot recall any such experiences, what do you believe is blocking your ability to successfully manifest? Explain.

34. The captain said that he had an instinctual feeling that led him to invite the author to his table. Do you believe there was a psychic or energetic connection between Claude Bristol's desires and the captain's thoughts? If so, why? If not, why not. Explain your perception of this experience.

35. Bristol quotes the old Latin proverb, *"Believe that you have it, and you have it."* Write a list of everything that you have in your life—big and small. Try to make the list as complete as possible.

36. Reflect on the list you just created. With each of the items, did you ever have a belief that you would not be able to have it? Why or why not?

37. Now write a comprehensive list of all the things that you would like to have in your life. Think about your body, mind and spirit. Do not hold back. List anything that you can think of.

38. Go through the list of your desires that you just wrote. Put an "x" beside anything that you currently believe you are not capable of having. Take some time to look deep within yourself. Ask yourself why you believe you cannot have the items you marked with the "x". Observe any emotional, physical or spiritual blocks you may have. List them and note if they change as you continue this learning process.

39. Regarding illness, Bristol asserts that if you believe you will recover, then you will. What are your beliefs around illness and recovery? Do you believe you can "think" or "believe" yourself into perfect health?

40. Bristol references British scientist, Dr. Alexander Cannon who likened the potential human experience to that of the crab. The crab can grow a claw that it has lost, while to date, man cannot grow another limb. Dr. Cannon declared that "while today a man cannot grow a new leg, he could if the mind of man hadn't rejected the possibility. Do you believe that man has the potential to grow limbs? Why or why not?

41. The author shares the story of how his neighbor got rid of warts on his hand through the power of suggestion. He then cites several case studies and experts who have believed this to be true. On a scale from one to ten (one being "not at all" and ten being "absolutely"), rate how much you believe in the power of suggestion.

1——2——3——4——5——6——7——8——9——10

42. The author makes reference to Dr. Carrel and his book, *Man the Unknown*. Are you familiar with this book? If so, write a brief summary of your response to it. If not, research the book and take some time to peruse through it. Write about your findings.

43. In her novel *The Life Everlasting*, Marie Corelli wrote, *"The very idea that any one creature (human) should be fortunate enough to secure some particular advantage which others, through their own indolences or indifference, have missed is sufficient to excite the envy of the weak or the anger of the ignorant...It is impossible that an outsider should enter into a clear understanding of the mystical spiritual-nature world around him and it follows that the teachings and tenets of that spiritual-nature world must be more or less a closed book to such a one—a book, moreover, which he seldom cares or dares to try and open. For this reason the sages concealed much of their profound knowledge from the multitude, because they rightly recognized the limitations of narrow minds and prejudiced opinions...What the fool cannot learn he laughs at, thinking that by his laughter he shows superiority instead of latent idiocy."* What are your thoughts on this quote? Write a response, whether you dispute or support her claim.

44. Bristol cites "belief" to be at the core of any supernatural powers. On a scale from one to ten (one being "very little" and ten being "a great deal"), rate how much you believe in the supernatural.

1——2——3——4——5——6——7——8——9——10

45. The author refers to mind power as a "science." Do you believe this to be true? Why or why not?

46. Bristol shares the story of Ashely C. Dixon as an example of how the power of belief works. With only $65 to his name, Dixon amassed $100,000 after working on the

science of belief. At that time, $100,000 was a great deal of money. How much money would you like to earn within the next 10 years? How much money would you like to have saved within the next 10 years?

47. In a letter to the author, Mr. Dixon states, *"It cannot be done in a moment, or a day or a month, but it can be done."* Do you believe it will take you 10 years to gain the fortune you desire? Why or why not?

48. Mr. Dorr Quayle turned his life around by following Claude Bristol's teachings. He stated, *"When you have that knowing inside of you, fear has vanished and the obstruction to a continued life of all good, removed."* Can you recall ever having a "knowing" about something that is sure to transpire so much that removes your fear and any obstructions from your life? If so, describe the situation. If not, what do you think is currently preventing you from experiencing it?

49. The author describes how the words, "cosmic consciousness" came into his mind. He studied the writings of Dr. Richard Maurice Bucke, and saw how much his experiences paralleled his own. He described *"brilliant white light."* Have you ever had an experience with white light? If so, describe it. If not, what do you think that the author is referring to?

50. Claude Bristol noted that his company was struggling—not because of external conditions, but because the staff were all succumbing to mass fear-based thoughts. He believed they were attracting disaster by fearing it. He realized that all he had to do was reverse the thinking of everyone connected with his organization. Have you ever noted fear in others and worked towards reversing it? If so, explain. If not, experiment with this exercise and journal about anything you note.

51. Have you ever noted your own thinking, and successfully reversed it? If so, explain. If not, next time you catch yourself immersed in fear, experiment with shifting it. Write about your findings.

52. What action steps could you currently take to reverse your fear? Some have tried imagining the worst case scenario, and in doing so, realize that it is not so bad. Others use distraction techniques. Many have found that when you allow yourself to fully experience any feelings (including fear), the feelings subside and eventually melt away. In this case, it is the resistance of the feelings which creates the anxiety. Experiment with various techniques. Then write at least three action steps you could take to alleviate any fears next time they arise in you.

53. The author emphasizes that you should never use the science he shares for harmful or evil purposes. He asserts that if you do, it will eventually boomerang and destroy you. Before you go any further, write a signed declaration, affirming that you will not do so.

Chapter 2

Mind-Stuff Experiments

In order to get a clearer understanding of our subject, the reader should give thought to thought itself and to its phenomena. No one knows what thought really is, other than it is some sort of mental action; but, like the unknown element, electricity, we see its manifestations everywhere. We see it in the actions and expressions of a child, in an aged person, in animals, and, in fact, to varying degrees in every living thing. The more we contemplate and study thought, the more we realize what a terrific force it is and how unlimited are its powers.

Glance around as you read this. If you are in a furnished room, your eyes tell you that you are looking at a number of inanimate objects. That is true so far as visual perception is concerned; but in reality you are actually looking at thoughts or ideas which have come into materialization through the creative work of some human being. It was a thought, first, that created the furniture, fashioned the window glass, gave form to the draperies and coverings.

The automobile, the skyscraper, the great planes that sweep the stratosphere, the sewing machine, the tiny pin, a thousand and one things—yes, millions of objects—where did they come from originally? Only one source. From that strange force—thought. As we analyze further, we realize that these achievements, and in fact all of our possessions, came as a result of creative thinking. Ralph Waldo Emerson declared that the ancestor of every action is thought; when we understand that, we begin to comprehend that our world is governed by thought and that everything without had its counterpart originally within the mind. It is just as Buddha said many centuries ago: "All that we are is the result of what we have thought."

Your very life is your thinking and the result of your thinking processes. Your flesh, bones, and muscles can be reduced to 70 per cent water and a few chemicals of small value, but it is your mind and what you think that makes you what you are. The secret of success lies not without, but within, the thoughts of man.

Figuratively, thought makes giants out of pigmies, and often turns giants into pigmies. History is filled with accounts of how thought has made weak men strong and strong men weak, and we see evidence of its working around us constantly.

You do not eat, wear clothes, run for a bus, drive your automobile, go for a walk, or read a newspaper—you don't even raise your arm—without a preceding thought-impulse. While you may consider the motions you make as more or less automatic, perhaps caused by some physical reflexes, behind every single step you take in life, regardless of its direction, is that formidable and powerful force—thought.

The very way you walk, the way you carry yourself, your talk, your manner of dress, all reflect your way of thinking. A slovenly carriage is an indication of slovenly thinking, whereas an alert, upright carriage is the outward sign of

inward strength and confidence. What you exhibit outwardly, you are inwardly. You are the product of your own
thought. What you believe yourself to be, you are.

Thought is the original source of all wealth, all success, all material gain, all great discoveries and inventions,
and of all achievement. Without it there would be no great
empires, no great fortunes, no great transcontinental rail
lines, no modern conveniences; in fact, there would be no
advance over life in the most primitive ages.

Your thoughts, those that predominate, determine your
character, your career, indeed your everyday life. Thus it
becomes easy to understand what is meant by the statement that a man's thoughts make or break him. And when
we realize that there can be no action or reaction, either
good or bad, without the generating force of thought initi-
ating it, the Biblical saying, "For whatsoever a man soweth,
that shall he also reap," and Shakespeare's words, "There
is nothing either good or bad, but thinking makes it so,"
become more intelligible.

Sir Arthur Eddington, the famous English physicist,
says that to an altogether unsuspected extent the universe
in which we live is a creation of our minds; while the late
Sir James Jeans, who was equally famous in the same field,
suggested that the universe was merely a creation that resulted from the thought of some great universal mind underlying and co-ordinating all of our minds. Nothing is
clearer than that the world's greatest scientists and thinkers
of our age are not only voicing the ideas of the wisest men
of old, but that they are confirming the fundamental principle of this book.

Almost since the beginning of the human race, the
molding of men has been done by those who knew some-

thing of thought's great power. All the great religious leaders, kings, warriors, statesmen have understood this science and have known that people act as they think and also react to the thought of others, especially when it is stronger and more convincing than their own. Accordingly, men of powerful dynamic thought have ever swayed the people by appealing to their minds, sometimes to lead them into freedom and sometimes into slavery. There never was a period in history when we should study our own thoughts more, try to understand them, and learn how to use them to improve our position in life, by drawing upon the great source of power that lies within each of us.

There was a time when I would have laughed at people who talked about the magnetic force of thought, how thought correlates with its object, how it can affect people and inanimate things, even at great distances. But I no longer laugh, nor do others who know something of its power, for anyone who has any intelligence sooner or later comes to the realization that thought can change the surface of the entire globe.

The late George Russell, famous Irish editor and poet, was quoted as saying that we become what we contemplate. Undoubtedly, we become what we envisage, and he certainly demonstrated it in his own life by becoming a great writer, lecturer, painter, and poet.

However, it must be borne in mind that many of our ideas, the thoughts we think, are not ours at all, or those of our own originating. We are molded also by the thoughts of others; by what we hear in our social life, what we read in newspapers, magazines, and books, what we hear in the movies, the theater, and on the radio; even by chance remarks from the conversation of bystanders—and these thoughts bombard us constantly. Some of them that accord with our own inmost thoughts and also open the way to greater visions in our life are helpful. But often there are thoughts that are upsetting, that weaken our self-confidence, and turn us away from our high purposes. It is these outside thoughts that are the trouble makers, and later I shall point out how you can keep free of them.

Few people give much thought to the law of cause and effect as applicable to the operation of the mind, or comprehend what is meant when they hear such thoughts as, "Everything is within; nothing is without" or "Mind is the source of all power," and so on. I believe that no better explanation of this can be given than appeared in an article published in the Commercial and Financial Chronicle (Dec. 10, 1932). This publication has been known for more than a hundred years as the "Bible of business and finance," and with the permission of Herbert D. Seibert, editor and publisher, I quote it in part. It is entitled "El Dorado."

El Dorado, a country rich beyond all precedent in gold and jewels, lies at every man's door. Your bonanza lies under your feet. Your luck is ready at hand. All is within; nothing is without, though it often appears that men and peoples by dumb luck or avarice or force or overreaching strike upon bonanzas and sail away in fair weather on the sea of prosperity . . . Man individually and collectively is entitled to life in all abundance. It is a most evident fact. Religion and philosophy assert it; history and science prove it. "That they might have life, and that they might have it more abundantly," is the law. What do you seek? Pay the price and take it away. There is no limit to the supply, but the more precious the thing you seek the higher

the price. For everything we obtain we must barter the
gold of our own spirits.

Where to find the gold of the All Powerful? One secures the gold of the spirit when he finds himself. When he finds himself, he finds freedom and all riches, achievement, and prosperity. High sounding talk? No, the most palpable evidence of American history and biography, of all history. The concrete proof is apparent even in current events if we but open our eyes. Nothing substantial, lasting, powerful, or moving was ever accomplished, nor ever can be, except by men discoverers in themselves of the gold of the spirit, which commands dominion, power, and accomplishment. Men who know themselves know at once that all material things and ideas have a spiritual counterpart or basis. They see it in money, in credit. The law of supply and demand is not to an awakened man merely an economic principle, but the material manifestation of spiritual law. Such freedom-seeking men see the same principle operating in gravitation, in chemical affinities, in macrocosm and in microcosm.

America has long been the greatest of El Dorados, the stage upon which the most numerous of self-found men worked their bonanzas and their miracles of thought to the enrichment of themselves and mankind at large. There is no exploitation, only a showering of gifts, easily bought by free spirits and generously scattered on all hands according to the expressed law of bargain of the Original, Permanent Owner, and First Producer. To the self-found man of action all the money, credit, and capital goods he can use. Mackay, O'Brien, Hearst, and Fair, brave young Americans of 1849, found gold in themselves before they struck it rich in California. They had to. "If there is gold there," they told one another, "we'll get our share." How great must have been the spiritual wealth of such a free-found man as James J. Hill, who built the Great Northern Railroad from nowhere to nowhere, in a wilderness where no one lives. His madness founded an empire. By spiritual force he turned forests and plains into a thousand El Dorados, and by the same force commanded all the gold and credit needed for the markets of Amsterdam and London and enabled millions of Americans to discover for themselves great bonanzas in the cold Northwest.

Thomas A. Edison said a few years before he died: "Ideas come from space. This may seem astonishing and impossible to believe, but it is true. Ideas come from out of space." Surely Edison should have known, for few men ever received or gave forth more ideas. Let each man seek the El Dorado within himself. Power is plentiful. The source is inexhaustible. As the Canonical Fathers of the church expressed it, that which is received is according to the measure of the recipient. It is not the power that is lacking, it is the will. When one finds oneself the will becomes automatically set toward El Dorado.

By a full and powerful imagination anything can be brought into concrete form. The great physician, Paracelsus, said: "The human spirit is so great a thing that no man can express it; could we rightly comprehend the mind of man nothing would be impossible to us upon the earth. Through faith the imagination is invigorated and completed, for it really happens that every doubt mars its perfection. Faith must strengthen the imagination, for faith establishes the will." Faith is personal, individual. Salvation, any way you take it, is personal. Faith comes in the finding of one's self. This self-finding establishes a clear realization of one's identity with the eternal. Strong, self-assertive men built up this El Dorado of America. "Man, know thyself," thine own individual self, is everlastingly the supreme command. Self-knowers always dwell in El Dorado; they drink from the fountain of youth, and are at all times owners of all they wish to enjoy.

The words of Paracelsus just quoted are well worth re-reading and further study, for once you grasp their meaning and discover how to apply the principle, you will certainly have more light on how to succeed in your undertakings. However, I would like to point out that hard work alone will not bring success. The world is filled with people who have worked hard but have little to show for it. Something more than hard work is necessary: it is creative thinking and firm belief in your ability to execute your ideas. The successful people in history have succeeded through their thinking. Their hands were merely helpers to their brains.

Another important point is that one essential to success is that your desire be an all-obsessing one, your thoughts and aims be coordinated, and your energy be concentrated and applied without letup. It may be riches or fame or position or knowledge that you want, for each person has his own idea of what success means to him. But whatever you consider it to be, you can have it provided you are willing to make the objective the burning desire of your life. A big order, you say. Not at all; by using the dynamic force of believing, you can set all your inner forces in motion, and they in turn will help you to reach your goal. If you are married, you remember the stimulating and emotional experience of courting the girl you wanted for your wife. Certainly, it wasn't nerve-racking work—quite the contrary, you'll admit—but what were you using, if not this very same science, even though unconsciously. The desire to win a helpmate was uppermost in your mind from the time you got the idea until your marriage. The thought, the belief, was with you every minute of the day and perhaps it was with you in your dreams. Now that you have a clearer idea of the part that thought and desire play in our daily lives, the first thing to determine is precisely what you want. Starting in with the general idea that you merely want to be a success, as most people do, is too indefinite. You must have a mental pattern clearly drawn in your mind. Ask yourself, Where am I headed? What is my goal? Have I visualized just what I really want? If success is to be measured in terms of wealth, can you fix the amount in figures? If in terms of achievement, can you specify it definitely?

I ask these questions, for in their answers are factors which will determine your whole life from now on. Strange as it may appear, not one out of a hundred people can answer these questions. Most people have a general idea that they would like to be a success, but beyond that everything is vague. They merely go along from day to day figuring that if they have a job today they will have it tomorrow, and that somehow they will be looked after in their old age. They are like a cork on the water floating aimlessly, drawn this way and that by various currents, and either being washed up on the shore, or becoming water-logged and eventually sinking.

Therefore, it is vital that you know exactly what you want out of life. You must know where you are headed, and you must keep a fixed goal in view. That, of course, is the over-all picture; it makes no difference whether you want a job or a better one, a new house, a place in the country, or just a new pair of shoes. You must have a fixed idea before you'll obtain what you are after.

There is a great difference between a need and a desire. For example, you may need a new car for business, and you may desire one in order to give pleasure to your family. The one for your business you will get as a matter of necessity. The one for your family you will plan to get as soon as possible. For this car you will make an extra effort, because it is something you have never had before, something that will add to your responsibilities, and something that will compel you to seek new powers within yourself and new resources outside. It is desire for something new, something different, something that is going to change your life, that causes you to make an extra effort; and it is the power of believing that alone sets in motion those inner forces by which you add what I call plus-values to your life.

So you begin with desire if you ever hope to achieve anything or gain more than you have now. It is the prime motivating force in all of us and, without an all-consuming desire, nothing can be achieved or gained. However, as we shall see, there is more to it than mere desire.

I am aware that metaphysicians claim that thoughts are things. They may be in a general sense; but, so far as the effect upon us individually is concerned, they do not become real to us until we give them life with our own thinking or through the workings of our imaginations.

At first reading, this may appear a little strange but it will perhaps become clearer if I cite a few examples. For instance, you are advised to wear rubbers when you go out in the rain. We've all heard the remark, "If you don't, you'll catch your death of cold." That thought has never had the slightest effect upon me. I haven't worn rubbers since I was a small child. I have had my shoes and feet thoroughly wet hundreds of times and often for hours at a time, yet I cannot recall the time I ever caught cold as a result. Some people have a tremendous fear of drafts, but I have often thought that if they did catch cold by being in a draft it was because of the fear thoughts rather than because of the drafts themselves. I sit in drafts for long periods daily, and at night I sleep in a corner room which has windows on both sides of the room that I raise in all sorts of weather, so that the wind often sweeps across me. Yet I've never had a cold as a result, because I never give it a thought.

However, I do not advise anyone accustomed to wearing rubbers to go without them, neither do I suggest to anyone afraid of drafts to stay in them. For lifelong habits and beliefs with their consequences are not going to change overnight.

For centuries outstanding thinkers have claimed that man through his mind could shape events and control matter, and the more you study this science, the more you will realize the amazing powers of your own mind.

A. Conan Doyle, creator of Sherlock Holmes, and for many years a member of the British Society for Psychic Research, declared that he believed there was a constructive and destructive power in thought alone which was akin to the "faith that can remove mountains." He said that while the results themselves were conclusive, he had no idea what power it was that came from a man's mind and that could separate the molecules of a solid object toward which it was directed. I know that materialists will scoff at such a statement. But just remember what is being done with radar and how radio waves go through wood, brick, steel, and other so-called solid objects. If thought waves, or whatever they are, can be tuned to even higher oscillations, why can't they affect the molecules of solid objects?

There are many professional gamblers who contend that a strong mental influence has much to do with achieving so called lucky results in games of chance, such as card playing, the calling of dice, the operation of a roulette wheel, etc. The writer knows one man who can step up to a cigar store punch board and with a few punches grab off the best prizes. Once I asked him about it and he said: "I never go near a punch board unless I am in the mood for it, and that means that I must be in the frame of mind that I'm going to win. I've noticed that if there's the slightest doubt in my mind, I don't win. But I can't recall the time that I didn't get winning numbers when the winning idea was firmly fixed in my mind before I started to play."

Hooey, you say—but wait. Do you know that departments of psychology in great universities have already undertaken experiments to determine whether the mind possesses the power to influence material objects, and that the experiments have already demonstrated the existence of such a power? While the experiments have not been too widely publicized, there have been stories appearing from time to time giving the general facts.

Perhaps the most outstanding work has been done at Duke University, where Dr. J. B. Rhine and his associates have demonstrated that psychokinesis, the name given to designate the power of mind by which material objects are influenced, is much more than idle theory. Dice (yes, the old army type of dice used in crap games) were thrown by a mechanical device to eliminate all possibility of personal influence and trickery. Since 1934 when experiments of this type were started, there have been many tests in which millions of throws of the dice have been made. The results were such as to cause Dr. Rhine to declare that "there is no better explanation than the subjects influenced the fall of the dice without any recognized physical contacts with them." By mentally concentrating upon the appearance of certain numbers, while at the same time they stood at a distance to avoid all physical contact with the mechanical thrower and with the dice, the experimenters were frequently able to control the dice. In a number of the experiments, the scores made under psychokinesis refuted some of the traditional mathematical odds of millions to one against the reappearance of certain combinations of numbers in repeated succession.

Meditate over this for a few minutes and then realize what it means to you. Those experiments give you some idea of what is meant by "Thought creates after its kind," "Thought correlates with its object," "Thought attracts that upon which it is directed," and similar statements that we have heard for years. Recall that it was Job who said: "For the thing which I greatly feared is come upon me." Our fear thoughts are just as creative or just as magnetic in attracting troubles to us as are the constructive and positive thoughts in attracting positive results. So no matter what the character of the thought, it does create after its kind. When this sinks into a man's consciousness, he gets some inkling of the awe-inspiring power which is his to use.

However, I cling to the theory that while thoughts do create and exercise control far beyond any limits yet known to man, they create only according to their pitch, intensity, emotional quality, depth of feeling, or vibratory plane. In other words, comparable to the wave length and wattage of a radio station, thoughts have a creative or controlling force in the exact ratio of their constancy, intensity, and power.

While many explanations have been offered, no one knows whether thought is a form of electrical energy or something else yet to be defined. But having been an experimenter in that branch of electricity known as "high-frequency," in which the great electrical genius, Nicola Tesla, pioneered, whenever I think of thought and its radiations or vibrations, I instinctively link them up with electricity and its phenomena. In this manner they become more understandable to me.

I find that I am far from being alone in holding this idea, for scientists have perfected apparatus that actually charts the oscillations of the vibration emanating from the human brain. The apparatus up to this time has been used primarily to indicate a person's mental health, but investigators declare that shadings of emotions, dreams, and remote disease are also considered and studied.

In 1944, Dr. H. S. Burr and his co-workers at Yale University, after experimenting for twelve years, reached the conclusion that an electrical aura of their own making surrounds all living things, and that life is connected electrically to the whole pattern of the universe. For years, mystics, occultists, and metaphysicians have claimed that each individual possesses such an aura, and there are countless cases in which these auras have been recorded as actually seen. However, in no instance, until the results at Yale were published, have I found an explanation in which these are linked with electrical phenomena.

Hermes Trismegistus and the ancient Hermetic philosophers all taught the theory of vibration, while Pythagoras, the great geometrician and philosopher, who lived in the sixth century before Christ, held that everything that exists is a vibration. This is the very essence of our scientific electronic theory of today—that all matter consists of electrons (negative) and protons (positive), that is, of particles or charges of electricity which are constantly acting and reacting upon each other. For lack of a better term, I use the word "vibration" or "oscillation," and when the "frequency" of the electrical particles is changed, the form of material object changes. The difference in matter and the so-called solids as we know them is the difference in the composition of the vibrations—the electrons and the protons. Herein we have a possible explanation of the forces used by the ancient alchemists who claimed to be able to transmute the lesser elements and metals into those of greater value: e.g., iron and lead into silver and gold. They claimed also to be able to heal all disease by the same forces. Rutherford, an English physicist, well known for his research into radioactivity, has thrown some light on this theory of transmutation of the elements and the lesser metals in connection with the theory of electronics.

When we realize that our nervous system is reached only through vibration, in other words, that our five known and defined senses record seeing, hearing, feeling, tasting, and smelling by means of the vibrations given off by the external things themselves, we get a better understanding of the nature of vibrations. For example, we hear a loud noise. It comes to us only via the sound vibration. We see a green leaf, but it is merely the color vibration as gathered by the eyes, and later transmitted to the brain. There are, however, many vibrations which are pitched at a much greater frequency than our five senses are attuned to, and of which we never have any conscious knowledge. By way of illustration, there is a dog whistle pitched so high that only a dog can hear it.

We have all heard of the power of "the laying on of hands," and most of us know how soothing hands stroking our temples can lessen the intensity of a headache. Can this be due to some form of electrical energy flowing from our finger ends? The Bible tells of numerous instances where healing was accomplished by the touch of Jesus' hand. Does the explanation he in this little-known field of electricity—the science of vibration? And does this electrical atmosphere, which Dr. Burr claims is of our own making and which surrounds all living things, enable us to cause certain impulses to pour forth literally from our fingers or from our minds—vibratory forces that can act upon others and upon so-called material objects? All persons living in high altitudes have felt and sometimes observed the electric spark resulting from walking across the room and then touching some metallic substance. That, of course, is a form of static electricity generated by friction, but it gives an idea of how one kind of electricity can be developed through the body.

Among pictures descriptive of the experiments of Yale investigators is one showing that when intact forefingers (that is, without cuts or other injuries) were dipped in salt-water cups connected with a galvanometer, there was a flow of electricity between the positive left hand and the negative right hand, measuring 1.5 millivolts. In another picture, two middle fingers, one with a slight cut at the tip, were partially immersed in the cups, but this time the polarity of the hands changed, the left hand changing from positive to negative and the right becoming positive, with the current stepping up to 12 millivolts.

As I looked at those pictures, I recalled an instrument known as a "biometre" perfected many years ago by a French scientist, Dr. Hippolyte Baraduc, consisting of a bell-shaped glass in which was suspended a copper needle fastened to a fine silk thread. Below the needle but inside the glass was a circular piece of cardboard marked off into degrees.

Two of these instruments were placed side by side and the fingers of both hands of the operator were held within half an inch of the glasses, his mind concentrated on the delicately balanced needle. By changing his mental attitude or the polarity of his thinking, the operator could cause corresponding changes in the direction of the needle, now in one direction and now in another, the needle following absolutely his changing directive thought currents.

Here is a simple experiment embodying similar principles. Take a piece of medium-weight paper, about three inches square, and fold it diagonally from corner to corner. Then open it and make another diagonal fold so that there will be two folds or creases forming intersecting diagonals. Again open the paper, which will now present the appearance of a low, partially flattened-out pyramid. Now take a long needle and force it through a cork so that the point extends an inch or so above the top side of the cork. Place the cork with its needle, point up, on top of an inverted water glass, so that there may be free movement of both hands and of the paper which is to revolve on the needle point. Then take the piece of paper and balance it, where the creases intersect, on the point of the needle, placing it so that the four sides of the pyramid point downward.

Place the glass, with the cork, needle, and paper on a table or desk in a room free from drafts, keeping away from heat registers or windows, thus avoiding possible heat waves or air currents. Then place the hands around the piece of paper in a semi-cupped position, keeping the hands or fingers a half inch or so away from the paper, so that it may revolve freely. Now order it to revolve upon the needle point. At first it will wobble—perhaps revolving slowly at first and in one direction or the other; but if your hands remain steady and you concentrate upon a certain direction of movement, the paper will revolve until it turns rapidly upon the needle point. If you mentally order a change in direction, the one-way movement will cease and the paper will start revolving in the opposite direction. Of course, it is essential that you do not breathe or exhale in the direction of the paper.

Many explanations of what causes the paper to revolve have been offered, such as heat waves from the hands, a body reflex of some kind, and the like. If the paper revolved in only one direction, then one of these explanations could be accepted. But when a person, with a little practice and confident and concentrated thinking, can cause the paper to revolve first in one direction and then in another by reversing the polarity of his thinking, it is clear that the principle is the same as that which governs the experiments with the biometre.

In carrying out another similar experiment, a small disc of cardboard known as the "dialette" bearing the facsimile of the face of a clock, with numbers from one to twelve, is used. (This is better known as the Rosicrucian Dialette and is issued by Amorc, Rosicrucian Brotherhood.) A sharp needle is pushed through its center and on top of it is balanced a sliver of thin cardboard fashioned in the shape of an arrow. The disc is placed on top of a glass filled with water in which the lower part of the needle is submerged. The operator places his hands around the top of the glass, the disc, and arrow; then orders the arrow to revolve, change its position, or stop at any desired position or number. However, it must be recognized in all these experiments that not everyone can immediately get satisfactory results, because the power of mind or thought concentration and projective influence varies in individuals.

If there is a form of electricity which emanates from our hands or fingers in particular and if there are waves, either dynamic or magnetic, caused by vibrations set up either consciously or unconsciously by our thinking, do we not then have an explanation of table-lifting, automatic writing, the performances of the planchette or ouija board, and many of the mediumistic or occult operations? Now that the Yale experimenters have concluded that all living things are surrounded by an electrical atmosphere of their own making, and the Duke experimenters are still exploring the field for further proof that thought or some similar force can affect material objects, we are beginning to receive verification of the idea expressed by Dr. Phillips Thomas, research engineer for the Westinghouse Electric Company. In 1937, according to newspaper dispatches, Dr. Thomas told the Utah session of the American Electrical Institute:

"We feel certain that whatever we do, say, or think is accomplished by some type of radiation. We think such radiations are electricity. In the near future we may be able to capture and interpret these radiations of personality and thought through electrical impulses. Prospects of an early solution are bright."

Since some of my readers may not have a clear understanding of the radiation of thought, I offer a simple explanation. A pebble tossed into a pond immediately upon striking the surface of the water sets up a series of ripples or small waves, which spread out circle-like and ultimately reach the shore line where they appear to stop. The larger the pebble, the higher the waves. Two stones of different sizes and weights tossed in simultaneously at different places but in close proximity will both set up a series of waves, converging upon each other. Where the two sets meet there appears to be a struggle as to which is to overcome or pass the other. As far as our physical vision is concerned, if the waves are of the same size, both seem to stop or merge at their meeting-point; but if one is larger than the other, the larger sweeps over the smaller and creates waves in the wake of the smaller ripples.

Think about this in connection with your own mental impulses—for example, how thoughts of one nature stop or overwhelm others—and you readily appreciate how the more powerful or concentrated the thought, the quicker its tempo, the greater its vibration, the more it sweeps aside the weaker vibrations, the more rapidly it does its creative work.

We hear and read much about various stages of thought, degrees of consciousness, thought concentration, the strength of our faith, all of which deals with the intensity or the degree of power we send forth. Creative force comes only when there is a completely rounded-out thought, when there is a fully developed mental picture, or when the imagination can visualize the fulfillment of our ambition and see in our mind a picture of the object we desire—a house, a car, a radio, etc.—just as if we already possessed them.

As a result of my studies of the so-called mystic teachings, the various mental sciences and the regular orthodox church teachings, I am convinced that they all work in varying degrees, but only to the extent that their followers believe. So it is with prayer, whether it be a part of a church service or the purely spontaneous and personal supplication of the individual.

However, I am forced to the conclusion that many people go through the lip-service act of saying their prayers without, the slightest belief that those prayers will be answered. Consequently, they are not answered. I am frequently reminded of the story of the old lady who, professing a belief in prayer, undertook to go shopping. The day before she prayed that on her shopping day the sun would shine. But upon completion of her prayer she glanced out of the window, saw some black clouds, and instantly declared: "But I know it's going to rain." In the late fall of 1944, the *Saturday Review of Literature*, which doesn't go in for hocus-pocus, contained an article by Thomas Sugrue. He declared that the mind-cure movement had grown so rapidly that it was now encountered everywhere. He cited several cases in which both men and women had secured phenomenal results. One woman, who at sixty-two had been partially crippled and whose fingers were bent with arthritis, had taken up a system of Yogi breathing and had entirely recovered from her physical ailments. Mr. Sugrue declared that after her restoration to health she was adjudged by those who saw her to be about forty. Another woman achieved excellent results under an occult system of metaphysics, and guesses as to her age were fifteen years under her real age. He told also of a retired missionary who for the past twelve years had experimented with psychic phenomena and had obtained most startling results.

We can come to only one conclusion, and that is that all the systems, creeds, and cults work as a result of the firm beliefs of the individual—and that brings us to the magic of believing.

Sigmund Freud, the famous Austrian psychoanalyst, whose works are today standard for psychiatrists, brought the world's attention to the hypothesis that there was a powerful force within us, an unilluminated part of the mind—separate from the conscious mind—that is constantly at work molding our thoughts, feelings, and actions. Others have called this division of our mental existence, the soul, and some metaphysical teachers claim that it is located in the solar plexus. Others call it the super-ego, the inner power, the super-consciousness, the unconscious, the subconscious, and various other names. It isn't an organ or so-called physical matter, such as we know the brain to be, and science hasn't located its tangible position in the human body.

Nevertheless, it is there, and from the beginning of recorded time man has known that it exists. The ancients often referred to it as the "spirit." Paracelsus called it the will, others have called it the mind, an adjunct of the brain. Some have referred to it as conscience, the creator of the "still, small voice within." Still others have called it intelligence and have asserted that it is a part of the Supreme Intelligence, to which we are all linked. Hence the name Universal Mind—that which embraces every living thing, all human as well as plant and animal life.

No matter what we call it—the writer prefers the word subconscious—it is recognized as the essence of life, and the limits of its power are unknown. It never sleeps. It comes to our support in times of great trouble, it warns us of impending danger, often it aids us to do that which seems impossible. It guides us in many ways and when properly employed performs so-called miracles.

Objectively, it does as it is told, that is, when it is commanded or besought by the conscious mind; subjectively, it acts primarily upon its own initiative, or appears to, although there are times when its activity appears to be the result of influences from the outside.

Sir Arthur Eddington is quoted as saying: "I believe that the mind has the power to affect groups of atoms and even tamper with the odds of atomic behavior, and that even the course of the world is not predetermined by physical laws but may be altered by the uncaused volition of human beings."

When this idea is fully comprehended, it becomes breathtaking. It is more understandable in the light of the electronic or vibratory theory.

Every student of the subject knows what may be accomplished by getting into direct contact with the subconscious mind—thousands have employed it to achieve wealth, power, and fame in this world, as well as to cure physical ailments and solve countless human problems. And its power is there for you to use. The only steps you have to take are to believe in its power and to use the technique set forth in this book, or else to devise a system of your own that will put it to work for you.

The late Dana Sleeth, whose syndicated column covering the observations of a hillbilly was well known to newspaper readers twenty years ago, once told me that he considered the subconscious mind one of his greatest aids not only in furnishing him with ideas but in assisting him to find lost tools and other articles. Mr. Sleeth at the time was living in the hills remote from cities and towns, alternating as a columnist and farmer. He had made an extensive study of the subject and we often discussed it as well as exchanged letters covering our ideas.

It's a wonderful thing—the subconscious mind, [said Mr. Sleeth], and for the life of me I can't see why more people don't learn about it and its use. I don't know how many thousands of times it has helped me with my problems. Ideas for feature stories have often come to me when I was engaged in such lowly tasks as stump grubbing. And as for locating lost tools—it's a knockout.

You know nothing is ever lost—it's just misplaced. It's right there to be found in the exact place where you left it or dropped it. I have found dozens of misplaced tools in the identical spot where my subconscious mind told me to look. This is the way it would work. Say for example it was a pocket knife—mine's a good-sized one—that I had misplaced or dropped. I would say, "Pocket knife, where are you?" Then I would close my eyes for a moment or I might gaze off into space—the answer might not always come immediately, but when it did it would come in a flash, and I would be led right to the spot where lay the knife. It always seemed to work unfailingly—even to such things as axes, rakes, and other tools that I was constantly leaving around somewhere—you know we newspaper people are not very methodical.

I used to have a great deal of difficulty in remembering names, but I have found that if I could visualize the man or woman whose name I had temporarily forgotten, and see an outline of his or her features, the color of the eyes, hair, manner of dress, etc., the subconscious would bring me the name without difficulty.

I don't know where I learned this but in trying to recall something, a certain story or certain fact that appeared at the moment to escape me, I would relax, elevate my head, put my right hand a couple of inches above my forehead, sometimes I might close my eyes or gaze off into space; but this little trick always seemed to get results.

Never forget: inventions, great musical compositions, poetry, fiction, and all other ideas for original accomplishment, come from the subconscious. Give it the thought or the material and keep it going with a deep-rooted desire for performance and you will get results. There is an old saying that once we start weaving, the Gods will furnish the skein, and how true that is.

When you start to operate with the aid of this power the bricks automatically fall into place as though a magical hand had touched them. Results will certainly follow in a most astounding manner. Ideas for accomplishment will pop here and they will pop there.

What may appear as coincidences are not coincidences at all but simply the working out of the pattern which you started with your own weaving. I am certain that thousands of successful men and women reach great heights and accomplish marvelous results without knowing anything about the subconscious mind and with no knowledge that it was the power which made for accomplishments.

Living here in the hills away from people and everyday influences, I have often felt that those who live close to nature were in a much better position to utilize the subconscious than others. I believe that day will come when science will prove that the great power of the subconscious is one of the most formidable forces in shaping and controlling our lives.

A passing or momentary thought-flicker dies almost aborning, although it may later reveal cumulative power. But the force that brings into play the great system of the subconscious is a sustained thought or, as previously stated, a fixed mental picture. There are many methods for stepping up the tempo of the vibrations of conscious thought in order to bring into action the subconscious forces, although sometimes just a single utterance, a momentary glance accompanying a word or two traveling from one person to another, has brought the subconscious into immediate play. So have catastrophic danger, moments of great peril and times of great stress, when, alone or in the company of others, a person is suddenly confronted with the necessity for immediate action. It comes to the aid of those in the habit of making quick decisions almost instantaneously, and it comes into operation when you have cleared your conscious mind of its multitude of conflicting thoughts. "Going into the silence" is another way of expressing it.

Perhaps the most effective method of bringing the subconscious into practical action is through the process of making mental pictures—using the imagination—perfecting an image of the thing or situation as you would have it exist in physical form. This is usually referred to as visualization.

However, most of the sustained and continuing manifestations come as a result of belief. It is through this belief with its strange power that miracles happen and that peculiar phenomena occur for which there appears to be no known explanation. I refer now to deep-seated belief—a firm and positive conviction that goes through every fibre of your being—when you believe it "heart and soul," as the saying goes. Call it a phase of emotion, a spiritual force, a type of electrical vibration—anything you please, but that's the force that brings outstanding results, sets the law of attraction into operation, and enables sustained thought to correlate with its object. This belief changes the tempo of the mind or thought-frequency, and, like a huge magnet, draws the subconscious forces into play, changing your whole aura and affecting everything about you—and often people and objects at great distances. It brings into your individual sphere of life results that are sometimes startling—often results you never dreamed possible.

There are countless references to it in the Bible. It is the first condition for membership in many religious, fraternal, and political organizations. Everywhere men are looking for people who have the kind of belief they will fight for, because it is the people who are charged with the vibrations of strong beliefs that sometimes do the miraculous, the things we so often say are "unbelievable." That kind of belief has the magic touch. It is also the basic principle in both white and black magic.

STUDY GUIDE

Chapter 2

The author opens this chapter by sharing practical exercises that will assist you in increasing your awareness of how mind power has been at the root of your experiences. He shares insights on just how powerful the mind is, emphasizing that thoughts have a magnetic force that draws upon the greater source of power that lies within each of us. He cites several examples of individuals who have amassed great success because of their commitment, passion and connection to the power of their minds. He asserts that your desires should be all encompassing, and that your thoughts do not become real until you give them life. He ends this chapter introducing the tool of visualization and emphasizes how powerfully it can support you in manifesting your desires.

1. Bristol asserts that *"No one knows what thought really is, other than it's some sort of mental action."* You are encouraged to contemplate "thought" as a phenomenon. Have you ever done so in the past? Take some time to describe what you believe "thought" to be. Describe it as if you were explaining the phenomenon to a being who is not human and has no relationship to our existing definition of it.

2. The author suggests that you glance around the room, and note that whatever you are looking at first came into existence through thought (the furniture, draperies, etc.). Anything created by man first started with a thought. In fact, all of your possessions came as a result of creative thinking. Take five minutes and look around you, noting all that has been created by thought. As you observe, allow yourself to feel gratitude for the magic of the mind.

3. Bristol asserts that *"The secret of success lies not without, but within, the thoughts of man."* Write a list of the external happenings that you have thus far blamed on your failures. Then reflect on this quote. With the new realization that these external circumstances are not the cause, but your mind is, do you see yourself as a victim? Explain.

4. According to the author, *"What you exhibit outwardly, you are inwardly."* Look in the mirror. What do you see? How do you carry yourself? Do you appear erect and strong, or hunched over and tired? Do you have frown or smile lines on your face? Are your eyes bright and cheery, or listless and depleted? Write a list of your observations. Then describe the impression that you believe you make on others.

5. Ask one or two trusted friends or family members about how you physicalize yourself, encouraging them to be honest and forthright. Write about your findings.

6. Reflect on the statement, *"Man's thoughts make or break him."* Write a list of how your thoughts have "made" you. Then write a list of the ways your thoughts have "broken" you. Then summarize what you learned in doing this exercise.

7. The author asserts that the world's greatest scientists and thinkers are confirming the fundamental principles of this book. List at least three famous figures who reflect this philosophy.

8. Irish editor and poet, George Russell coined the phrase, *"We are what we contemplate."* Imagine that you thought yourself into being. You pre-determined the way you look, feel, speak, and relate to others. How does this change your perspective on your life, especially with those things in which you find yourself dissatisfied?

9. You should also note that we are molded by the thoughts of others around us. For the next 24 hours, take note of what you hear from others, on the media (radio, television and newspapers). Take some time to list all of the messages that come from outside of you.

10. Bristol cites the Commercial and Financial Chronicle (Dec. 10, 1932) as an exemplary example of how the "Mind is a source of all power." In the "El Dorado" article, the author states "one secures the gold of the spirit when he finds himself." Do you believe that the "gold of the spirit" rests in you? Why or why not?

11. On a scale from one to ten (one being "very little" and ten being "a great deal"), rate much you feel you have "found" yourself.

1——2——3——4——5——6——7——8——9——10

12. The author shares several examples of those in American history who found themselves and created massive empires: MacKay, O'Brien, Hearts, Fair (1849 California gold rush success stories), and James J. Hill (founder of the Great Northern Railroad). Choose at least one of these men who "found" themselves and learn more about his story. Write about your findings and how they impact you.

13. Bristol asserts that *"it is not power that is lacking, it is the will"*. Do you believe the struggles you have met with manifesting your desires thus far lie in your lack of will or lack of power? Please explain.

14. Do you believe that the obstacles you are currently facing involve more than a lack of "will" on your part? Please explain.

15. The author states that *"Faith must strengthen the imagination, for faith establishes the will."* Sometimes we assume that we have faith, but upon further investigation,

we realize that we may not be as faithful as we think. Do you trust and have faith that you will be successful, or do you worry, fret and believe that you will experience struggle before any success comes your way? Honestly reflect on this and then write about your faith or lack thereof.

16. According to Bristol "self-finding establishes a clear realization of one's identity with the eternal." On a scale from one to ten (one being "very little" and ten being "a great deal"), rate how much you identify yourself with the eternal.

1——2——3——4——5——6——7——8——9——10

17. The author encourages you to study the words of Paracelsus. Take some time to research him and the message that he shares. Write about your findings and how they relate to your life's journey.

18. Bristol asserts that it takes more than hard work to succeed. Many work hard, but do not succeed. He states that you need *"creative thinking and firm belief in your ability to execute your ideas."* On a scale from one to ten (one being "very little" and ten being "a great deal"), rate how much you use your creative mind:

1——2——3——4——5——6——7——8——9——10

19. What do you do the develop your creativity?

20. What further steps can you take to develop your creative mind? Note them, and then take immediate action on at least one item from your list.

21. Bristol also shares that *"essential to success is that your desire be an all-obsessing one, your thoughts and aims be coordinated, and your energy be concentrated and applied without letup."* Do you give 100% to each of these three imperatives? Why or why not? Where is your enthusiasm lacking?

22. Bristol emphasizes that you must have a mental pattern of what you want clearly drawn in your mind. Ask yourself "Where am I headed? What is my goal? Have I visualized just what I really want? If success is to be measured in terms of wealth, can you envision the specific amount in figures? In terms of achievements, can you be specific and definite?" Take time to answer each of these questions in as much detail as possible.

23. Take some time to create a representation of your desires—whether a video montage, a vision board, a written declaration or some other form of expression. Use as much of your senses in your creation as possible. What do they look like? Smell like? Taste like? Sound like? Feel like? Have fun doing this exercise. Then put your representation somewhere where you can observe it often. Take time each day to look at it. Take time to feel into experiencing those desires manifesting here and now.

24. Bristol asserts that it is important that you have a fixed idea of what you want. For example, do you want "a job, or a better one, a new house, a place in the country, or just a new pair of shoes?" Go through you goals and make them more specific. Provide as much detail as possible. Then set an intention for "this or even better." This allows for the magic to extend beyond your imaginings.

25. The author states *"it is desire for something new, something different, something that is going to change your life, that causes you to make an extra effort."* Are there any new items that you don't yet have on your list? If so, add them to your list providing as much detail as possible.

26. Bristol maintains that thoughts do not become real to us *"until we give them life with our own thinking or through the workings of our imaginations."* Do you believe in this statement? Why or why not? Explain, giving an example.

27. Do you want more financial abundance in your life? If so, exactly how much more money do you want, and what date do you wish to have it? Take some time to see the money in your bank account or investment account. Make the reality of the experience as strong as possible for yourself, and do so in the present; as if you already have it.

28. Bristol asserts that our lifelong habits and beliefs cannot be changed overnight. What lifelong habits would you like to change? Write a list.

29. What lifelong beliefs do you look forward to shifting? Write a list.

30. Take some time to work through each of the lifelong habits and beliefs you wish to change. With each, focus on what you want to believe, and avoid focusing your energy on what you don't want. Write about your experience as you practice this. Are you noting any blocks? If so, what are they and how did you work through them?

31. Based on Sir Arthur Conan Doyle's observations, referencing radar and radio waves, the author queries, *"If thought waves, or whatever they are, can be tuned to even higher oscillations, why can't they affect the molecules of solid objects?"* What would your response to this question be? Can you provide an example that supports your claim?

32. Discussing a punchboard game winner's achievement, the individual chose to play the game only when he had no doubt in his mind that he would win. He stated, *"I can't recall the time that I didn't get winning numbers when the winning idea was firmly fixed in my mind before I started to play."* Have you ever noted a similar experience, where a belief in an outcome started with an absolute knowing that ultimately transpired? If so, explain. If not, why do you believe you have not yet experienced this? Explain.

33. The author cites the 1934 studies done with psychokinesis and dice with Dr. J.B. Rhine at Duke University as evidence of the power of the mind. He asks you to meditate over this and realize what it means to you. What does it mean to you? Write about any impressions you received while meditating on this study.

34. Have you or anyone you have known experienced or witnessed psychokinesis in action? If so, please describe the experience.

35. Bristol emphasizes that our fear-based thoughts are just as powerful as the positive. Have you noted situations where your fearful thoughts were so strong that what you feared actually manifested in your life? If so, please explain. If not, why do you think you have been able to avoid such experiences?

36. The author states *"While thoughts do create and exercise control far beyond any limits yet known to man, they create only according to their pitch, intensity, emotional quality, depth of feeling, or vibratory plane."* What do you think he means by this? Explain.

37. The author questions as to whether thoughts are linked to electrical current. Don't forget that Claude Bristol had these observations during the 1930's before technology was able to do what it can today. He really was a man before his time. Use your imagination and cast yourself ahead 100 years. What could you imagine is possible as time, technology and the human mind evolve? Write about your imaginings.

38. Bristol references the aura that surrounds all things as being linked to electricity or vibration. He links the science of transmutation and alchemy to this phenomenon. Do you believe one could change iron to gold? Why or why not? Please explain.

39. Based on the theories Bristol discussed, all that we experience come to us through vibration. He cites the laying on of hands as one such example. Do you believe in energy healing? Why or why not?

40. The author suggests that you do an experiment that is similar to the biometre. To do so, you need a cork, needle, three-inch square piece of paper and a glass. If you haven't already done so, try this experiment and then write about the outcome.

41. Based on the concept of the "Magic of Believing", what is the message that comes to you in response to the results of this experiment?

42. Another experiment that the author suggests is one in which you create a dialette. Try this experiment and note anything in particular that you observe.

43. Bristol emphasizes that not everyone can immediately get satisfactory results because *"the power of the mind or thought concentration and projective influence varies in individuals."* If you don't get immediate results, take some time to try the experiment again. Note any shifts. If there are none, why do you think this is so? Please explain.

44. The author likens the effect of radiation to the ripples or small waves that appear in response to a pebble hitting water. He suggests you consider this image in relation to your mental impulses and how *"thoughts of one nature stop or overwhelm others—and you readily appreciate how the more powerful or concentrated the thought...the more rapidly it does its creative work."* Pay attention to your thoughts today. You will likely discover that many of them are repeated. You may find that you have many more negative thoughts than you realized. Write about your experience as you concentrate on your thoughts today. Did you learn anything new about them?

45. Claude Bristol asserts, *"Creative force comes only when there is a completely rounded-out thought, when there is a fully developed mental picture, or when the imagination can visualize the fulfillment of our ambition and see in our mind a picture of the object we desire—a house, a car, a radio, etc.—just as if we already possessed them."* Close your eyes and visualize your perfect day, focusing on it as if it is happening in the present. Use all of your senses. What do you taste? Smell? Feel? Hear? See? Then write about your experience in the present with as much detail as possible.

46. The "mind cure" moment was growing in popularity during the 1940's. On a scale from one to ten (one being "very little" and ten being "a great deal"), rate how much you believe in an abundant, benevolent universe.

1——2——3——4——5——6——7——8——9——10

47. The author cites the findings of Sigmund Freud and others, referencing the *"illuminated part of the mind, the soul, the super-ego, the inner power, the super-conscious, the unconscious, etc."* He also references it as the *"universal mind."* Close your eyes and take some deep breathes. Then ask your soul for a message. Sit quietly and wait to receive it. Remain open and curious. Write the message you receive and what it means to you.

48. Sir Arthur Eddington is quoted as saying: *"I believe that the mind has the power to affect groups of atoms and even tamper with the odds of atomic behavior, and that even the course of the world is not predetermined by physical laws but may be altered by the uncaused volition of human beings."* Do you believe this statement to be true? If so, what evidence do you see of it in the world today?

49. The author shares the story of farmer and columnist, Mr. Sleeth and the power of his subconscious mind to find things. Have you ever found misplaced items by calling

on the power of your subconscious mind? If so, describe the incident(s). If not, do you believe that you could use your subconscious mind to do so?

50. Mr. Sleeth also used his subconscious mind to remember names. Do you have trouble remembering names? If so, next time you forget, practice his technique of seeing an outline of the person's features and allowing your subconscious mind to remind you of his or her name. Write about your findings next time you practice this technique.

51. Another technique that Mr. Sleeth shared was placing his right hand a couple of inches above his forehead when he wanted to recall something. Try this technique and write about any discovering you make while doing it.

52. You are reminded *"inventions, great musical compositions, poetry, fiction, and all other ideas for original accomplishment, come from the subconscious."* Have you ever had an idea for an invention come into your thoughts? If so, what was it? Did you take any action on it? Why or why not?

53. Sleeth encourages you to *"give it the thought or the material and keep it going with a deep-rooted desire for performance and you will get results."* Are there any creative endeavors that you are passionate to manifest? What are they? Take some time to commit to manifesting and look forward to results appearing. Write about your findings.

54. Mr. Sleeth stated, *"What may appear as coincidences are not coincidences at all but simply the working out of the pattern which you started with your own weaving."* Do you believe in coincidences or intentional manifestations? Explain.

55. Sleeth believed that those living in nature and away from people were more apt to connect with their subconscious. What are your beliefs about this?

56. *"Once we start weaving, the Gods will furnish the skein"* is a quote that Mr. Sleeth referenced in his writings about the power of the subconscious mind. Close your eyes for a couple of seconds, and ask your subconscious, *"What weavings do I need to start at this time in my life?"* A response may come in the form of a symbol, a song or some other method of communication. Write about the message(s) you receive and what they mean to you.

57. Mr. Sleeth asserts that *"sustained thoughts"* or *"fixed mental pictures"* have a great deal of manifesting power in our lives. For the next week starting paying attention to where your thoughts go, and any mental pictures that continue to be fixed in your mind. Write them down, and note: are they positive or negative? Are they faith or fear-based? Do they energize me, or lower my energy?

58. Central to the success of hearing the voice of your sub-conscious mind is, as Sleeth puts it, *"Going into the silence"*—meditation and visualization. Do you practice either of these modalities on an ongoing basis? Why or why not?

59. More powerful, however, is to believe in something *"through every fiber of your being; heart and soul."* Sleeth claims that such a belief changes the tempo or thought-frequency of the mind. He notes that there are several references to it in the Bible and other religious documents. Do you believe that yogis can levitate, that Moses parted the sea, or that Christ walked on water? If so, do you think that they were super-human, or simply that they believed that they could? If you believed it possible, do you think that you could you do the same? Explain.

Chapter 3

What the Subconscious Is

There is no artist, man of science, or writer of any distinction, however little disposed to self-analysis, who is not aware by personal experience of the unequalled importance of the subconscious," wrote Gustave Geley, distinguished French psychologist and author of From the Unconscious to the Conscious. He said also that the best results in life were obtained by close harmony and cooperation between the conscious and subconscious minds, and he pointed out that up to the nineteenth century the psychology of the subconscious was completely ignored, and it was then considered only as the abnormal outcome of disease or accident.

As the subconscious plays a very important part in the magic of believing, it will bring you to a quicker understanding of this science if you have a clear and detailed picture of what the subconscious mind is, where it is located, and how it functions, both by itself and in collaboration with the conscious mind. Some of the material in this chapter you will find referred to or even repeated in succeeding chapters; but as repetition is an essential part of the technique of this science, it will be equally effective in presenting the knowledge of the science itself; and furthermore, the quicker you get an understanding of it, the quicker you will be on your way to getting what you desire.

In giving you this picture of the subconscious mind, it is necessary for me to use scientific terms here and there, for practically all the knowledge of the subconscious has come as a result of the study and experimentation of some of the world's greatest psychologists. But even if you find it a little difficult to understand at first reading, repeated readings will make it clear and you will thus have a solid foundation upon which to proceed with the active part of the science.

In the first chapter I told you that it was The Law of Psychic Phenomena by Thomson Jay Hudson that first got me to thinking about the subconscious mind and its great possibilities for helping individuals in their everyday life. Since that time there have been other books, such as The Sub-Conscious Speaks by Erna Ferrell Grabe and Paul C. Ferrell, The Source of Power by Theodore Clinton Foote, The Unconscious by Morton Prince, M.D., and Common Sense and Its Cultivation by Hanbury Hankin, which have greatly added to the knowledge of the subject. It will be my aim to give you not only a mental picture of the conscious and subconscious minds in the light of modern findings concerning their relations and functions, but also definite instructions as to the method by which you can bring them under your control and direct their energies toward assisting you to fulfill your desires.

"There is dormant in each human being a faculty, whether it is developed or not, which will enable that particular individual to succeed if the desire for success is present in his conscious mind." Thus wrote the authors of The Sub-Conscious Speaks.

This "faculty" has always been known and recognized for its strange and unusual powers, but it was not until about a century and a half ago that psychologists who made it the subject of their special investigation and experimentation, called it the subconscious mind. Emerson was certainly aware of the dual character of the human mental organization when he wrote in his Journals: "I find one state of mind does not remember or conceive of another state. Thus I have written within a twelve-month verses ('Days') which I do not remember the composition or correction of, and could not write the like today, and have only for proof of their being mine, various external evidences, as the MS in which I find them, and the circumstances that I have sent copies of them to friends, etc., etc."

Today the words conscious and subconscious are widely understood, and it is recognized that we all have two minds, each one endowed with separate and distinct attributes and powers, and each one capable, under certain conditions, of independent action. There is no difficulty in your comprehending that the conscious mind operates in the brain, for whenever you do any concentrated thinking you feel it in your head. Sometimes the thought is so intense and prolonged that your head aches, or your eyes become tired, or your temples throb. Also, you can generally trace the source of the thought. It may be suggested by something you have seen or heard or read; perhaps it is a new idea for your business or your home; maybe it is the continuation of some thought you have been pondering for a long time past. The point is that you can connect it with something already related to your consciousness. Sometimes your thought is concerned with trying to solve a difficult problem, and you have become so exhausted and so discouraged at failing to arrive at the solution that you "give it up," "let the whole thing go," "dismiss it from your mind," a state of feeling you often have at night when you can't sleep because of the thought that is pounding and gripping your brain. The moment you "let it go," it begins to sink, as though it were moving downward somewhere inside of you. The tension in your conscious mind then decreases and you are soon asleep. The next morning when you wake up, your conscious mind begins to think again about the problem, when suddenly there appears before your mind's eyes a mental picture of your problem—completely solved and with all the necessary directions for appropriate action on your part.

Where did the thought go when you released it from your conscious mind and through what power inside of you was the problem solved? It is well known that many writers, orators, artists, musical composers, designers, inventors, and other creative workers have long made use of their subconscious minds either consciously or unconsciously. In this connection Merton S. Yewdale, well-known book publisher's editor, called the writer's attention to a recent statement by Louis Bromfield, the American novelist. Mr. Bromfield was quoted as saying:

One of the most helpful discoveries I made long ago in common with some other writers is that there is a part of the mind, which the psychologists call the "subconscious" that works while you are sleeping or even while you are relaxing or engaged in some other task far removed from writing. I have found it possible to train this part of the mind to do a pretty organized job. Very often I have awakened in the morning to find a problem of technique, or plot, or character, which had long been troubling me, completely solved while I had been sleeping. The judgment of the "subconscious mind" which represents inherited instincts and the accumulation of experience, is virtually infallible, and I would always trust its decisions over any judgment arrived at through a long and reasonable process of conscious thinking.

No doubt you already have a mental picture of your two minds: the conscious mind in your head, above the line of consciousness; and the subconscious mind in your body, below the line of consciousness—with a means of communication between them.

Now it is the conscious mind that is the source of thought. Also, it is the mind that gives us the sense of awareness in our normal waking life: the knowledge that we are ourselves here and now: the recognition and understanding of our environment: the power to rule over our mental faculties, to recall the events of our past life, and to comprehend our emotions and their significance. More concretely, it enables us to have a rational understanding of the objects and persons about us, of our own successes or shortcomings, of the validity of an argument, or the beauty of a work of art.

The chief powers of the conscious mind are reason, logic, form, judgment, calculation, conscience, and the moral sense. By it we take cognizance of the objective world, and its means of observation are our five physical senses. Our conscious mind is the outgrowth of our physical necessities and likewise our guide in the struggle with our material environment. Its highest function is that of reasoning, and by all methods—inductive and deductive, analytic and synthetic. For example, suppose you are undertaking to discover a new serum. You use your conscious mind and employ the inductive method of reasoning. That is, you first collect the facts and elements that are presented to your sense perceptions; then you compare them one with another, noting similarities and dissimilarities; then you select those which are alike in qualities, in uses, or in function, after which you proceed to form a generalization or law, that certain things which have such qualities will function in such a way. This is the scientific method of arriving at knowledge, and it forms the basis of modern education in schools and colleges. But in some form or other we all use it to help solve our problems, whether personal, social, business, professional, or economic. Many times the solution of our problem results from this use of our conscious mind. But now and then when the solution is not forthcoming, we become exhausted with continued trying, we begin to lose confidence in ourselves, and we often resign ourselves to the idea that we have failed and that nothing can be done about it. Here is where the subconscious mind comes in—to help us to renew our belief in ourselves, to assist us to overcome our difficulty, and to put us on the road to achievement and success.

Just as the conscious mind is the source of thought, so the subconscious is the source of power. Also, it is one of the greatest realities in human life. It is rooted in instinct, and is aware of the most elemental desires of the individual, yet it is always pressing upward into conscious existence. It is a repository of spontaneous impressions of men and nature, and a memory vault in which are kept the records of facts and experiences that are sent down to it from time to time by the conscious mind for safekeeping and future use. Thus the subconscious mind is not only a mighty storehouse of ever-ready material which can be placed at the disposal of the conscious mind, but also a powerhouse of energy with which the individual can be charged, thus enabling him to recover his strength and courage, and also his faith in himself.

The subconscious mind is beyond space and time, and it is fundamentally a powerful sending and receiving station with a universal hookup whereby it can communicate with the physical, mental, psychic, and, according to many investigators, spiritual worlds, past, present, and future, as well. Such is the power of your subconscious mind. In brief, the subconscious embodies the feeling and wisdom of the past, the awareness and knowledge of the present, and the thought and vision of the future. Emerson, though he wrote of instinct, endowed it with so many superior attributes that he undoubtedly was thinking of the subconscious mind when he wrote: "All true wisdom of thought and of action comes of deference to this instinct, patience with its delays. To make a practical use of this instinct in every part of life constitutes true wisdom, and we must form the habit of preferring in all cases its guidance, which is given as it is used."

The powers of the subconscious are many, the chief of which are intuition, emotion, certitude, inspiration, suggestion, deduction, imagination, organization, and, of course, memory and dynamic energy. It takes cognizance of its environment by means independent of the physical senses. It perceives by intuition. It operates most successfully and performs its highest function when the objective senses are quiescent. But it can function during the waking hours as well as during sleep. It is a distinct entity, it possesses independent powers and functions, with a unique mental organization all its own, and it sustains an existence that is closely allied to the physical body and the life of the individual, and yet that also operates independently of the body.

Now the subconscious mind has three primary functions. First, with its intuitive understanding of the bodily needs, it maintains and preserves (unaided by the conscious mind) the well-being and indeed the very life of the body. Second, as pointed out in the previous chapter, in times of great emergency it springs into immediate action (again independently of the conscious mind) and takes supreme command, acting with incredible certitude, rapidity, accuracy, and understanding, in the saving of the life of the individual. Third, it is operative in the psychic world in which the psychic powers of the subconscious are manifested in such phenomena as telepathy, clairvoyance, and psychokinesis. But, also, it can be summoned to help the conscious mind in time of great personal necessity, when the conscious calls upon the subconscious to use its powers and resources to solve a vital problem or bring to pass that which is sought or desired by the individual.

In this book we are concerned particularly with the last part of the third primary function of the subconscious mind, and especially with the technique by which it operates for your benefit. Accordingly, to draw upon the resources and powers of the subconscious and awaken it into action, you must first be sure that you are asking for something that is rightfully yours to have and is within your ability to handle, for the subconscious manifests itself only according to the capabilities of the person. Then you must have patience and absolute faith, for, as Théodore Simon Jouffroy, the French philosopher, said, "The subconscious mind will not take the trouble to work for those who do not *believe* in it." Next, in conveying your need to the subconscious, it must be in the spirit—that the work has *already been done*. Thus, while it is necessary for you to *feel and think* yourself successful, it is important for you to go one step further and actually see yourself as already successful, either in the performance of some selected task or as actually occupying the position to which you are aspiring. For the next and final step, you must wait patiently while the subconscious is assimilating the elements of your problem and then goes about its own way to work it out for you.

In due course, with the flowing of the ideas and plans of the subconscious into your waiting conscious mind, the solution of your problem will be revealed to you and the correct course of action indicated, which you must follow immediately and unquestioningly. There must be no hesitation on your part, no mental reservation, no deliberation. You must receive the message from the subconscious freely, and after understanding it you must act on it at once. Only by so doing will you make your subconscious serve you and continue to respond whenever you call upon it.

However, your problem may be one that cannot be solved in the above manner; instead of receiving the solution in the form of a "blueprint," as it were, to guide your steps to the final fulfillment, you may, instead, feel some mysterious force urging you at intervals to do certain things that seem to have no special significance or logical connection. Nevertheless, you must continue to believe in the power and wisdom of the subconscious, and obediently perform the seemingly irrelevant things; one day you will find yourself in the position you sought through the aid of the subconscious, and doing the work you envisioned for yourself. Then, when you look back, you will see how the things you were called upon to do all formed a logical line of events, the last one of which was your final arriving—the reward of your sincerest hopes and desires—your own triumphant personal success!

STUDY GUIDE

Chapter 3

When the subconscious is in harmony with the conscious mind, it plays an important role in the magic of believing. In this chapter, the author shares research, insights and information on the workings of the subconscious mind, especially in relation to how it supports extraordinary phenomenon. He references the research and writings of several early experts in this area of human nature and mind power development. He lists the powers of the subconscious mind, focusing particularly on its primary functions (the third being most significant in relation to mind power). He ends this chapter with some specific suggestions on the traits and practices you should follow in order to nurture a growing, trusting relationship with your mind.

1. This chapter opens with a quote from Gustave Geley, a distinguished French psychologist. He stated, *"the best results in life were obtained by close harmony and co-operation between the conscious and sub-conscious minds."* He referenced "harmony" between the two as being key. Do you believe that having a harmonious life also supports your ability to manifest your desires? Why or why not?

2. Do you believe your life is harmonious? On a scale from one to ten (one being "very little" and ten being "a great deal"), rate how much harmony you currently experience in your life.

1———2———3———4———5———6———7———8———9———10

3. What action steps could you take to increase the harmony in your life? List at least two that you can act upon, and then create an action plan. Keep a journal of your experiences as you implement this action plan.

4. He also references *"co-operation.* On a scale from one to ten (one being "very little" and ten being "a great deal"), rate how much co-operation you currently experience in your life.

1———2———3———4———5———6———7———8———9———10

5. How might you cultivate greater co-operation in your life? List at least two things you could do to increase the sense of co-operation you experience, then follow up and integrate them into your life. Write about your findings in doing so.

6. The author asserts that having a *"clear and detailed picture of what the subconscious mind is, where it is located and how it functions"* will bring you to a quicker understanding of this science. What is your current understanding of the sub-conscious mind?

7. Where do you believe the sub-conscious mind is located?

8. How do you believe the sub-conscious mind functions?

9. The author mentions that there will be repeated messages throughout the book, but asserts that repetition is an essential part of the technique of this science. Often, with our sense of urgency, we can be impatient, especially with repetition. How do you feel about repetition?

10. On a scale from one to ten (one being "extremely impatient" and ten being "extremely patient"), rate how impatient you are.

1———2———3———4———5———6———7———8———9———10

11. Do you believe your impatience supports or detracts from manifesting your desires in your life? Explain.

12. The author references several books: The Sub-Conscious Speaks by Erna Ferrell Grabe and Paul C. Ferrell, The Source of Power by Theodore Clinton Foote, The Unconscious by Morton Prince, M.D., and Common Sense and

Its Cultivation by Hanbury Hankin. Do some research on these books and choose one to read. Of course, complete this course first, and then take some time to do so. Write about your findings.

13. Erna Ferrell Grabe and Paul C. Ferrell wrote, *"There is dormant in each human being a faculty, whether it is developed or not, which will enable that particular individual to succeed if the desire for success is present in his conscious mind."* On a scale from one to ten (one being "not at all" and ten being "very much so"), rate how "dormant" you believe this faculty to be in your mind.

1———2———3———4———5———6———7———8———9———10

14. The author described the process where your conscious mind agonizes over a challenge for hours before you go to sleep. You finally let go of the thoughts and drift into sleep, only to wake up and find an answer to your problem appear within your mind's eye. Have you ever experienced this phenomenon? Write about your experience(s) and the revelation(s) you made.

15. The author writes that *"The judgment of the 'subconscious mind which represents inherited instincts and the accumulation of experience, is virtually infallible, and I would always trust its decisions over any judgment arrived at through a long and reasonable process of conscious thinking."* Do you currently trust the judgments of your sub-conscious mind over your conscious thinking mind? Why or why not?

16. The author states that the conscious mind is in the head, while the subconscious mind is in the body. Is this how you perceived the location of your conscious and sub-conscious minds? If not, how have you perceived them?

17. Bristol asserts *"the chief powers of the conscious mind are reason, logic, form, judgment, calculation, conscience, and the moral sense."* Go through each of these functions and list examples of how you use your mind with each.

18. The highest function of the conscious mind is reasoning—inductive and deductive, analytic and synthetic. The author provides the example of discovering a new serum, as "the scientific method of reasoning" to describe the various functions. Create your own example and include each of the listed elements of scientific reasoning in your description.

19. According to the author, at the point where you give up on relying upon your conscious mind to find solutions, you subconscious mind kicks into play. He states that as the conscious mind is the source of thought, the subconscious mind is the source of power. Have you viewed your subconscious mind as the source of your power? If not, how does this new perspective change your perception?

20. According to the author, *"the subconscious mind comes in—to help us to renew our belief in ourselves, to assist us to overcome our difficulty, and to put us on the road to achievement and success."* This statement portrays the subconscious as our savior and best friend. Think of your best friend; the individual who you feel truly has your back. Then consider someone that you greatly respect, who is a worldly and esteemed genius. If you perceive your subconscious as being a combination of these two individuals, how would you relate to it?

21. On a scale from one to ten (one being "very little" and ten being "a great deal"), rate how much you trust in your subconscious mind, given this new perspective.

1——2——3——4——5——6——7——8——9——10

22. The author refers to the subconscious mind as rooted in instinct, aware of your most elemental desires, a memory vault, and a repository of spontaneous impressions of men and nature. Why do you believe such a powerful aspect of yourself is not something you can consciously wrap your head around?

23. Bristol states that the subconscious mind is not only a *"mighty storehouse of ever-ready material...but also a powerhouse of energy with which the individual can be charged . . . enabling him to recover his strength, courage and faith in himself."* What do you think is preventing you from fully utilizing the expansiveness of your subconscious? If you don't already do so, try quieting your mind and connecting with your subconscious through meditation at least 5 minutes each day. Write about your findings.

24. *"The subconscious embodies the feeling and wisdom of the past, the awareness and knowledge of the present, and the thought and vision of the future."* With this description, the subconscious mind appears to have infinite power and genius. Write a note of appreciation for this powerful aspect of yourself, and then read it aloud.

25. Louis Bromfield stated," *The judgment of the "subconscious mind" which represents inherited instincts and the accumulation of experience, is virtually infallible, and I would always trust its decisions over any judgment arrived at through a long and reasonable process of conscious thinking."* Humankind places such importance in our conscious minds. Do you believe that you can better trust your unconscious mind? Why or why not? Please explain.

26. Reflect on your life. Have you ever taken an initiative that was not conscious (i.e. likely came from your subconscious mind), and later realized that it did not serve your best interest? Explain.

27. You can often get impulses that come from fear-based thinking, and sometimes it is difficult to decifer whether these thoughts are subconscious messages or fear-based conditioning. Do you have a clear distinction between the two? Please explain.

28. Do you believe you get your power from other sources that are not rooted in the subconscious mind? If so, where do you believe these powers come from? Please explain.

29. Bristol states that the subconscious mind is rooted in instinct. Have you ever make an instinctual decision that, in reflection you believe did not best serve you? Explain.

30. He further describes the subconscious mind as *"a repository of spontaneous impressions of men and nature, and a memory vault in which are kept the records of facts and experience that are sent down to it from time to time by the conscious mind for safekeeping and future use."* Have you considered your subconscious mind a *"repository"*? Why or why not?

31. The subconscious mind is *powerhouse of energy with which an individual can be charged."* On a scale from one to ten (one being "very little" and ten being "a great deal"), rate how depleted of energy you find yourself on a regular basis.

1———2———3———4———5———6———7———8———9———10

32. The author claims that you can recover your strength, courage and faith in yourself by accessing your subconscious mind. Do you believe this to be true? Why or why not?

33. *"The subconscious mind is beyond space and time, and it is fundamentally a powerful sending and receiving station with a universal hookup whereby it can communicate with the physical, mental, psychic, and, according to many investigators, spiritual worlds, past, present, and future, as well."* Believing this to be the case, if you could access any information from any time and space, what would you be interested in learning? Write a list.

34. Bristol asserts that "you must have patience and absolute faith, for as Theodore Simon Jouffroy, the French philosopher, said, 'The subconscious mind will not take the

trouble to work for those who do not believe in it.'" Do you believe this to be true? Why or why not? Do you believe your subconscious mind works whether you believe in it or not? Please explain.

35. The next tenet that the author asserts is that *"in conveying your need to the subconscious, it must be in the spirit—that the work has already been done."* Do you take time each day to visualize your desires? If so, do you see them as if they are in the present, already manifested? Take a few moments now to visualize the perfect day, and be sure to experience it in the here and now.

36. The final step is to wait patiently while the subconscious assimilates the elements of your problem and then *"goes about its own way to work it out for you."* Have you ever wanted something, only to find that it did not manifest in the way that you planned? If so, what do you believe was at play when this occurred?

37. Claude Bristol then asserts that when the correct course of action is revealed to you, you must *"receive the message from the subconscious freely, and after understanding it, you must act on it at once."* Some believe that once an invention or idea appears in the consciousness to one, it will appear to many, thus immediate action is important. Do you believe this to be true? Why or why not?

38. If you act on the impulses of your subconscious, it will continue to serve you. Do you think that the author is suggesting that if you do not act upon its suggestions, it will stop serving you? Please explain.

39. The subconscious may hand you solutions in the form of "blueprints", however it may also urge you at intervals to *"do certain things that seem to have no special significance or logical connection. Nevertheless, you must continue to believe in the power and wisdom of the subconscious, and obediently perform the seemingly irrelevant things; one day you will find yourself in the position*

you sought through the aid of the subconscious, and doing the work you envisioned for yourself. Then, when you look back, you will see how the things you were called upon to do all formed a logical line of events, the last one of which was your final arriving—the reward of your sincerest hopes and desires—your own triumphant personal success!" Write about a situation you have had where you followed your inner guidance, despite your doubts, and experienced fortuitous ending to the events. If you have not experienced this, why do you believe you have not? Please explain.

Chapter 4

Suggestion Is Power

How many times have you heard it said, "Just believe you can do it and you can!" Whatever the task, if it is begun with the belief that you can do it, it will be done perfectly. Often belief enables a person to do what others think is impossible. It is the act of believing that is the starting force or generating power that leads to accomplishment. "Come on, fellows, we can beat them," shouts someone in command, whether in a football game, on the battlefield, or in the strife of the business world. That sudden voicing of belief, challenging and electrifying, reverses the tide and—Victory! Success! From defeatism to victory—and all because some mighty believer knew that *it could be done.*

You may be shipwrecked or tossed into the water near a rocky shore, and momentarily you may fear that there isn't a chance for you. Suddenly a feeling comes that you will be saved or that you can save yourself. The moment you have that feeling it begins to take the form of belief, and along with the belief comes the power to assist you. You may be in a fire, surrounded by flames and enveloped in smoke, and frantic with fear. This same power asserts itself—and you may be saved. Emerson explains it by saying that in a difficult situation or a sudden emergency our spontaneous action is always the best. Many stories have been told of the great reserves of the subconscious mind, how under its direction and by imparting its superhuman strength frail men and women have been able to perform feats far beyond their normal powers. Great orators and writers are often amazed at the power of the subconscious mind to furnish them with a steady flow of thoughts.

After studying the various mystical religions and different teachings and systems of mind-stuff, one is impressed with the fact that they all have the same basic modus operandi, and that is through repetition—the repeating of certain mantras, words, formulas, or just plain mumbo-jumbo, which William Seabrook declared witch doctors, Voodoo high priests, "hexers," and many other followers of strange cults, use to invoke the spirits or work black magic. One finds the same principle at work in the chants, the incantations, litanies, daily lessons (to be repeated as frequently as possible during the week), the frequent praying of the Buddhists and Moslems alike, the affirmations of the Theosophists and the followers of Unity, the Absolute Truth, New Thought, Divine Science; in fact, it is basic in all religions, although here it is white magic instead of black magic. When one seeks further, one sees the same principle at work in the beating of tom-toms or kettledrums by savages in all parts of the globe, the sound vibrations of which arouse similar vibrations in the psychic nature of these savages, so that they become stimulated, excited, and emotionalized to the point where they defy death. The war dances of the American Indians with their repeated rhythmic physical movements, the tribal ceremonies to bring rain, the dancing of the whirling dervishes, even the playing of martial music at critical times, as well as the spirited music that is played for the workers in many industrial plants, embody the same principle.

Some interesting facts as to the repetition of certain mystical chants and prayers are recounted by Theos Bernard in his book, Penthouse of the Gods, published in 1939. When he wrote it, he claimed to be the first white person to enter the mysterious city of Lhasa in Tibet, high in the Himalaya mountains, where dwell in monasteries thousands of lamas—followers of Buddha. On reading the book one gets the impression that when the lamas or monks are not eating or attending to the material wants of the body, they are constantly and continuously engaged in their mystical chants, using their prayer wheels. Bernard declared that in one temple the monks spent the entire day repeating prayers they had started at daybreak, the exact number of repetitions being 108,000. He told also of how lamas accompanying him repeated certain fixed chants for the purpose of giving him additional strength.

It is obvious that in all similar religions, cults, and orders there is a prescribed ritual in which the repetition of words, mystical or otherwise, plays an important part. And this brings us to the law of suggestion, through which all forces operating within its limits are capable of producing phenomenal results. That is, it is the power of suggestion—an autosuggestion (your own to yourself) or heterosuggestion (coming to you from outside sources)—that starts the machinery into operation or causes the subconscious mind to begin its creative work—and right here is where the affirmations and repetitions play their part. It's the repetition of the same chant, the same incantations, the same affirmations that leads to belief, and once that belief becomes a deep conviction, things begin to happen. A builder or contractor looks over a set of plans and specifications for a bridge or a building, and, urged by a desire to get the contract for the work, declares to himself: "I can do that. Yes, I can do that." He may repeat it silently to himself a thousand times without being conscious of doing it; nevertheless, the suggestion finds a place in which to take root, he gets the contract, and the structure is eventually built. Conversely, he may say that he can't do it—and he never does.

This is the identical force and the same mechanics that Hitler used in building up the German people to attack the world. A reading of his Mein Kampf will verify that. Dr. René Fauvel, a famous French psychologist, explained it by saying that Hitler had a remarkable understanding of the law of suggestion and its different forms of application, and that it was with uncanny skill and masterly showmanship that he mobilized every instrument of propaganda in his mighty campaign of suggestion. Hitler openly stated that the psychology of suggestion was a terrible weapon in the hands of anyone who knew how to use it. Let's see how he worked it to make the Germans believe what he wanted them to and once that belief took hold, how they started their campaign of terror. Slogans, posters, huge signs, massed flags appeared throughout Germany. Hitler's picture was everywhere. "One Reich, one Folk, one Leader" became the chant. It was heard everywhere that a group gathered. "Today we own Germany, tomorrow the entire world," the marching song of the German youths, came from thousands of throats daily. Such slogans as "Germany has waited long enough," "Stand up, you are the aristocrats of the Third Reich," "Germany is behind Hitler to a man," and hundreds of others, bombarded them twentyfour hours a day from billboards, sides of buildings, the radio, and the press. Every time they moved, turned around, or spoke to one another, they got the idea that they were a superior race, and under the hypnotic influence of this belief, strengthened by repeated suggestion, they started out to prove it. Unfortunately for them, there were other nations who also had strong national beliefs that eventually became the means of bringing defeat to the Germans.

Mussolini, too, used the same law of suggestion in an attempt to make a place for Italy in the sun. Signs and slogans such as "Believe, Obey, Fight," "Italy must have its great place in the world," "We have some old scores and new scores to settle," covered the walls of thousands of buildings, and similar ideas were at the same time dinned into the people via the radio and every other means of direct communication by the spoken word.

Stalin, too, used the same science to build Russia into what she is today. The Institute of Modern Hypnotism in November, 1946, recognizing that Joseph Stalin had been using the great power of the repeated suggestion upon the Russian people in order to make them believe in their strength and power, named him as one of the ten persons with the "most hypnotic eyes in the world," rating him as a "mass hypnotist."

The Japanese war lords used it to make fanatical fighters out of their people. From the very day of their birth Japanese children were fed the suggestion that they were direct descendants of Heaven and destined to rule the world. They prayed it, chanted it and believed it; but here again it was used wrongly.

For forty-four years, ever since the Russo-Japanese war, the Japs immortalized Naval Warrant Officer Magoshichi

Sugino, fabled as one of Japan's early suicide fighters and greatest heroes. Thousands of statues were erected to his memory and in repeated song and story young Nipponese were taught to believe that by following his example, they could die in no more heroic manner than as a suicide fighter. Millions of them believed it and during the war thousands of them did die as suicide fighters. Yet Sugino, who was supposed to have gone to his death while scuttling a ship to bottle up the Russian fleet at Port Arthur, didn't die. He was picked up by a Chinese boat, and upon learning that he was being lauded by his people as a great suicide fighter, decided to remain forever obscure and became an exile in Manchuria. Associated Press dispatches from Tokyo in November, 1946, tell how he was discovered after all these years and was being returned home. Although he was alive and well, it continued to be dinned into the ears of young Nipponese that there was no greater heroic act than to die as Sugino had. This terrible and persistent deeply founded belief, though based entirely on a fable, caused thousands of Japanese to throw away their lives during the war.

We, too, as Americans, were subjected to the power of suggestion long before and during World War I; we got it again in a big way under the direction of General Hugh Johnson with his N.R.A. plan, and in World War II it inspired us to increase our effort, to buy bonds, and so forth. We were constantly told that Germany and Japan had to be defeated unconditionally. Under the constant repetition of the same thought all individual thinking was paralyzed and the mass mind became grooved to a certain pattern—win the war unconditionally. As one writer so ably said: "In war the voice of dissension becomes the voice of treason."

So again we see the terrific force of thought repetition—it is our master and we do as we are ordered.

This subtle force of the repeated suggestion overcomes our reason, acting directly on our emotions and our feelings, and finally penetrating to the very depths of our subconscious minds. It is the basic principle of all successful advertising—the continued and repeated suggestion that first makes you believe after which you are eager to buy. In recent years we have enjoyed a vitamin spree. Vitamins for this and vitamins for that have come to us from all sides, and millions buy them in capsule form, so potent is the repeated suggestion of their value.

For centuries tomatoes were looked upon as poisonous. People dared not eat them until some fearless person tried them and lived. Today millions of people eat them, not knowing that less than a hundred years ago they were considered unfit for human consumption. Conversely, the lowly spinach may go into the discard, because our own United States Government declares that it does not contain the food values attributed to it for centuries. It is easy to see that millions will believe this and refuse any longer to honor Popeye's favorite dish.

Nothing is clearer than that the founders of all great religious movements knew much about the power of the repeated suggestion and with it gained far-reaching results. Religious teachings have been hammered into us from the time of our birth, into our mothers and fathers before us and into their parents and their parents before them, and likewise back through the centuries. There's certainly white magic in that kind of believing. Such statements as "What we do not know will not hurt us" and "Ignorance is bliss" take on greater significance when we realize that the only things that can harm us or bother us are those of which we become conscious. We have all heard the story of the man who didn't know it couldn't be done and went ahead and did it. Psychologists tell us that as babies we have only two fears: the fear of loud noises and the fear of falling. All of our fears come with knowledge or develop as a result of our experiences; they come from what we are taught or what we hear and see. I like to think of men and women who, like staunch oak trees, can stand firm amid the many crosscurrents of thought that whirl around them. But far too many people are like saplings that are swayed by every little breeze and ultimately grow in the direction of some strong wind of thought that blows against them.

The Bible is filled with examples of the power of thought and suggestion. Read Genesis, chapter 30, verses 36 to 43, and you'll learn that even Jacob knew its power. The Bible tells how he developed spotted and speckled cattle, sheep, and goats by placing rods from trees, partially stripping them of their bark so they would appear spotted and marked, in the watering troughs where the animals came to drink. As you may have guessed, the flocks conceived before the spotted rods and brought forth cattle, "ringstraked, speckled, and spotted," and incidentally Jacob waxed exceedingly rich.

Moses, too, was a master at suggestion. For forty years he used it on the Israelites, and it took them to the promised land of milk and honey. David, following the suggestive forces operating on him, slew the mighty, heavily armed Goliath with a pebble from a slingshot.

The frail little Maid of Orléans, Joan of Arc, heard voices (?), and under their suggestive influences became imbued with the idea that she had a mission to save France.

She was able to transmit her indomitable spirit to the hearts of her soldiers and she defeated the superior forces of the British at Orléans.

William James, father of modern psychology in America, declared that often our faith [belief] in advance of a doubtful undertaking is the only thing that can assure its successful conclusion. Man's faith, according to James, acts on the powers above him as a claim and creates its own verification. In other words, the thought becomes literally father to the fact. For further illumination of faith and its power, I suggest that you read the General Epistle of James in the New Testament.

Let us go into the field of sports where everyone who has ever witnessed a football or baseball game has actually seen this power of suggestion at work. The late Knute Rockne, famous coach at Notre Dame, knew the value of suggestion and used it repeatedly. But he always suited his method of applying it to the temperament of the individual team. A story is told that on one Saturday afternoon Notre Dame was playing in a particularly grueling game, and at the end of the first half was trailing badly. The players were in their dressing room nervously awaiting the arrival of Rockne. Finally the door opened and Rockne's head came in slowly. His eyes swept inquiringly over the squad—"Oh, excuse me, I made a mistake. I thought these were the quarters of the Notre Dame team." The door closed and Rockne was gone. Puzzled and then stung with fury, the team went out for the second half—and won the game.

Other writers, too, have explained the psychological methods used by Rockne and have told how the late Fielding Yost of Michigan, Dan McGugin of Vanderbilt, Herbert Crisler of Princeton, and dozens of others, used the "magic" of suggestion to arouse their teams to great emotional heights.

Before the Rose Bowl game of 1934, the "wise" tipsters rated the Columbia team as "underdogs." They reckoned without Coach Lou Little and his stirring talks to his players day after day. The game started and everyone knew that Columbia "was in there." When the whistle blew for the end of the game, the Columbia men were the top dogs over the "superior" Stanford team.

In 1935 Gonzaga University beat powerful Washington State 13 to 6 in one of the most upsetting games ever seen in the West. Gonzaga was a non-conference team, while the Washington State team, because of its great record, was thought to be unbeatable. Newspaper stories at the time reported Sam Dagley, assistant coach, as having declared that Gonzaga played inspired football, and he revealed that Coach Mike Pecarovich for half an hour before the game played "over and over" a phonograph record of one of Rockne's most rousing pep talks.

Mickey Cochrane of the Detroit Tigers a number of years ago literally drove a second-division-minded group of baseball players to the top of the American League by using the same power of the repeated suggestion. I quote from a newspaper dispatch: "Day after day, through the hot, hard grind, he [Cochrane] preached the gospel of victory, impressing on the Tigers the 'continued thought' that the team which wins must go forward."

You see the same force actively at work in the fluctuations of the stock market. Unfavorable news immediately depresses prices, while favorable news raises them. Intrinsic values of stocks are not changed, but there is an immediate change in the thinking of the market operators, which is reflected at once in the minds of the holders. It is not what will actually happen, but what security holders believe will happen that causes them to buy or sell.

In the depression years—and there may be years like them in the future—we saw this same suggestive force working overtime. Day after day we heard the expressions, "Times are hard," "Business is poor," "The banks are failing," "Prosperity hasn't a chance," and wild stories about business failures on every hand, until they became the national chant, and millions believed that prosperous days would never return. Hundreds, yes thousands, of strong-willed men go down under the constant hammering, the continuous tap, tapping of the same fear vibratory thoughts. Money, always sensitive, runs to cover when fear suggestions begin to circulate, and business failures and unemployment follow quickly. We hear thousands of stories of bank failures, huge concerns going to the wall, etc., and people believe them readily and act accordingly.

There will never be another business depression if people generally realize that it is with their own fear thoughts that they literally create hard times. They think hard times, and hard times follow. So it is with wars. When peoples of the world stop thinking depressions and wars, they will become non-existent, for nothing comes into our economic scheme unless we first create it with our emotionalized thinking.

Dr. Walter Dill Scott, eminent psychologist and long president of Northwestern University, told the whole story when he said: "Success or failure in business is caused more by mental attitudes even than by mental capacities."

Human beings are human beings the world over, all subject to the same emotions, the same influences, and the same vibrations, and what is a big business, a village, a city, a nation but merely a collection of individual humans controlling and operating it with their thinking and believing? As individuals think and believe, so they are. As a whole city of them thinks, so it is; and as a nation of them think, so it is. This is an inescapable conclusion. Every person is the creation of himself, the image of his own thinking and believing. As King Solomon put it, "For as he thinketh in his heart, so *is* he."

Recall the panic on the night of October 20, 1938, when Orson Welles and his Mercury Theater players put on the air a dramatization of H. G. Wells' novel, The War of the Worlds. It was a story of an invasion by some strange warriors from the planet Mars, but it caused fright among millions of people. Some rushed out-of-doors, police stations were besieged, eastern telephone exchanges were blocked, New Jersey highways were clogged. In fact, for a few hours following the broadcast, there was genuine panic among millions of listeners because they believed our earth was being attacked by invaders from Mars. Yes, indeed, belief can and does cause some strange and unusual happenings.

Rallies held in schools and colleges just before important athletic contests are based on the same principles— speeches, songs, and yells become the means of creating suggestion and arousing the will to win. Many sales managers employ the same principle in their morning sales meetings when frequently music from an orchestra, radio, or phonograph is used to emotionalize the salesmen and to get the idea over to them that they can beat all their previous sales records. The same principle with varying technique is basic in the army—in fact, in all armies. The commands and formations constantly repeated in close-order drill develop in the men instant obedience, which ultimately becomes instinctive; the commands and formations become so fixed in their minds and bodies that their movements are almost automatic—all of which in turn creates that self-confidence which is absolutely necessary in active conflict.

It is very important to remember that while the subconscious will get into action at once under the impetus of the commands or suggestions which it receives from the conscious mind, or which come from outside sources and are transmitted to it via the conscious mind, it gets results quicker if the conscious mind accompanies its message with a mental picture of the desired goal. It may be faint, sketchy, or even unfinished, but even if it is only an outline, it will be sufficient for the subconscious to act upon.

And this brings us to rituals and ceremonies which are performed amid dramatic settings in churches and secret orders, all designed to appeal to the emotions and to create a mystical picture in the minds of the beholders. These rituals, no matter what the setting, are there to hold your attention and to link the hidden meanings of these symbols with the particular ideas that are to be implanted in your mind. Various fighting arrangements, different paraphernalia, often a special garb for those directing the operations, all to the accompaniment of soft, often religious, music, help to create a mystical, or what some term a spooky, atmosphere in order to put you in the proper emotional, and incidentally receptive, state. The idea is as old as history. Not only the most civilized peoples but also the most primitive savage tribes have their characteristic ceremonials. Similar methods for impressing the individual are employed at mediumistic séances and crystal-gazing performances; even the gypsy phrenologist considers it a part of her "props."

Without this atmosphere, which tends to make our conscious mind drowsy and even temporarily puts it to sleep, we would not be so easily convinced, for the desire to satisfy completely our longings for the mystical and miraculous is often not sufficient by itself to permit conviction.

This is not said with any idea of being sacrilegious, but to present a picture of the historic method of appealing to the masses, and to point out how awakening and stirring their emotional interest prepares the way to approach their reasoning mind. Appeal by drama is the first step in arousing the emotions of the people, no matter for what purpose.

Could the late Aimee Semple McPherson, she with the long flowing white robe and picturesque auburn hair-do, have put over her great act of saving souls as well as achieving healings, without her superb understanding of the power of the dramatic? It's something to wonder about, because Billy Sunday in his best table-sliding act was a novice compared to Aimee when it came to showmanship or a matter of plain impressiveness. She with her many artifices and stage settings put on a most solemn performance, and her followers, on the Pacific Coast at least, declare that the results she got were real and lasting. This is no reflection on the memory of Mrs. McPherson, for her followers were very sincere and believed in her work, her teachings, and the results—and that's all that matters.

However, there are men and women with strong personal magnetism, and great orators, who can get the same emotional effect without "props" or stage setting to aid them. They are masters of tone effects, emotional appeal, gesticulations, bodily movements, eye magnetism, etc., by which your attention is held and you yourself are thrown wide open to their driving appeal.

Let's consider charms, talismans, amulets, good-luck pieces, four-leaf clovers, old horseshoes, a rabbit's foot, and countless other trinkets which thousands of people believe in. By themselves, they are inanimate harmless objects without power, but when people breathe life into them by their thinking they do have power, even though the power isn't in them per se. The power comes only with the believing—which alone makes them effective.

Two outstanding illustrations of this are found in the stories of Alexander the Great and Napoleon. In Alexander's day, an oracle proclaimed that whoever unloosened the Gordian knot would become ruler of all Asia. Alexander, as you may remember, with one stroke of his sword cut the knot—and rose to tremendous heights and power. Napoleon was given a star sapphire when a child, with the prophecy that it would bring him luck and some day make him Emperor of France. Could it have been anything but the supreme belief in the prophecy that carried these two great men to a place in the hall of fame? They became supermen because they had supernormal beliefs.

A cracked or broken mirror isn't going to bring you bad luck unless you believe in it, and as long as the belief is fertilized, nurtured, and made a part of your inner self, it's going to bring you bad luck—believe it or not, because the subconscious mind always brings to reality what it is led to believe. One of our presidential candidates of a few years back, a man of high attainment and regarded by many as a man of great intelligence, was pictured as standing before the door of his barn above which was nailed an old good-luck horseshoe. The story goes that it was upside down. He was defeated. However, I mention this chiefly to show that beliefs in charms and symbols are not confined to simple, naturally superstitious people, but are frequently held by even the most enlightened.

It is claimed that there are people with certain mind powers which, when directed at plant life, such as grain, vegetables, flowers, and trees, can make them grow more abundantly. A number of years ago we had an old Swiss gardener who insisted that we replace in our yard a number of small trees and shrubs. At first I couldn't see the reason for digging up the old ones and replanting others, but the old man's insistence prevailed. I observed that in planting them, just after he got the small trees in the soil and covered the roots, he engaged in some sort of audible Mumbo Jumbo. He did the same with the shrubs. One day, my curiosity piqued, I asked him what he was "mumbling about" as he placed the trees and shrubs in the ground. He looked at me searchingly for a moment, then said: "You may not understand, but I'm talking to them, telling them they must live and bloom. It's something I learned when I was a boy from my teacher in the old country, Switzerland. Anything that grows should have encouragement and I'm giving it to them."

It is a long way from Switzerland to British Columbia, but in that Canadian province is a tribe of Indians, the members of which always talk to their halibut and salmon lines, hooks, and so forth, before actually starting to fish, claiming that if they didn't, the fish wouldn't bite. Many are the tales of South Sea Islanders who offer food to their tools and implements, talking to them as though they were alive, and beseeching them to get results. It isn't a great jump from those customs to the blessings offered at ship launchings or at sailing times of large fishing fleets in all civilized countries even today, where prayers are offered for successful voyages or ventures.

Observers have often declared that there appears to be a kind of affinity between certain humans and plants, which the plants seem to feel. There are thousands of professional gardeners who will plant seeds only at certain times of the moon. Superstition, you say? Perhaps it is practical mysticism. The Yale investigators referred to previously have also concluded that electrical fields play a major part in plant life, and certainly that is scientific.

When I think of those who plant only at certain times of the moon, I recall a thrifty neighbor of mine who, although a man of intelligence and mature years, had his hair cut at only certain times of the moon. I don't remember whether it was when the moon was waxing or waning that he would visit the barber, but whatever the phase of the moon, the time he selected, he maintained, caused his hair to grow less abundantly than if he had it cut at other times. I asked him once where he got such an idea and he glared at me as though I were belittling his intelligence. I never did get an answer to my question.

What has been said about plant and animal life may cause a lot of materialistic people to take violent issue, but it must be remembered that there are many forces at work in the world of which we know little or nothing. Consider how many new principles were developed in World War II. As this is written, the American Rocket Society has made application to the United States Government for land on the moon. Perhaps the application was made in a spirit of facetiousness, but who knows when some "Buck Rogers" will pilot a rocket plane to the moon? I, for one, wouldn't say it couldn't be done some day, for I don't know and neither do those who say it is impossible.

Without question human imagination or visualization and concentration are the chief factors in developing the magnetic forces of the subconscious mind. You have often heard the statement, "Hold the picture," and that, of course, means holding the mental picture or vision. Here again is where suggestion—repeated suggestion—plays its part. For example, you would like a new home and your imagination goes to work. At first you have only a hazy idea of the kind of house you would like. Then, as you discuss it with other members of your family or ask questions of builders or look at illustrations of new houses, the picture becomes clearer and clearer, until you visualize the house in all its particulars. After that the subconscious mind goes to work to provide you with that house. It may come into manifestation in any number of ways. You may build it with your own hands, or it may come to you through purchase or from the actions of outsiders. Its manner of coming is of no great consequence.

The process is the same when you are after a better job or planning a vacation trip. You've got to see it in your mind's eye, see yourself as holding that job, or actually taking the trip. Some of our fears become realities through our imaginations, just as Job's did. Fortunately, many of them do not, if we hold the mental picture only temporarily, or at least not long enough to have it focused fully upon the screen of our subconscious. The Biblical warning, "Where there is no vision, the people perish," is a fundamental truth, whether it be considered individually or collectively. For without the mental picture of accomplishment, little is done. You want a better job? You'll get it when you give your subconscious mind a mental picture of yourself holding that job.

As I write this, I think of the many experiences related to me by those who have used this science during the years, and I want to give you some of the stories, for in them you may perhaps find clues to an even more effective use of the principles and the mechanics of applying them, which I am setting forth.

A friend got the idea of building a boat. He knew nothing about boat construction, but believed that with some simple instructions he could build one. So he went ahead. In the course of the construction he found that he needed an electric drill, but he didn't want to spend $75 or $80 for the kind he wanted, especially when it would be used only a few months. First, he tried renting a drill, but inasmuch as it could be used only at night and had to be returned early the next morning, he found such an arrangement very inconvenient.

Then he told me: "I got thinking one night that somewhere there was a drill for me and I would have it placed in my hands. The more I thought about it, the more I thought it possible. However, nothing happened for several days; then one evening a friend who owned a sizable garage—a man I hadn't seen for a couple of years—came to see me. He, too, was interested in boats, and hearing that I was building one, said he'd like to look it over. He saw me floundering around with the heavy half-inch drill I was using and asked me where I got it. I told him I had rented it and he laughed, saying, 'Come over to the shop tomorrow and I'll lend you a smaller one which you can handle much easier.' Needless to say, I got it and kept it during all the period I was constructing the boat.

"A somewhat similar experience happened when I was cutting the ribs. I had a small jig saw, but found that it wouldn't cut through three-quarter-inch lumber. Then I found myself wishing for a band saw—that thought led me to a place a few blocks away from my house where I knew there was a woodworking shop. I could use the band saw if I paid the owner fifty cents an hour for its use. However, I found that I was running to and from my home, first to fit the ribs and then to shape them, and losing too much time in the process. I frequently said to myself during those days that there was some easier way to get the use of a band saw, and there was.

"The following Sunday another friend came to see how the boat was getting along and when I told him that I had been slowed down without the use of a band saw, he too laughed, saying, 'I bought one Thursday and I will not be using it for some little time. Got to get my shop fixed up and in the meantime you're welcome to use it.' As a matter of fact, he delivered it to me that same day and I kept it a number of months. I finished the boat!"

Another man told me the story of how he got the use of a thirty-foot extension ladder with which to paint his house. "I thought I would undertake the painting in my spare time," he told me, "and began looking around to find where I could get the use of a ladder. I found places where I could rent one, but they fixed time requirements which didn't fit into my plans. I don't know how many times I said to myself: You're going to find a ladder. And I did. It was Memorial Day, and while in my back yard I happened to notice that a neighbor across the street from me was using a long ladder to wash off the walls of his house. I called to him, asking where he got the ladder. He told me he had bought it when he purchased the house. That afternoon it was in my back yard, and I had the loan of it for several weeks!"

Another man told me that shortly after the United States entered the war, he wanted a garbage can of a certain size, but because of priorities he was unable to locate what he wanted. He said he visited second-hand stores, junk-shops, bakeries, and garages, in an endeavor to find the kind of container he wanted, but without success. He was about to give up hope when one morning he noticed workmen who were making repairs on a concrete building across from his home. They were using some waterproofing material from a can, exactly the kind of can he had pictured for his own use. He said he asked the man in charge of the work what would be done with the container when the work was finished and he was told that it would be left on the ground to be hauled away. He then explained his wants, and a couple of days later the container was in his garage—the workmen had not only emptied it but had washed and scrubbed it before delivery!

I had taken my car to a shop owner for repairs to the ignition system, after several had failed to locate the trouble. I told him how the car had been acting, and after listening he said, "I believe I can fix it." I casually remarked, "Belief is a great thing, isn't it?"

"You bet it is. Thought is the greatest force in the world and the dumb ducks laugh when you talk about it," he answered rather caustically.

"I don't, I'm interested," I replied. "Tell me of some instances where you have demonstrated the power of thought."

"I could keep you here all day telling you of its power—at least in my own life."

"Tell me a few. When did you first become aware of it?"

"Oh, I guess about twelve years ago when I fell and broke my back. I was in a cast for a long time and the doctors told me that even if I recovered I would be crippled the rest of my life. As I lay on my back in the hospital worrying about my future, I frequently thought of the words used by my mother to the effect that 'One just has to believe.' One day it dawned on me that if I could hold on to the mental picture I was going to be all right, and if I believed in it sufficiently, I could get well. To make a long story short, here I am crawling over and underneath cars, and far from being a cripple as you can see for yourself."

"Very interesting. Tell me of more cases," I urged.

"Well, I've used it frequently to get more business. As a matter of fact, this present location is a result of it. As you know, I was burned out at my old place a few weeks ago and, owing to the war, space like this in the city is well-nigh impossible to find. For two or three days, worrying about my possible inability to get another location, I deliberated whether I should attempt to continue with the business or go to work for someone else. Then one night I made up my mind I would continue in business for myself. That was the turning point, and just before I went to sleep I said to myself, 'Oh, you'll find a place within the next few days. This thought power hasn't failed you yet.' I went to sleep with full confidence that the place would be forthcoming. The very next day I went over to see the painter where I had taken the car I saved from the fire, and mentioned that I was looking for another place. 'That's funny,' he commented, 'you can rent this space, for I've just bought the building in the next block from an owner who wanted to retire.' And here I am on a main thoroughfare and with more business than I can possibly handle!"

I know that some readers will say that these are merely coincidences, but my files are filled with similar "coincidences." To some of you they may be just that, but those who are acquainted with this science know that these things have come about as the result of intensified thought or mental picture-making. However, we come again to a matter of opinion—the difference in conclusions between those who think this is all nonsense and those who know that the things we think materialize after their kind.

Again we are reminded of what Paracelsus said: "Men who are devoid of the power of spiritual perception are unable to recognize anything that cannot be seen externally."

It is pretty well agreed that the subconscious mind works as a result of images thrown upon its screen, but if there is something wrong with your projection apparatus or the original slide, then the projected image is blurred, inverted, or a total blank. Doubts, fears, counterthoughts, all have a part in blurring the pictures you consciously desire to project.

Those who have well-developed imaginations, such as great artists, writers, and inventors, possess the ability to visualize or to make mental pictures almost at will. However, with the mechanics which will be enlarged upon later and the explanations already given, anyone following them should have no difficulty in being able to see in his mind's eye the things, objects, or situations as he desires them to be in reality.

One of the greatest fishermen I ever knew used this visualizing method. He could sit in a boat with one or two others and pull trout after trout out of the water, while his companions using the same kind of bait or fly and with apparently the same mechanical technique, cast or dropped their flies or hooks in the same places repeatedly, but without results. I asked him about it one time and he laughingly replied: "I put the old 'squeeza-ma-jintum' [his word for magic] on them. I figuratively or mentally get down there where they are, and tell them to hook the bait or fly. In other words, I see them snapping at the hook and believe that it will work. That's all I can give you in the way of an explanation."

This story was told to another fisherman not blessed with the first fisherman's luck, and he scoffed at it. "Ridiculous," he declared. "Any good fisherman must know the stream, the holes, the habits of fish, the type of bait or flies to use, and he'll catch them if they are there." However, he couldn't explain how others skilled in fishing technique could fish in an identical spot and still not catch them like the man who used the old "squeezama-jintum." The writer is not a fisherman, but surely if this law of attraction works in other ways, there is no reason why it could not be used advantageously in fishing.*

Now, let's go into the field of golf. For many years I was interested in the game and was a member of several clubs. I frequently played with a man who in his younger days had been one of the world's tennis champions. This man was one of the most amazing short-shot players on the Pacific

---

* Ben Hur Lampman, associate editor of The Oregonian, author of many articles and books on fishing and kindred subjects, twice an O. Henry Memorial Award winner, and a recognized naturalist, upon reading the foregoing said: "The man who says that it is ridiculous to consider your fishing friend as claiming there's some sort of magic or attraction at work when he catches fish where others fishing in the same spot get mediocre results, merely makes himself ridiculous by displaying his ignorance. I can't explain how your friend is always so fortunate in making his catches beyond saying that there is decidedly something psychic about successful fishing. Any one who has studied the habits of fish and tried to catch them sooner or later realizes that there is more to successful fishing than merely throwing a lure or bait into a place where the fish are supposed to be. Just what the relationship is between mind and fish—if any—I can not explain, but having been a student of fish, their ways and habits practically all my life, I do know that in successful fishing there is an unexplainable element or factor at work—call it what you please. I say it is something psychic and undoubtedly in the realm of psychic phenomena lies the explanation of the so-called fisherman's 'luck' or the 'squeeza-ma-jintum' or magic of your successful fisherman friend."

Coast. With his mashie or mashie niblick he could place the ball on any desired spot on the green with a dead stop, as close to or as far from the pin as he desired, and he was usually down in one putt. His putting, too, was an art to marvel at.

"How did you do it, George?" I asked him one day when he amazed everyone in our foursome with what could be called phenomenal shots. "Well," he replied, "you've played handball and squash, and you know what it means to place your shots on the front wall. You intuitively place it high or low or so it will rebound to a side wall or result in a kill or an extremely low ball. I learned placement years ago in tennis. You have sort of a mental picture where you want the ball to go or land before you hit it with your racquet or hand. I use the same principle with my short shots and putting. In other words, when I face the green and before I swing my club, I have an instant mental picture of where I want the ball to land, and when I putt I actually see the ball dropping into the hole. Of course, a proper stance, knowledge of handling the clubs, and so forth, are vital. But most golfers have that and still don't get results. It is true that I spend many hours in practice, so do others; but the main thing is that I just seem to know where the ball is going to land before the club hits it. There's a confidence or a belief existing that I can do it and with a mashie or mashie niblick I cause a backspin that will bring the ball to a dead stop when it lands."

For you who may raise your eyebrows at this, let's examine the facts given in a newspaper story written by the famous sports writer, Grantland Rice. It appeared in the middle 'thirties and had to do with the phenomenal amateur golf player, John Montagu. Rice declared that Montagu could run rings around anyone and that the ball always landed where he wanted to place it, whether 300 yards down the fairway or a chip shot to within two or three feet of the cup, and then when he putted it was like the crack of doom. Rice said that the ball went where Montagu wanted it to go. Now let's read Montagu's own explanation as given in the same newspaper story. He said: "Golf to me is played with the head, mind or brain or whatever you wish to call it. Of course, there are fundamentals of stance, grip, swing; but I must have a clear, clean mental picture of what I am doing before I play the shot. That mental picture takes charge of the muscular reaction. If there is no mental picture—what happens is a mere guess. This means almost endless concentration of thought if you are under pressure and there is no thrill in any game unless you are under pressure."

Gene Sarazen, who was one of the greatest golf professionals of all times, used similar methods in his matches, and if you read his little book *Golf Tips*, you will find that he has much to say about mental pictures, objectives, concentration, and confidence.

All golfers have heard of "mental hazards." In reality, they are bunkers, traps, water hazards, etc. But in the imaginations of many players they are formidable handicaps to put fear into the hearts of the players. On one course where the writer often played there was a water hole. The distance from the tee to the hole was about one hundred feet spanning a small lake or pond approximately fifty feet wide, an easy shot with a mashie or a mashie niblick for the average player. One member of the club who had been a great baseball and football player in his younger days, for a long time could never get over this water hazard. Invariably with his irons he would put ball after ball into the water, to the accompaniment of profanity on his part and laughter on ours. Finally, as the months went by he took to using his spoon and hitting the ball far beyond the green. One day I said to him, "I know, the water fools you, but the next time just blot out of your mind the picture that there is water between the tee and the green and see instead, mentally, an easy short fairway before you." The first time he followed the suggestion his ball fell a few inches from the pin, and from that time on, he later told me, as long as he followed the blotting-out technique, he never had any trouble; but when he was unable to concentrate on his own mental picture, due to the joshing from other members of his foursome, he landed into difficulties.

In observing many pool and billiard games, I am convinced that certain skilled players influence the direction and fall of the balls by mind control, although they may be completely in ignorance of the power they are using. If it can work on a golf ball, it certainly can work on a billiard ball.

Roy Chapman Andrews tells the story of a San Antonio, Texas, man, who with a twenty-two calibre rifle fired more than 14,500 shots at small blocks of wood tossed into the air without a single miss. Mr. Andrews emphasized perfect timing and remarkable accuracy. Nothing was said of the mindpictures; but if you have ever done any prolonged trap or target shooting, you know the part visualizing plays.

One finds the same sort of "magic" at work in all fields of sports. Great baseball batters, expert forward-passers in football, accurate drop-kickers—all consciously or unconsciously picture connecting with the ball and placing it where they want it to go. Certainly, practice, timing, and so forth, all have their primary importance, but the mental side must never be overlooked.

In this connection, I was impressed by several statements made by Dr. Marcus Bach in his recent book, They Have Found a Faith. Dr. Bach tells of bowling with Father Divine, and of observing from the way Father Divine selected a ball, and from his stance and delivery, that he was no bowler. Yet Father Divine made a strike on his first try and, according to Dr. Bach, it was one of the prettiest strikes he ever saw. Dr. Bach says: "Father's nonchalance was characteristic. He rubbed the soft palms of his hands together as if to say, 'Well, what do you expect when the Lord rolls one!'"* Again Dr. Bach speaks of an interview with Rickert Fillmore, manager of Unity City and son of one of the founders of the Unity movement, in which he asked if the works of Unity could be applied to a real estate venture. Mr. Fillmore replied, "If it works at all, it works everywhere."

Many readers of this book may not be golfers or billiard players, but here's a simple experiment that will demonstrate to you this strange power of attraction through visualizing or making the mental picture actually work. Find a few small stones or pebbles which you can easily throw and locate a tree or a post of six to ten inches in diameter. Stand away from it twenty-five or thirty feet or any convenient greater distance and start throwing the pebbles in an endeavor to hit it. If you are an average person, most of the stones will go wide of their mark. Now stop and tell yourself that you can hit the objective. Get a mental picture of

* From They Have Found a Faith by Marcus Bach, Copyright, 1946. Used by special permission of the Publishers, The Bobbs-Merrill Company.

the tree figuratively stepping forward to meet the missile or of the stone actually colliding with the tree in the spot where you want it to strike, and you'll soon find yourself making a perfect score. Don't say it's impossible. Try it and you'll prove that it can be done—if you will only believe it.

In the early days of wartime gasoline rationing when most people didn't consider getting additional coupons a criminal offense, a friend found he didn't have enough gas to take him to his duck lake. One Sunday while in his home he told me how he had secured sufficient coupons to make several trips to the shooting grounds. Said he: "I had just about given up the idea of duck shooting this fall when the thought occurred to me that I could put this Mind Stuff to work and get some more gas. Of course, everyone around the office knew that I wanted to go duck shooting and most of them knew of my problem. Whether they passed out word to their friends I do not know, but I got more coupons than you could shake a stick at. I had a constant picture of going hunting and using my automobile and of someone giving me coupons. It may be hooey, but I got the gasoline coupons. Even a farmer friend gave me gas out of his allotment."

Now let's take this same science into the kitchen. Did it ever occur to you that the so-called good cooks use this same science, some consciously and others unconsciously? Two people can attempt to make the same kind of pie. Identical ingredients will be used and instructions followed to the letter—one will be a failure while the other will be the last word in culinary achievement. Why? In the first case, the one cook approaches pie-making with trepidation. She knows she has had pie failures in the past and wonders how this one is going to come out. She doesn't have a perfect mental picture of an appetite-satisfying golden brown crust with a wonderful zestful filling. She's upset and nervous, and, without her knowing it, her uneasiness is communicated to her pie-making. The second one knows that she knows that the pie is going to be "tops"—and it is. That primary mental picture—her belief—makes it so.

If you are a mediocre cook and you like to cook—that's a very necessary requisite too—sell yourself on the idea that you can prepare superior dishes and you can do it, for you have the forces inside of you and they will come to your aid if you will only believe in them and call upon them. So put your heart and soul into the next pie you make and even you will be surprised at the result when you see the realization of your mental picture of the perfect pie.

The same law will work no matter where it is applied, and that goes for everything from fishing to money-making or success in business. Let's take an example out of the war. General Douglas MacArthur declared when he left the Philippines: "I shall return." With our Pacific Fleet in ruins at Pearl Harbor, practically no airplanes or transports at the time, and with the Japanese in control of most of the South Pacific, MacArthur had no physical evidence that he would ever return. However, he must have had a mental picture of his return or he would have never made the statement. It was a statement of confidence or belief, and history relates his triumphant return. Thousands of similar cases happened during the war and are happening today.

Chapter 4

The author opens this chapter with an assertion about the power of your beliefs. He speaks of the great reserves that exist in your subconscious mind, and shares every examples of where ritual and repetition have played a significant role in affecting the behaviors of the masses. He takes us on a short journey through history, showing how the power of suggestion has been used to create great shifts in humankind throughout the ages. He shares examples of mind power from political leadership to athletic coaching success; from business leadership pioneering to successful sales campaigns. He shares how important imagination, visualization and concentration are in enhancing your ability to manifest your desires into your life. He takes you through an exercise in visualization, and shares powerful anecdotes of how others have successfully used their to manifest wonders into their lives.

1. Bristol opens this chapter asserting that if you believe you can do something, then it will be done perfectly. Do you believe this to be true? Why or why not? Please explain.

2. Have you ever believed you could do something and failed? If so, what do you think happened?

3. According to the author, once you have a belief, the power to assist you then follows. Have you ever had a situation where you felt you were not qualified to do a certain task, but were then overcome with a sense of *"I can do this!"* Thereafter, the task was completed quickly and with ease? Please explain. If not, why do you believe you haven't had such an experience?

4. The author uses the example of great orators who are often amazed at how the subconscious mind furnishes

them with a steady flow of thoughts. List one or more orators that you admire. Then do some research on how they became such powerful speakers. Was this miraculous access to information a part of their experience? Explain.

5. Thought repetition in the spiritual realm is referenced as *"white magic."* Bristol emphasizes that sound vibration stimulates and emotionalizes individuals to the point where they can even defy death. Do you believe in such phenomenon? Why or why not? Please explain.

6. The law of suggestion is exemplified in prescribed rituals, such as repeated mantras or prayers that are practiced in religions, cults and orders. List the rituals or repeated practices that you experience in your life.

7. Autosuggestion is suggestion that is your own, in which you are the source. What autosuggestions do you practice?

8. Often the thoughts that we think are repeated and automatic. Unfortunately, very often those thoughts are negative. For one hour, pay attention to the thoughts in your head and list them on paper. How many are positive? How many are negative? How many are thoughts that you often repeat to yourself?

9. Heterosuggestions come to you from outside sources. Reflect on which heterosuggestions you receive on an ongoing basis. Write them down and note whether or not they are positive or negative.

10. Do you watch the news and a lot of television? If so, what are you watching? Are the contents mostly positive or negative? If a great deal of the contents is negative, consider abstaining from watching it for at least a week. Then note any changes in your thoughts and feelings.

11. Do you consciously practice positive affirmations? If so, do you note any results? If not, consider a positive

affirmation that you could repeat to yourself for at least 28 days. Practice is regularly and note any shifts in your thoughts or feelings. Write about your experience.

12. Bristol cites Hitler and his ability to build up the German people to attack the world as an example of the power of suggestion. Hitler openly stated that the psychology of suggestion was a terrible weapon in the hands of anyone who knew how to use it. He used flags, signs, plastered posters of himself throughout Germany. He used slogans, songs, billboards, radio and the press to hypnotize the masses. Write a list of present day initiatives that use these same tactics to affect the masses.

13. Have you ever used any of these tactics to promote yourself or something you believed in? If so, what did you do and was it effective? Please explain.

14. Joseph Stalin was a mass hypnotist who was named as one of the ten persons with the *"Most hypnotic eyes in the world."* Have you ever been in the presence of such a powerful hypnotist? If so, describe their power and how they swayed your thoughts and beliefs.

15. Bristol explains that the power of hypnosis can be used for both good and evil. List ways in which you have noted it being used for evil through history and into present day.

16. List ways in which you note hypnosis being used for good through history and into present day.

17. Thought repetition is often used in advertising. Make note of popular advertisements throughout your life that come to mind. Were they using repetition as a means of influence? If so, explain how. If not, what do you believe made them so impactful?

18. According to the author, *"babies only have two fears: the fear of loud noises and the fear of falling."* He claims that *"our fears come with knowledge or develop as a result of our experiences: they come from what we are taught or*

what we hear and see." Do you believe this to be true? If so, what is the evidence of it in your life?

19. There has been research done with tribes that have been in isolation and have not been exposed to the thoughts and beliefs of the rest of the world. In these tribes children were given a great deal of freedom, almost from birth. They often played near deep wells, however they never fell in. The argument of the researcher was that they were not conditioned to fear falling in. In your opinion, does this theory align with Bristol's theory referenced in #18? Why or why not?

20. The bible is filled with examples of the power of thought and suggestion. Moses, David (of David and Goliath), and Joan of Arc were each potent examples of such power. Can you think of modern day versions of how the power of suggestion is used by leaders to bring good into the world? If so, list them and describe how they use this tool.

21. According to William James, *"often our faith [belief] in advance of a doubtful undertaking is the only thing that can assure its successful conclusion. Man's faith acts on the power above him as a claim and creates its own verification."* What does he mean by it *"acts on the power above him as a claim and creates its own verification"*?

22. The author shares stories about the famous Notre Dame coach, Knute Rockne and how he aroused his teams to great emotional heights, often through the repetition of his pep talks. Have you ever been coached by such an inspiring and powerful person? If so, describe how. If not, which coaches come to mind?

23. Claude Bristol also cites the power of the repeated negative media messages during the great depression. Consider more recent financial downturns and how they were repeatedly portrayed in the media. Do you believe the portrayal had an effect on the negative outcome? Please explain.

24. The author asserts, *"when the world stops thinking depressions and wars, they will become non-existent, for nothing comes into our economic scheme unless we first create it with our emotionalized thinking."* Do you believe this statement to be true? Please explain.

25. Can you imagine a world without wars? Do you believe that if you can imagine it, it can happen? If so take 2 minutes each day for at least a month, and imagine a world that is free of wars. Write about your experience.

26. Dr. Walter Dill Scott said *"Success or failure in business is caused more by mental attitudes even than by mental capacities."* On a scale from one to ten (one being "very little" and ten being "a great deal"), rate how much you believe your thoughts have attributed to the successes or failures you experienced in business.

1———2———3———4———5———6——— —7———8———9———10

27. Bristol asserts *"As individuals think and believe, so they are. As a whole city of them thinks, so it is; and as a nation of them think, so it is. This is an inescapable conclusion."* What messages are prominent in your city? What messages are prominent in your nation? Do these messages resonate within you as well?

28. What messages do you want to resound in your city? Nation? List them.

29. When Orson Wells presented the H.G Wells radio show, *War of the Worlds,* he created mass hysteria. His performances were so powerful, they convinced thousands to believe that they were real. Have you ever experienced something that was a performance, yet was so real that it profoundly impacted you? If so, write about your experience and why you thought it was so powerful.

30. The author stresses that you get quicker results if your conscious mind accompanies its message with a mental picture of the desired goal. Thus *"rituals and ceremonies*

which are performed amid dramatic settlings appeal to the emotions." Props like symbols and potent music are used to further stir emotions. List three situations that stirred you most in your life. What were the elements involved? Were they dramatic? Powerful? Was music involved in any way? What made them so powerful?

31. The author makes reference to the phenomenon of superstition. An example being that a broken mirror will bring you bad luck. Do you avoid walking under a ladder, or throw salt behind your shoulder if the shaker falls on the table? These are examples of popular superstitions. Are you superstitious? If so, how?

32. Bristol makes reference to a Swiss friend who spoke to his plants in order to make them grow healthier and faster. Do you do such things? Do you believe that they work? Why or why not?

33. While the tenets of this book are timeless and universal, the author makes reference to man piloting a rocket to the moon someday. What "someday" visions do you have for humankind when you think of the evolution of consciousness? Write about them.

34. One of Bristol's friends shared a story that he imagined seeing the drill that he needed in his hands, and soon after an old friend visited and ended up lending him a drill at no cost. The author shares other similar stories.

Have you ever experienced such synchronicities? If so, describe them. If not, why do you believe you have not?

35. The author shares the stories of his auto mechanic and how he experienced several instances where his needs manifested when he needed them to. Of course, he believed in the power of his mind. Has your own belief in the power of your mind ever disappointed you? If so, please explain.

36. Paracelsus said, *"Men who are devoid of the power of spiritual perception are unable to recognize anything that cannot be seen externally."* Who are the greatest skeptics that you know? List them. Do they struggle with manifesting their desires in their lives? Please explain.

37. The author cites many instances where athletes use the power of their minds to gain success at their sport. What sports do you enjoy the most? Have you ever used the power of your mind when enjoying the sport? If so, please explain. If not, why not? Next time you play, be sure to practice seeing the outcome that you wish to produce. Write about your experience.

38. One golfer claimed that the mental picture in his head took charge of his muscular reaction. This sounds scientific. Does this statement make sense to you? Why or why not. Please explain.

39. During a golf game, the author encouraged a friend to blot out the water trap from his mind when making his shot. It worked. What technique do you use with the "water traps" that arise in your mind? Explain.

40. The author references the studies of Dr. Bach and several instances where he noted mind power at work. Whether making a pie or winning at war, the mind has extraordinary power. Write about the most poignant way in which you used your mind power to create change in your life.

Chapter 5

The Art of Mental Pictures

When I was in the investment banking business, one of the salesmen, a young chap, came into my office for advice.

"I wish you would tell me how I can overcome my fear of _____. I know I can sell him if I can get in to see him and talk with him on his own level. As it stands, he's got the life scared out of me and every other salesman."

The man the salesman referred to is a millionaire with a very imposing office organization. He is a portly type, with a heavy shock of hair and beetle-browed; because of his growling manner, he easily scares timid folks. However, I knew he liked people who talked up to him.

The salesman had been picturing this man as he saw him and momentarily I was puzzled, but the answer soon came and I said: "You know he's not going to hurt you physically. Suppose you saw him at the beach in a bathing suit, you wouldn't be afraid of him there, would you, even though he did appear to be a pretty hairy fellow?"

"Certainly not," replied the salesman. Then the idea of a hairy body came to me and I asked the salesman: "Bob, did you ever see one of those clownish dancing bears, tied to a grind organ, wearing a fez or a dunce cap? You know they can growl, but most of them are toothless and can't bite."

"Sure," responded the salesman.

"Well, you have an imagination. Just picture our friend as one of those harmless old bears, fez, collar, and all, and the mental hazard is gone, isn't it?"

The salesman, laughing heartily, went out. A few days later he sold the man $20,000 worth of securities, and this executive may still be wondering how the young salesman ever got in to see him, to say nothing of selling him. At last accounts, the young fellow was still selling this wealthy man.

A couple of weeks later the same salesman was back in my office, telling me how he had used similar methods in making another sale, this time to a gruff old man who wore white whiskers, had a patriarchal and stern appearance, and used a vitriolic tongue that was feared by most salesmen.

"That old goat had me buffaloed for a long time. I knew he had money, but every time I passed his store and saw him scowling—he was always scowling—I couldn't get up courage to go in and tackle him. A few days ago I got thinking of the picture-making plan you told me to use on _____ and the idea popped into my head of a picture of Santa Claus. I said to myself, 'Sure, the old goat could be Santa Claus and who's afraid of that kindly old boy?' Well, it worked there too. The old man was swell to me—sort of flattered that a young fellow like me dared approach him. I got a $5000 order out of him and he told me to come back next week as he wanted to go over his whole security list with me. That means more business."

There are many men holding executive positions who assume an importance that causes some people to hold them in awe. With their elaborate office surroundings and their numerous secretaries and clerks, they put on a show that proves impressive to some people. Just bear in mind that these executives are mere human beings with the same fears, the same frailties, the same faults that are common to millions; at home they are often docile little souls. When you do this and picture them as they really are, rather than as they appear or pretend to be, the mental hazard immediately disappears. The genuinely great man is usually easy to approach and seldom barricades himself from callers. If you are a salesman, this should give you a clue to how to eliminate the mental hazards that crop up when you call upon someone who puts on a show of being superior.

A lawyer told me of an experience that nicely illustrates my point.

"I once found myself pitted against a lawyer who had a great reputation and was generally feared by younger men. For a little while in the courtroom, I admit I was frightened, but I closed my eyes and said to myself, 'I'm just as good as he is; as a matter of fact, I'm better. I can lick him and I will.' I repeated words and phrases like that for several seconds and when I opened my eyes, I could have licked two like him. I now go through the same little ritual whenever I get a tough case or the jury doesn't look favorable. Maybe it's luck, maybe it's all illusory, but it always works."

People who act and appear hard-boiled are usually "softies at heart, and once an interviewer eliminates the mental hazard, he has licked the situation. Take a couple of deep breaths the next time you call on one, convince yourself he'll be a "push-over," and he will.

During the depression days of the 'thirties, a group of managers and assistant managers, including the butchers of a large grocery chain store, came on their initiative to me for help. After a six weeks' course of lectures, the men decided to put the lectures into effect. It was agreed that each store one day a week would use the science I had expounded to push the sale of certain items. After considerable debate, among the items selected for the test were cheese, rolled roasts, salmon, and just plain Hubbard squash. (The manager of a store in one of the outlying districts had said he could make a good buy of squash from a farmer customer.) The day before each sale the managers carefully coached their clerks to make a mental picture of each customer coming into their stores and buying the selected items. Of course, prominent displays were made of each item, and each clerk was instructed to think of selling the special item during the day whenever a customer appeared. The results were astounding. The store specializing in cheese sold more cheese in that one day than had passed over the counter in a six months' period; the shop which on Saturday specialized in the rolled roasts had them sold before noon; the store which on Friday had featured fresh salmon sold more salmon than all the other stores of the group combined; the one where squash had been selected had to call upon the farmer twice during the day to replenish the supply.

Today, with only one exception and he is a war casualty, each man who took the lecture course is either in business for himself or has a much better job. As a matter of fact, one of the men now owns three stores of his own, while another is manager of a chain of stores in a neighboring state.

I think of a recent conversation with the head of a large Pacific Coast advertising agency, who for a number of years handled the sales promotion work for a well-known coffee manufacturer who had recently sold his business.

"If there was ever a man who used this stuff to tremendous advantage," declared the advertising executive, "it was old man _____. He came to this section as a kid and learned the coffee roasting and blending business. He concluded that he could do better if he were in business for himself. He thoroughly believed that he could blend the best coffee, and even up to the time of his retirement, after years in the business, he thoroughly believed that his coffee was the best on the market. Of course, that belief made a millionaire of the old man."

Once I had given a printer a small manuscript that I wanted to get out in pamphlet form which dealt with the subject we are now considering. The next morning he popped into my office, almost out of breath and visibly shaking. Naturally, I asked if there were anything wrong, and he spluttered: "Just had the oddest experience. I took your manuscript home last night and read it, and I said to myself, 'If the stuff actually works as the author claims, then I ought to be able to find a parking space close to his office when I go to see him.' I thought no more about it until I was driving from our plant to your office just a few minutes ago, and then the thought again occurred to me that it might work. Well, I turned the corner and there wasn't a space to be seen on Sixth Avenue, and I was going to dismiss it all as bunk. But as I slowed down to let some pedestrians pass, I saw a machine pull away from the curb right in front of this building and there was my place. It gives me goose-pimples. Maybe it's just one of those things."

"Perhaps," I said, "but why not try it again?"

He did, and had similar results over a period of years. Call them coincidences if you like. But this printer never would, especially when shortly afterward he was able to more than treble his business while most printers were having a difficult time to get any orders.

Now and then I told acquaintances about the experiences of the printer and I was astounded to learn that others seemed able to find parking space as had this printer. One woman, a Unity student, told me that she and her sister never drove downtown without saying that they would find a parking space in or near a spot that they desired—and they always found it.

A woman, a dietician and instructor in a large hospital, said to me: "The working of this power, or whatever it is, often frightens me. As an illustration, this happens with continued frequency. Every morning on my way to work when I enter the business section, the traffic lights always turn green and I get through all of them without a stop. I cannot recall the time that the lights have shown red against me. Now I just take it all as a matter of course." A few months ago a woman was arrested for violating the traffic signals, but according to the newspaper stories at the time, she convinced the judge that the green light was on when she crossed the intersection. She was a motherly woman and the judge freed her when she told him, "Judge, the light just had to be green, and it always is for me because I keep repeating as I near an intersection 'Green light be on, green light be on.'"

The police maintained, however, that there were no signals at this intersection—only the flashing intermittent red light. But here was the motherly old lady convincing the judge of her belief, and obviously she believed in her ability to have the signals the way she wanted them.

A woman told me of an automobile trip made from Washington, D. C., to join her husband who had been assigned to duty in a Pacific Coast city. "I was frightened in the beginning," she said. "I had never driven any such distance alone in my life. One day I got thinking of my grandmother who had been one of the pioneers to the Pacific Northwest and who had done many things alone. My fear was gone at once. However, the garage man who looked over my car before I started told me not to go without getting new tires; he said the old ones would blow out any time. If I hadn't been so intent on making the trip and without delay, I might have listened to him; but the thought again came to me that they would last until I got across the country—and last they did. While I do not use the car much now, the original tires are still there, though in pretty bad shape. But no blowouts ever occurred."

Another case that reinforces my contention involves an oil refining company and more than a million dollars of investors' money. In its early days the company experienced great financial difficulties brought on by suits and marketing problems, and it became necessary to reorganize the whole financial structure, with the security holders taking new securities but foregoing interest for a number of years. The stockholders were told to make a mental picture of the oil turning into money and coming from every still and every spigot—in short, to visualize the company as a money-maker. Incidentally, this company was in a field dominated by strongly intrenched major companies. Nevertheless, not only did the company become a substantial money-maker, but it was subsequently sold and all the security holders got back their money with interest in full.

Jimmy Gribbo, well known to sports fans as a manager of prizefighters, has made winners out of many boxers by teaching them how to visualize themselves as winners—and they became winners.

The writer is aware that some of his readers, especially those who know nothing about Mind Stuff, will question these stories but those who related them are of undoubted veracity, and the writer also thinks that there are many of his readers who from their own experiences could relate much stranger tales.

G. N. M. Tyrrell, a well-known English investigator and writer, declares that if while dwelling upon the activity of the subconscious mind we determine upon an intention to do a certain thing, we may subconsciously initiate a train of events likely to bring this thing about. The statement is credited to Dr. Shailer Mathews, long associated with the University of Chicago, "that we influence events by very great desires, and there is psychological proof on ourselves of the effects of our own desires."

Here are two cases directly in point.

The woman head of a large antique shop, a recognized authority on antiques whose advice concerning them was much sought after by other women, happened to dislike social activities. She was constantly bothered by a woman to accompany her to luncheons and teas. This second woman merely wanted to be seen in the company of this authority on antiques, and invitation after invitation had been declined by the authority. A well-known lecturer was scheduled to talk before a woman's club, and under the insistent pleas of the second woman the head of the antique shop finally agreed to go with her.

"She caught me in an off moment," she told me, "and no sooner had I agreed than I began to regret that I had made the promise to go. I hate those would-be highbrow affairs and this was going to be one, I was certain. Actually at night I would have cold sweats thinking about what I had done and how I could get out of going without offending the woman, who was a fairly good customer of the store, and who, incidentally, I knew would have a lot of mean things to say about me should I fail to keep my agreement.

"I thought about it and thought about it, figuring on making up excuse after excuse—none of which seemed good enough or plausible. I was nearly beside myself. The woman and I had nothing in common. As a matter of fact, she bored me. The day of the meeting was drawing near and I had about concluded to phone her, telling her that an important engagement had come up making it impossible to attend the lecture, when in she came.

"She was all apologies when she informed me that the lecture had been canceled. Did I draw a sigh of relief? I thoroughly believe in what you preach and I think that my thought had something to do with what happened. I know that some will say it was a coincidence—let them call it that if they please. But stranger things than that happen, and they're not all coincidences."

The second story involves the manager of a company manufacturing a hay fever remedy. He had recently arrived in town, found an apartment near his office, and sought a telephone for his apartment. At that time, just after the war, the telephone company had a long waiting list and was installing telephones only on very high priorities, such as service for doctors, police, fire officials, and those engaged in public emergency work.

He had tried for two months, without success, to get a telephone, seeking out everyone he could to help him.

Through a mutual friend he learned that I knew the manager of the company and he came to see me. I quickly disillusioned him of the idea that I could get the manager to give him a telephone ahead of several thousand others, but I did tell him that if he could establish his rights to a priority, he shouldn't have any trouble.

I asked him whom he had talked with and he gave me the names of several people occupying both major and minor positions with the company. Then he explained that it was imperative that he have a telephone, for he was the only one connected with his own company who could handle after-office-hour business.

"Do you have many long-distance calls?" I asked. "And how much does your company telephone business amount to a month?"

He gave me an unusually high figure for his monthly bills. "Take your last few months' bills with you and see the man you saw first, look him straight in the eye and tell him that you've just got to have a telephone without delay," I told him, "but don't go near him until you can convince yourself that you can convince him. Otherwise, your task is futile. You've just got to make up your mind that you're going to have a telephone installed in your apartment, and you must believe it."

"I'll try it," he said, then quickly catching himself said, "No, I'll do it. I'll get that telephone."

He came to see me several days later.

"It certainly worked. I must tell you about this, for it's very funny how a positive thought brings about such a series of happenings. I went to see the man I had first talked with, and he was rather amazed that I had come back to him. I explained in detail this time why it was imperative that I have a phone, I showed him the bills as you suggested, and it was only a matter of minutes before I had him convinced. He was just about to call the manager to plead my cause when, lo and behold, the manager called him on some other matter. Then this man told the manager of my troubles and the manager agreed I was entitled to a priority. He suggested that I see a Mr. _____ in charge of priority ratings. I had never heard of this man before and prior to that time had known nothing of the priority system. I saw this man, told him my story and considerable about our business, referring to the product which we manufactured. I nearly collapsed when he told me that he was bothered by hay fever and had tried various remedies without results. It was a natural from then on. It all gives me a sort of spooky feeling. How did it happen that the manager called the man I was talking with at that particular time and how did it happen that the man with the final say-so was a hay fever victim and one I could help? From now on send me the scoffers."

Of course, we all know that our thoughts determine our carriage, our facial expression, our conversation, for what we are outwardly comes as the result of what we think habitually. There are many women who have improved their appearance by continuing to feel the delights of beauty, by thinking thoughts of the beautiful, by wearing stylish clothes, by adding things of beauty to their surroundings, by developing poise and easy carriage, and by constantly telling themselves that they are going to win out. You have seen in movie plays how a badly dressed, ordinary-looking girl can be transformed into a most attractive woman by beautiful clothes and the latest style of hair-do. You can do the same thing—and you will speed up the process if you will continue to hold the mental picture of your new self and never relax for a second.

Most people dread going to a dentist. It isn't so much what happens as what the patients think will happen that brings on the jitters. Again we have thought creating conditions which we would go a long way to avoid. The American Weekly, in its issue of July 7, 1940, told of a Pittsburgh dentist specializing in handling children, who fixed up a children's playroom adjoining his operating room and had it fitted up with toys, sandboxes, blocks, etc. The idea was to get the children interested in playing and thus get their thoughts off the work on their teeth. Once in the chair, the children were encouraged to talk about anything but their teeth. The dentist even attached a button switch to his electric drill line which the children themselves could turn on and off, the dentist assuring them before he started to work that they might turn off the current at the slightest indication of pain. His practice was enormous.

A barber who has built up a large clientele among small children has on his stands numerous children's books, all well illustrated, which he puts in the hands of his little patrons as he places them in his chair. He gets them interested in the pictures before he starts cutting their hair. "Once in a while it doesn't work," he said, "especially if the child hasn't been taught to look at pictures. Then I have to bring out the mechanical toys, such as those that utter throaty sounds or squeaks when they are squeezed. But the trick is to get the kids to forget about their hair being cut. Once that is done I have no trouble."

Imagination or mental picture-making can often produce queer results. Fear is basically an imaginary factor, as millions of men who went through the war will testify. You suddenly receive a telegram or a long-distance telephone call and before you open the envelope or answer the phone you fear you'll hear bad news—and you promptly get a sinking feeling in the pit of your stomach. The news may be good but for the moment you are shaken with fear and only the good news relieves you of that nervousness.

The story is often told of two men who got the only room left in the hotel. It was ordinarily a storage room, but the hotel, when crowded, used it as a bedroom. During the night one of the men complained of lack of air, and upon arising he groped through the dark to what he thought was the window. He couldn't open it, and, after finding a shoe, knocked out the pane of glass. Then they slept comfortably the rest of the night, only to discover at dawn that the window was intact. What had been smashed was the glass door to a closet!

A somewhat similar story was related during the war by Margaretta West in *This Week* magazine. She told of returning on a troopship from the South Pacific where she found herself packed into a cabin with seventeen other women. Because of the black-out rules the portholes had been closed, and the cabin was stifling. Inasmuch as the ship was not sailing until morning, permission was granted to open the portholes after everyone was in bed. Miss West tells how she undertook to open the portholes and how everyone was pleased that they could then sleep, and sleep they all did, related Miss West. But, on awakening in the morning, they found that Miss West had opened only the inner porthole, the outer one remaining closed and shutting out both light and air during the night.

During food rationing, thousands of people ate margarine in the home of friends, thinking it to be butter.

During prohibition days, it was a common practice to put moonshine whiskey into bottles with labels purporting to be genuine, and many did not know the difference. Sometimes the lowly carp has been served as red snapper, without anyone's being the wiser.

Science has proved in countless ways the effects of the workings of the imagination. Postage stamps have been placed on the skin of patients who believed that they were small mustard plasters; blisters developed under the stamps. By ringing a bell when food was offered to dogs, scientists soon had the animals associating the ringing of the bell with the thought of food, and it was only a short time before it was discovered that the mere ringing of the bell was sufficient to cause their stomachs to secrete digestive juices. Sit at a restaurant counter and notice an enticing dish placed before your neighbor. At once you are hungry and your mouth begins to water.

The peeling of onions often causes tears to flow from the person doing the peeling. Yet the mere sight of an onion being peeled by another person several feet away and with no odor permeating the air will bring tears to the eyes of others in the room. Some people cannot eat warmed-up leftovers, declaring that they make them sick. Undoubtedly, some leftover food that was eaten years before (perhaps it was partly spoiled) did upset their stomachs, and the mental picture never left them. Others claim that they have to take soda after every meal to help digest their food. Medical authorities say that this is often merely the working of their imaginations.

The writer has been across the Atlantic and Pacific Oceans several times and has never been seasick, even in the most severe storms and violent pitchings and rollings of the ship, except once; this was when he had to help another passenger who was violently ill. However, early in his travelings he learned to look away from those who were seasick, realizing that there was a suggestive force that could make him run for the rail. A sudden shock under the pressure of your imagination will cause your skin to turn cold and may even be followed by alternate sweats and chills. Emotional shocks resulting from something your physician has told you have a terrifying effect when your imagination goes to work.

Try whistling sometime when a friend is near you sucking a lemon. The mere sight of it will stop you, and all because the thought of the sour lemon puckers up your mouth and makes whistling impossible.

Often in lecturing, in order to prove the power of the imagination, I would hold up two small bottles, both containing different colored fluids. I would tell my audience that one contained lilac perfume and the other attar of roses, explaining that my experiment was for the purpose of determining the difference in the perceptive powers of my listeners. I would then turn my back on the audience so that they could not see which bottle I was partially emptying into the air; at the same time I called upon them to identify the odor. Some would say lilac, others attar of roses. Of course, there was always great chagrin when both groups discovered that their imaginations had led them astray, and that both bottles contained nothing but colored water, and neither had an odor.

Mark Twain in his little essay, Concerning Tobacco, says that a man thinks he can tell what he regards as a good cigar from what he regards as a bad one—but he can't. He goes by the brand, yet imagines he goes by the flavor. Twain, who had the reputation of smoking the worst cigars, tells how he borrowed from a wealthy friend a double handful of forty-cent cigars which bore red-and-gold labels signifying their quality. Twain removed the labels and put the now unbranded cigars into his own box. He passed them out to friends at the end of a dinner and they were all tossed away after two or three whiffs, because his friends believed they were the cheap cigars that Twain smoked. Unquestionably, there is a difference in the taste of even domestic brands of cigars and cigarettes, but the imagination plays an important part in determining it.

When we realize that inventors, artists, scientists, architects, as well as builders of great businesses, employ the imagination, we get some idea of its magnitude. Shakespeare said: "Assume a virtue if you have it not." Now let's take this great truth and follow some of its implications. In assuming a virtue, you are assuming it via your imagination. To become the person you would like to be, you create a mental picture of your newly conceived self, and if you continue to hold it the day will come when you are in reality that person. So it is with the accomplishment of desires.

But here we must make a distinction between daydreaming and a true mental picture, or the proper use of the imagination. Perhaps there is some genie who will drop $100,000 into your lap or overnight provide you with a mansion luxuriously furnished, though the writer has never had the pleasure of meeting one. But daydreaming or mere undirected wishful thinking doesn't have the power to release the latent forces within you that will bring you the one hundred thousand dollars or the mansion. When you employ your imagination properly, you see yourself doing a thing and you go ahead and do it. It's the doing the thing you have pictured to yourself that brings it into actual existence. In this connection, think about the use of a magnifying glass. When properly focused, it will gather the light from the sun and concentrate it, so that the heat will burn a hole in the object upon which the rays are focused. It must be held steady before the heat power is developed. So it is with the holding of the image or the mental picture.

Dr. Emile Coué, the little French doctor who threw so much light on the power of suggestion, declared that imagination was a much stronger force than will-power; when the two are in conflict, he said, the imagination always wins. In explanation, let's say you are an inveterate smoker of good cigars and decide to break yourself of the habit. You grit your teeth, shove out your chin, and solemnly declare that you are going to use your will-power to break yourself of the habit. Then suddenly comes the idea of the taste of a good cigar, its aroma and its soothing effects—the imagination goes to work and the resolution to break the habit goes out the window. The same holds true of efforts to break the drinking habit and other bad habits.

Charles Fourier, a French philosopher of more than a century ago, declared that the future of the world would grow out of the brain of man, shaped, controlled, and directed by the desires and passions by which men are moved. His prophecy is coming true, yet man through his mind has barely started shaping and controlling the world.

All of this brings us to the topic of desire and what you actually want in life. There are comparatively few people with great desires. Most are content to go along filling the tiny niches in which they find themselves. They accept their positions in life as something that fate has fixed for them, and very seldom do they make either a mental or physical effort to extract themselves from those positions.

They never raise their sights or realize that it's just as easy to shoot at a bird on a limb thirty feet above the ground as it is to shoot at it on the ground the same distance away. Many engage in wishful thinking, but wishful thinking in itself is without effect simply because the power factor is missing.

But when you run across a person who is "going to town"—and there are many—you realize that the great power behind it all is projected by desire. The way seems easy for those people— and to a great degree it is—because they are putting to use the powers of their subconscious minds which in turn magnetize, co-ordinate, and then transmit to their conscious minds the electrifying vision of the object of their desire.

So let's be reminded that whatever we fix our thoughts upon or steadily focus our imaginations upon, that is what we attract. This is no mere play of words. It is a fact which anyone can prove to his own satisfaction. Whether the results come through magnetic or electrical energy is something still undetermined; while man hasn't been able to define it, manifestations of thought-attraction can be seen on every hand. It is like the electrical field itself—we do not know what electricity is, although in a material sense we know how man can generate it through various kinds of energy-producing apparatus; we see electricity manifest every time we turn on a light or snap a switch.

However, it is very difficult for the average person to concentrate for any length of time, to say nothing of holding on to a mental picture for any great period. You can prove this to yourself in countless ways. You will find that thoughts, ideas, fantasies will ebb and flow through your mind with astonishing rapidity. You are constantly being swayed by what you read, see, and hear, and as a result the co-ordinating part of this creative force turns to gathering together all these scattered elements in a confused mass, instead of devoting itself to making a clear and dynamic picture of your desire.

That brings us to a system of mechanics by which anyone can focus thoughts so that they will penetrate to the deepest depths of the subconscious mind.

The writer has been in the private offices of a great many industrial leaders, business men, great bankers, and others, and long before this science of belief was understood by him, he was impressed with the pictures, photographs, slogans, bits of statuary, and so forth, which were to be found in the inner sanctums of great firms. In the office of the head of a great utility concern are hung the photographs of the early leaders in the industry; in another office are pictures of the great financiers of history; in some there are busts of Napoleon; in others little shrines, goodsized statues of Buddha; and I saw offices where there hung on the walls such slogans as "We do the impossible—any place, any time", "If it can be done, we can do it", "Do it now", "Be a self-starter—don't wait to be cranked." It is reported that F. W. Woolworth, who became known as the Napoleon of business, had his private office in quarters that were a replica of Napoleon's study. Undoubtedly many of you have seen or heard of such displays, but has it ever occurred to you what their purpose was?

There can be only one answer, and that is that they serve as a constant reminder—getting the picture over to the occupant of the room that he too can succeed as did those before him. He has a motto or a slogan to meet his gaze every time he looks around the room. He sees and feels the eyes of Napoleon upon him when he sits at his desk, or he feels a touch of the spiritual as he gazes at the little shrine. In other words, they are a form of mechanics that the executive uses to excite his imagination, a picture to inspire him, or a series of suggesting forces that reach his subconscious mind. In many a doctor's office (and in some of those who would scoff at the great power of suggestion) hang the photographs of great men of medicine, or famous teachers in medical schools. I have often wondered if the doctors realized the underlying power of these portraits.

When we realize that the subconscious mind is sensitized to the point that it works accurately to externalize the suggestion which is most greatly impressed upon it, we then get a better understanding of the necessity for concentration and for constant repetition of the one suggestion.

In common with other great men, Thomas A. Edison obviously knew the value of the repeated suggestion and made use of it. When his desk, sealed at his death, was opened February 8, 1947, as a part of the ceremonies celebrating the hundredth anniversary of the great inventor's birth, conspicuous among the articles found in it was a piece of paper which bore the legend, "When down in the mouth, remember Jonah, he came out all right." Edison must have thought well of that expression and perhaps reflected much upon it; otherwise he would not have kept it on his desk before him.

Often I have thought of this matter of desire and suggestion in connection with the planting of vegetable or flower seeds. Once the soil is prepared and the tiny seeds are placed in it, it is but a short time when they put forth roots and sprouts begin to appear. The moment they start upward through the soil in search of light, sunshine, and moisture, obstacles mean nothing to them. They will push aside small stones or bits of wood, and if they can't do that, they'll extend themselves and grow around them. They are determined to emerge from the ground. They blossom and give forth fruit, vegetables, or flowers, and they succeed unless some greater force destroys them. While we are not aware of the details of nature's secrets, we observe the seed buried for a long time in the dark gradually expanding and exerting itself until it becomes a thing of beauty or usefulness. Cultivate it, attend it, give it sunshine and water, and it grows into full life. Remember it always produces after its kind, be it single or hybrid.

So with you and the suggestions you impart to your subconscious mind. The result will be pure or complex, depending upon the original seed and the attention which you give it. In other words, plant the right kind of seed— thought of a pure strain—and habitually feed it with strong affirmative thought always directed toward the same end, and it will grow into a mighty force, finding ways and means of overcoming all obstacles. It will reach forth with its roots to find more food on which to grow and expand its foliage to gather more sunshine.

It was desire that brought progress to the world. Without it, we all would still be living in a primitive age. Everything we have in our modern world is the result of desire. Indeed, desire is the motivating force of life itself. You see it all around you—in the animal kingdom, in all forms of plant life, and in all acts and operations of human beings. Hunger promotes a desire for food, poverty a desire for riches, cold causes us to desire warmth, inconveniences a desire for better things.

It's the generating power of all human action, and without it no one can get very far. The keener, the more urgent the desire, the sooner its consummation. It marks the difference between the uneducated ditchdigger and the person of accomplishment, between the clerk and the executive, between the failure and the success. So you must start with desire, keeping in mind that with the magic of believing you can obtain what you picture in your mind's eye. The mechanics are for the purpose of helping you to focus sharply your desire-picture on the screen of your subconscious mind, as well as enable you to shut off and keep out all distracting thoughts, negative ideas, or any fear or doubt projections that might otherwise penetrate to your subconscious. So let's get down to the mechanics. Secure three or four cards.

Ordinary business-size cards will do. In your office, your home, your room, or any other place where you can have privacy, sit down and ask yourself what you desire above everything else. When the answer comes and you are certain that it is your uppermost desire, then at the top of one card write a word picture of it. One or two words may be sufficient—a job, a better job, more money, a home of your own. Then on each card duplicate the word picture on the original. Carry one in your billfold, or handbag, place another alongside your bed or fasten it to your bedstead, place another on your shaving mirror or dressing table, and still another on your desk. The whole idea, as you may have guessed, is to enable you to see mentally the picture at all hours of the day. Just before going to sleep at night and upon waking in the mornings are highly important moments of the twenty-four hours in which to concentrate upon your thoughts with added force. But don't stop with merely those two periods, for the more often you can visualize the desire by this method (or by one of your own devising), the speedier the materialization.

At the start you may have no idea of how the results are to come. Yet you need not concern yourself. Just leave it to the subconscious mind, which has its own ways of making contacts, and of opening doors and avenues that you may never have even thought of. You will receive assistance from the most unexpected sources. You will find that ideas useful in the accomplishment of your program will come at most unexpected times. You may be suddenly struck with the idea of seeing a person you have not heard from for a long time, or calling upon a man you have never seen before. You may get the idea of writing a letter or making a telephone call. Whatever the idea is, follow it. Keep a pad and pencil on a stand near the head of your bed, and when these ideas come during the night, note them on a pad, so they will not be forgotten by morning. Many successful people get ideas during the night that are immediately transcribed to a pad so they will not be lost.

For many years, before I thoroughly understood this science, I was associated with an executive who, after reaching his desk in the morning, would begin pulling notes out of his pocket. In a few minutes things would begin to hum. These notes might contain comments on various advertising media, an outline of a sales campaign, new purchases, or a rearrangement of the sales organization; but all of them contributed to the success of his operations.

If you bear in mind what I told you about successful executives and their custom of keeping in their offices pictures, mottoes, slogans, busts, and statues, you will appreciate that in using the cards you are utilizing the same forces, only in much more concentrated form.

As I write this, my memory goes back to the time when I put this science to work in order to pull off the rocks the firm of which I was then vice-president. All of the employees sat around in a half-circle, and as I began my remarks I asked each man to provide himself with paper and pencil. Most of them thought that I wanted them to take notes. But there was considerable surprise when I told them to write down what they most wanted in life. I explained that if they would do this, I would point out the way to obtain it. Two or three of the younger men laughed, but the older men, realizing that I was deadly earnest, did as I suggested. To the younger men I said simply: "If you want to hold on to your jobs, you'll do as I ask. For if this stuff doesn't work, we'll all be out on the street." They complied. I told them to show no one what they had written. After the meeting one of the younger men came to me to apologize for having laughed.

"That's all right, Bob," I told him.

"But it sounded so silly at first," he explained. "Imagine me getting a new automobile by simply writing it down. But after you explained the science of it all, I guess it does make sense."

Several years later this chap came to my home and said he wanted to show me something. He did. There along the parking strip was parked his expensive new automobile.

In the years that followed, I found occasion to ask those who attended that meeting if they had obtained what they had written down. Without exception, every man had. One had wanted a wife of a certain nationality. He got her, and there are two fine boys in the family. Another put down the figures of a very sizable fortune. He got it. Another man wanted a beach cottage. Another a better home, and so on. Steadily through the years every one of these men has constantly made money, many of them averaging monthly more than they had ever made before in their lives, much to the astonishment of many others in the same line of business. It cannot be too strongly emphasized that you should tell no one just what the words on the cards mean nor give anyone an inkling of what you desire. To do so may end disastrously for you. When you get a better understanding of this science, you can understand how thought vibrations, consciously or unconsciously, because of envy or some other cause, may be set up to counteract your own.

To illustrate this, I am reminded of a doctor friend who during the early war days applied for a commission in the navy. He closed his office, told everyone that he was joining the navy, and found himself the recipient of many parties and gifts. "It taught me a lesson never to tell anyone of my plans or desires," he laughingly told me later. "It was two years before I received notice of assignment, and during those years I found I had to go back into private practice. It certainly was embarrassing to both myself and family to get various farewell gifts and invitations, only to find that I was to cool my heels at home for two years."

The truth is that when you talk about what you're going to do, you scatter your forces. You lose the close connection with the subconscious, and you frequently find that unless you do as here directed, you will have to start all over again in your program of achievement.

"Go and tell no man" still holds true.

My readers will recall what I said previously about Mumbo Jumbo, chants, incantations, affirmations, etc., and I explained that by engaging in them you put the suggestive forces to work to stimulate your subconscious.

These repetitive words and phrases said silently or aloud are merely methods of convincing the subconscious mind, for autosuggestion, no matter what the form, is the only way of molding its pattern. The subconscious is extremely receptive, and it can be convinced of the propositions you present to it, be they true or false, positive or negative; once they are imbedded in the subconscious mind, it goes to work with all of its faculties and energies to materialize them, to make them real in life. The simpler the words to express the ideas you wish conveyed to the subconscious, the better. For example, if you are unhappy, use the words, "I am happy." You don't need the cards for this. Just repeat them to yourself twenty or thirty times. "I am strong," "I am happy," "I am convincing," "I am friendly, "Everything is fine" are a few simple affirmations that you can use to change your mental point of view for the better. But if the effects are to be permanent, the affirmations must be continued until the desired results are obtained.

The person with a fixed goal, a clear picture of his desire, or an ideal always before him, causes it, through repetition, to be buried deeply in his subconscious mind and is thus enabled, thanks to its generative and sustaining power, to realize his goal in a minimum of time and with a minimum of physical effort. Just pursue the thought unceasingly. Step by step you will achieve realization, for all your faculties and powers become directed to that end.

Suppose you want a better job or a promotion. Not only use the cards, but keep telling yourself constantly and continuously that you are going to get that job. You have already visualized it if you have accepted this science, but the repetition will be the means of driving the suggestion deeply and firmly into the subconscious mind. This may be compared to driving a nail into a board. The first tap puts the nail in place, but it is only by a number of heavy strokes that the nail is driven home. Never forget that the subconscious mind will accept and carry out whatever it is powerfully instructed to do. A great example of power developed by repetition is the story of Milo and the calf. Every day he lifted the calf, and then came the day when he was lifting a full-grown bull.

Think of all of this in terms of the so-called material things. You know that two objects cannot fill the same space at the same time. Your mind can be compared to that space: you can't keep your mind filled with negative thoughts or doubts if you have it filled with positive, powerful, and creative thoughts. Consider your mind a room with but a single door and you have the only key. It rests with you to decide who is to come through the door, that is, whether you are dominated by positive or negative thoughts, and which ones you are going to admit, for your subconscious mind will respond to the vibrations of the thoughts that are strongest in you.

Again, compare your mind to a tank filled with clear, unadulterated water. You cannot put any object into that tank without displacing some of the water and causing the tank to overflow. When you permit negative thoughts of doubt or fear to enter your consciousness, it is obvious that the forceful, positive, creative thoughts will have to give way, and consequently you lose your positive state. Thus, so long as you do not permit unfavorable vibrations to reach your subconscious mind, it will not be hindered by anything you may hear, see, or experience. In other words, you must at all times keep your mind filled with positive thoughts so that their strong vibrations will ward off all negative and destructive thoughts that might come from the outside.

For years philosophers have taught that if we are to be happy we must be busy, working or doing something that holds our attention. The explanation lies in the fact that when we are concentrated on some task, our minds are then not open to roving and undesirable vibrations. That is why many doctors advise business and professional men to take up hobbies, in order that their minds may be diverted from worry and trouble thoughts. Others advise trips, new scenes, new personal associations away from the familiar places where it is difficult to get away from disturbing thought vibrations and associations.

As I write, I think of an elderly couple who lost their only son in the Normandy invasion. For months after news of the boy's death was received, the couple kept his room intact just as it was when he left. On Sundays they would spend hours rearranging the furniture and fondly handling his belongings. Was it any wonder, with minds so constantly occupied with the memories of their son, that they became embittered old people? I know what it means to lose loved ones, but I have also learned that it is necessary to close the door on yesterday and keep it closed. We live today, not yesterday.

Now that you have an understanding of how circumstances, environments, and material objectives come into your life through your thinking, it's up to you to make your cherished dreams come true.

Suppose you want a new home. After you've got the first glimpse of the picture, start your affirmations going. Use any expressions you wish, or something like this: "I'm going to have that new home. I'm going to have that new home. I'm going to have that new home." And one day the way will be found and the new home will be yours.

If you're a salesman and want to increase your sales, use the cards, as already suggested, and tell yourself as frequently as possible that you are going to increase your sales. Do it with emphasis.

Strange as it may sound, we usually get what we anticipate, and if we anticipate increasing our sales and believe that we are going to do it, our sales will mount just as though some invisible friend were helping us. The idea of anticipation holds in everything we do.

An insurance man who had increased his business more than 200 per cent within a year after he began using this science, related this story to me: "The sales manager told me to call upon Mr. Blank and not come back to the office until I got an order out of him. This prospect was a hard nut to crack, as everyone knew. He had the reputation of being a very stubborn and cranky individual with little time for salesmen, to say nothing of us in the insurance business. However, I knew that he had lots of property and had to carry all sorts of fire and liability coverage. As I went down the stairs from our office and all the way up the street to this prospect's office, I kept repeating to myself: 'Fred, you're going to sell him, you're going to sell him. You're going to find him a fine old fellow, no matter what anyone says. He's going to be friendly and he's going to accept what you have to offer.' Maybe I repeated those ideas a couple of hundred times. Not only did he turn out to be very cordial, but I came away with an order for a $25,000 policy, the first our company had ever secured from the old man."

This insurance man has long since left the agency with which he was connected and now has a firm of his own, with a country estate he is rapidly developing into a showplace. A short time ago he told me that he was "fixed financially for life."

Dale Carnegie has told of the great success of Howard Thurston, the magician. According to the story, in going out on the stage Thurston would repeatedly say to himself that he loved his audience and that he was going to give them the best that was in him. He made two million dollars!

Another man—he's seventy-eight but doesn't look more than sixty—who is a profound student of this subject, and who used it to make a tremendous fortune for himself, but whose interests today are along other lines, declares that he still orders his subconscious mind to "get busy for him."

"I talk to it just as I might be talking to some individual to whom I was giving orders. And I never have any doubts or fears that it will not do as ordered. If I get an upset stomach, I simply tell it to be itself and act naturally; so with other ailments that arise. If I want to awaken at five o'clock in the morning without using an alarm clock, I peremptorily order my subconscious mind to awaken me. It has never failed in anything so far.

"I have long had a theory that the subconscious mind controls our age—what I mean is that for centuries the subconscious mind has been led to believe that a man should be old when he is sixty. For most people who have accepted the thought, it can't be otherwise, for that is what the subconscious mind believes. However, in my case I refuse to accept it and, as you know, I am as active as I was when I was fifty years old—and I expect to carry on for some years to come."

All of which shows the advisability of not implanting in your subconscious mind the idea that you are becoming old and incapable merely because the years are passing; it also shows that by keeping the subconscious free from the fixed idea of a decline, you improve your chances of prolonging your life far beyond the so-called allotted span.

Repetition is the fundamental rhythm of all progress, the cadence of the universe. It's the chuff-chuff of the locomotive that takes a train across the continent, it's the repeated explosions that generate power in the automobile engine, the airplane, the rocket gun, the robot bomb. It's the constant surging of the water against the turbine blades that generates electrical power. It's the tap-tap of the hammer that drives the nail into place. It's the deadly put-put of the machine gun that mows down everything before it. It's the constant and determined effort that breaks down all resistance, sweeps away all obstacles. It's the repeated auto- or heterosuggestion that makes you and others believe. It's the tap-tap of the same conscious thought that causes it to be impressed upon your subconscious mind and on the subconscious minds of others.

While anyone can demonstrate the efficacy of the repeated suggestion, whether it be used either constructively or destructively, the words of Professor Hugo Münsterberg, Harvard psychologist, throw considerable light on its value. He said: "The value of repetition must distinctly be understood in the relation of the inner-setting and the inner mental attitude."

Before World War II there was in Paris a famous institute devoted to the teaching of suggestion by means of phonograph records. They were played over and over again, and the listeners could hear any record they wanted—records that gave them the repeated suggestion that they were in good health, that they had the power to overcome their difficulties, that they could receive help in other ways.

For years mothers have been taught to talk to their babies and small children while they were asleep, repeating such suggestions as that they were going to grow well and strong, that they were to develop certain good habits, that they were to become good citizens. In view of the fact that the children were asleep, obviously the suggestions were directed to their subconscious minds.

In the destruction of Carthage, the greatest maritime power of the ancient world, we have an instance of the power of the repeated suggestion at work. Cato, the great Roman statesman, convinced that Rome and Carthage could not both survive, ended every speech in the Senate with the words, "Carthage must be destroyed!" He kept it up until the Romans were saying in their sleep, "Carthage must be destroyed"—and Carthage was destroyed.

Many people become confused and frustrated because they allow themselves to be influenced by negative thoughts of others—this is a weakness of many salesmen—when they absorb too much of what the prospect says about his reasons for not doing something such as buying. Repetition of negative thoughts will discourage even the most powerful if continued long enough, and unless your mind is closed against them and you counteract them by constantly thinking and radiating positive thoughts, you will sooner or later find yourself sunk. Some people wear themselves out trying to combat these negative forces by superhuman effort and sheer will-power, never realizing that their own minds, operating in accordance with the suggestive influences, are causing all the trouble.

Whether we know it or not, we are all victims of suggestion, in many cases almost to the point of being hypnotized. We follow along a beaten path of living just because we've been doing it for decades. We wear certain styles of clothing, hold to certain customs, all because we have been led to believe, through the never-ending suggestive thoughts that come to us from all sides, that that is the thing to do. Houses, churches, office buildings, automobiles, buses, streetcars for years followed a certain pattern, and yet, when someone gets off the beaten path with a new way of doing things, he is considered a crank or an eccentric. What I refer to, on close analysis, as mass hypnosis is seen around us in every human activity.

It has been my observation that those who consciously use this science (as well as those who may be using it unconsciously) are people of tremendous energies, virtually human dynamos. There are people who not only use their imaginations and hold strong beliefs and convictions, but they are great doers in action. And that brings me to this most important statement: "Faith without action is dead."

Unquestionably, there are people on this earth who by concentrated thought and by thought alone—without moving from their offices or making any contacts, personal or otherwise, with other people—can achieve remarkable things. But in the main, this so-called material world of ours is controlled by men of action—great dynamos of energy that energize others. Nicola Tesla, who probably understood the laws of vibration better than any other man of his time, declared that he could, with a machine that could be slipped into his pocket, cause the Empire State Building in New York to disintegrate and fall apart. (As a matter of fact, the operation of a somewhat similar bit of apparatus did cause buildings to shake, windows to break, furniture to move, in lower New York when Tesla was first experimenting with it during the eighteen-nineties.) That machine came out of Mr. Tesla's mind. His thoughts created it. Here is an example of a man who coupled his "faith with action."

There are metaphysicians and teachers of the occult who claim that a person can sit in his own office and visualize orders pouring on to his desk—and the orders will quickly materialize; but to accomplish it, the mental picture or thought projection must be definite and unwavering, and that requires great practice and concentration. Stranger things have been recorded. But for the person who has not yet developed this mind-power, it is well to add action and energy to his efforts by doing the things, following out the ideas, and by making the contacts which are dictated by his subconscious mind.

Many years ago I read that Franklin D. Roosevelt constantly made use of his subconscious mind, and I am certain that he knew much about the use of the repeated suggestion. He never looked "backward," but always "forward"—"yesterday" was a closed book. On April 17, 1945, Kirke L. Simpson, an Associated Press Staff Writer and an intimate of the late President, told of a party given Roosevelt after he had been stricken with infantile paralysis. Mr. Simpson said that Mr. Roosevelt was determined to walk again, somehow, anyhow, without crutches. His intimates, according to Mr. Simpson, decided to give him a cane as a token that they, too, expected him to walk again, and after it was presented the President sat all evening with the cane cuddled against his shoulder. Mr. Simpson said that he would reach up to pat its crook now and then, and "we knew that he was saying to himself: 'You'll walk again, Frank Roosevelt; you will walk again!'"

Roosevelt firmly believed in the power of believing, as is apparent in an article in Time magazine (March 4, 1946). It told of a letter written by him in 1924 to a doctor seeking advice on the treatment of infantile paralysis. Mr. Roosevelt pointed out that he thought gentle exercise, massage, and sun-bathing were essential. "But," he added, "more important than most therapy is a 'belief on the patient's part that he will eventually recover.'" Here we have a wonderful example of the magic of believing at work, and, as I have pointed out, of the part the "repeated suggestion" plays in establishing belief.

STUDY GUIDE

Chapter 5

This chapter opens with a delightful and engaging story of how the author used the art of mental pictures to calm a friend's fears and feelings of intimidation. He shares several cases where individuals have used visualizations in order to overcome obstacles and achieve great success. He warns that you should stay away for skeptics and nay-sayers, as ultimately they can affect your energy and that of those around you. He clarifies how mind power is different than daydreaming, and reminds us that many great inventors, artists, scientists, architects and business-builders have employed their imaginations to achieve their successes. To instruct you on the mechanics of mental picture, he takes you through some experiential exercises that can assist you in developing your power through mental imaging. He describes how repetition is key to the success of this technique. He ends this chapter with the statement that *"repetition is the fundamental rhythm of all progress; the cadence of the universe"* and emphasizes how we are all victims of suggestion whether conscious of it or not.

1. Claude Bristol describes the successes that his colleagues experienced after doing the "Picture-Making Plan" exercise with them. With this exercise, when the salesman found himself feeling intimidated by someone, he would see them in a less-frightening role—for example, Santa Claus. List at least three people that you find intimidating. Then consider each. What animal or characters do they remind you of? Might they be apes, frogs or cartoon characters? Imagine each of them at four years old. How did they behave? Where they intimidating then? Write about your findings.

2. Go to each person from #1, and the related less-intimidating impression you have of them. Imagine engaging with them as that character, or animal. What happens to your fear when you do so? Practice this with each, and then write about your experience in doing this exercise.

3. When discussing people who can achieve remarkable things by concentrated thought alone, the author cites Nicola Tesla as an example of a man who coupled his *"faith with action."* Can you think of other such individuals who have been unwavering in their faith, and committed in their actions? Write about them and why you believe they were so successful. What makes them different that you or I, or are they?

4. Bristol shares the potent story of Franklin D. Roosevelt's commitment to walk again. While Roosevelt instructed a doctor that *"gentle exercise, massage, and sun-bathing"* were essential, he added, *"more important than most therapy is a 'belief on the patient's part that he will eventually recover.'"* On a scale from one to ten (one being "not at all" and ten being "most definitely"), rate how much you believe that your thoughts can heal your physical ailments.

5. Have you ever "believed" yourself into physical recovery? If so, describe the circumstances around your ability to heal. If not, do you know of someone who has? Explain.

1———2———3———4———5———6———7———8———9———10

6. You are reminded that everyone in so-called "high places" have fears, frailties and faults, just like you. Another example that the author shares is with a lawyer. When he was up against a lawyer that was feared by many, he would simply close his eyes and say to himself, *"I'm just as good as he is; as a matter of fact, I'm better."* He claimed that it worked every time. Try this exercise with someone who you fear, or who you believe always wins over you. Write about your experience after doing so.

7. The author asserts, *"People who act and appear hard-boiled are usually 'softies and heart'"*. Write a list of individuals you know that appear gruff on the exterior, but are actually "softies."

8. Why do you think people put on an air of hardness? Do you think that they could be consciously or unconsciously keeping people at bay because they, themselves are fearful? Why or why not?

9. Do you ever find yourself having a hard edge in certain situations? If so, when and why?

10. Bristol suggests that the next time you encounter someone with an edge, take a couple of deep breaths and convince yourself that he or she will be a *"push-over."* Practice this next time you have such an encounter, and note whether or not it works for you.

11. After the author spent six weeks of lecturing to store owners, they all conducted experiments at their shops where they would have their staff see mental pictures of selling particular products to customers on certain days. The experiment was a huge success in each of the shops. If you have a successful business transaction, what would it look like? Like the store clerks, imagine it, seeing an outstanding outcome. Write about your experience in doing so, and any outcome that comes in response to doing this exercise.

12. Whether visualizing a parking spot or traffic lights that all remain green until you reach your desired destination, how do you use routine creative visualization in your life? If you don't, take some time and experiment. Imagine no line-ups at the movie theater, or your parking spot opening up for you. Write about your visualizations and any consequent experiences.

13. One woman shared her account of driving across the U.S.A., from Washington D.C. to the pacific coast. While a

mechanic suggested that her tires would not last, she felt that they would and consequently took the trip despite his warnings. Her "feelings" of getting there without problem overrode the mechanic's negative warnings. Why do you believe her will was stronger than his warnings? Please explain.

14. Do you have nay-sayers, or individual who always anticipate the worst case scenarios in your life? If so, who?

15. Do the negative people in your life affect the decisions you make? Why or why not?

16. What tactics do you use to override negative influences of those around you? List them.

17. English investigator, G.N. M. Tyrrell declared that *"If, while dwelling upon the activity of the subconscious mind, we determine upon an intention to do a certain thing, we may subconsciously initiate a train of events likely to bring this thing about."* The author continues by sharing an example of a man who manifests a priority phone. What percentage more business successes do you believe you could acquire if you practiced these techniques?

18. If you haven't yet practiced the techniques, what do you believe is stopping you?

19. What further steps can you take to overcome any blocks to your success?

20. The author also states that women who see themselves as beautiful and surround themselves with such beauty, will continue to experience it. Do you believe this to be true? Why or why not?

21. Who do you believe to be the most beautiful women in the world? List them.

22. Have these women maintained their beauty as they aged? If so, do you believe they did so through visualizing themselves as such? Why or why not?

23. On a scale from one to ten, (one being "not at all" and ten being "very"), rate how attractive you believe yourself to be.

1——2——3——4——5——6——7——8——9——10

24. Do you tend to focus on what you like, or what you do not like about your looks?

25. Do you believe that seeing yourself as more attractive will make you so? If so, spend 5 minutes each day for at least 28 days in front of the mirror, acknowledging your attractive attribute. List any changes you note in doing this exercise.

26. The author shares the remarkable story of a dentist who had a playroom in his office. He also had a button in which the child could stop the drilling process at will. His business was a huge success. Why do you believe that it was?

27. The method that both the dentist and the barber used was distraction. They took the children's' minds off of their teeth or hair, and onto something else. Do you ever use this technique with children? Do you ever use it with yourself or others? If so, how? Is it a success?

28. The author cites several examples of how powerful the mind can be. From upset stomachs to seasickness, he claims that the mind can have great power over how you react to things. He suggests that you try whistling while a nearby friend is eating a lemon. Try this exercise, and explain why it does or doesn't work.

29. The author quotes Shakespeare, *"Assume a virtue if you have it not."* What do you believe this quote means in relation to the power of the mind? Please explain.

30. According to the author, *"Daydreaming or mere undirected wishful thinking doesn't have the power to release the latent forces within you. When you employ your imagination properly, you see yourself doing a thing and you go ahead and do it. It's the doing the thing you have picture*

to yourself that brings it into actual existence." In your own words, describe the difference between daydreaming and properly using your imagination. Explain why one works and the other does not.

31. According to Dr. Emile Coue, with will-power and imagination are in conflict, imagination always wins. On a scale from one to ten (one being "very little" and ten being "a great deal"), rate how much emphasis you put on your willpower.

1——2——3——4——5——6——7——8——9——10

32. On a scale from one to ten (one being "very little" and ten being "a great deal"), rate how much emphasis you put in your imagination.

1——2——3——4——5——6——7——8——9——10

33. If you spend more time focusing on your willpower, what specific steps can you take to focus your attention and trust more in your imagination?

34. The author asserts that few actually possess great desires for themselves. They accept their positions as fate and fixed. Do you believe this to be the case in your life? Why or why not?

35. What evidence do you have that supports your believe in #32? Write about it.

36. "Power" is the factor that is missing from wishful thinking. How can you shift your own wishful thinking so that it has more power behind it?

37. We are often swayed by what we read, see and hear. This can weaken the power of our imaginations. Do you spend a great deal of time listening to the news, or watching television? Do you believe that doing so deters you from focusing on that which you desire? Explain.

38. The author cites examples of displays such as quotes, statues and photos of great leaders that are used by suc-

cessful businesses to support success. They serve as constant reminders, the mechanics that the executives use to excite, or inspire their imaginations. Do you have any quotes, statues or displays around your home or office that support your deepest desires? What are they? How do they work?

39. Are there any statues, quotes or other reminders that you really love? If so, make a plan to find them and display them. Then note any changes as you see these constant reminders.

40. The author shares the evolution of seeds. Unless great forces destroy them, they will naturally grow. Perhaps our nature is to "naturally grow" to manifest our dreams; we need only believe and get out of our way. What steps can you take to "get out of the way" of your growth?

41. Like a seedling, do you trust that you will grow naturally into your abundant birthright? Why or why not? Please explain.

42. Bristol affirms that, *"desire is the motivating force of life itself."* It exists in all things. *"The keener, more urgent the desire, the sooner its consummation."* Share an example of a time that you had an incredibly urgent desire that subsequently manifested very quickly into your life.

43. To support the mechanics of your desires, the author suggests that you get 3-4 business-size cards. Then sit down and write a list of everything you desire above all else. Once you are clear about what you desire above all else, on the top of one card, write a word picture that represents it.

44. The author asserts that you need to not only possess wishful thinking, but you also have to have power behind it as well. What do you think he means by "power" in this context? Please explain.

45. The author likens the evolution of manifesting your desires to the life cycle of plants, from seed to full growth. With cultivation, attention, sunshine and water, they grow. Imagine your desires as a growing plant. Think out of the box, and write about which plants your desires would be represented by—a flower, vegetable, fruit, tree, or weed. Use your imagination and visualize them. Then explain why you imagined that particular plant to match each specific desire.

46. The author asserts that *"the keener, more urgent the desire, the sooner its consummation."* In general, how fast are you in moving your thoughts into actions?

47. What steps might you take to become more proactive when you have an innovative thought or idea come to mind? For example, could you have a buddy you rely upon who could encourage you and hold you accountable? List some ways in which you can expedite moving forward more quickly.

48. The author encourages you to do the Card Exercise: *"Secure three or four cards. Ordinary business-size cards will do. In your office, your home, your room, or any other place where you can have privacy, sit down and ask yourself what you desire above everything else. When the answer comes and you are certain that it is your uppermost desire, then at the top of one card write a word picture of it. One or two words may be sufficient—a job, a better job, more money, a home of your own. Then on each card duplicate the word picture on the original. Carry one in your billfold, or handbag, place another alongside your bed or fasten it to your bedstead, place another on your shaving mirror or dressing table, and still another on your desk. The whole idea, as you may have guessed, is to enable you to see mentally then picture at all hours of the day."* Do this exercise.

49. Make a list of the places where you have placed the cards.

50. It is important that you focus on your desires just before you go to bed, and when you awaken. He asserts that the more often you can visualize the desire by this method, the faster it will materialize. Spend at least one month practicing this exercise. Write about how doing so affected you.

51. Spend at least one week tracking how many times each day you note your desires. Write about how doing so affected you. Note anything that manifests in your life, and be sure to be grateful for the shift.

52. The author warns that you show no one your lists. There are two contrary philosophies on this. While some suggest sharing your ideas elicits support from others to cheer you on, others suggest keeping your desires secret. What are your thoughts and beliefs on this?

53. The author shares a story where he takes several staff aside and encourages them all to write their desires on cards. Without exception, each man's desires were eventually manifest. Do you believe there was more power because of the group dynamic, or the presence of Bristol himself? Why or why not. Please explain.

54. Bristol asserts that when you talk about what you are going to do, you lose connection with your subconscious and often have to start all over again. How do you believe sharing information scatters the energy?

55. To shift your energy, you can repeat phrases to yourself such as, *"Everything is fine"* or *"I am happy."* For these phrases to be effective, you must continue repeating them until the desired results are obtained. What phrase do you feel you need to repeat to yourself today? Repeat that phrases until you feel you have attained your desired results. Write about your experience in doing so.

56. The story of Milo and the calf is an example of how repetition is effectively used. Have you ever followed a repet-

itive task, and discovered that because of the repetition, the task became very easy? If so, please explain.

57. It is important that you do not allow negative thoughts to penetrate your subconscious mind. If any such thoughts arise, try saying to yourself, *"Cancel, cancel"* and see the negative thoughts melting away.

    Whenever negative thoughts arise, try this exercise and write about your findings.

58. At the time that this book was written doctors recommended hobbies to busy businessmen in order to divert their thoughts. What hobbies do you practice?

59. Does practicing your hobbies relax you, or shift your energy into a more positive place? Please explain.

60. Bristol shares the story of a couple who became embittered because they continued to focus all of their energies on their son who died in the war. He asserts that it is important to let the past go. Write a list of those experiences from the past that you are holding onto.

61. Go through each of the experiences you listed. With each, make a decision. Will you choose to let it go? Why or why not?

62. The author shares the story of Howard Thurston, the magician. He constantly repeated to himself how much he loved his audience and his commitment to give the best that was in him. He subsequently became a millionaire. Try repeating a similar positive phrase when doing your the work. Note any subsequent changes.

63. When Bristol wrote this book, man was considered old at the age of 60. Times have changed and the ages anticipated for dying have expanded. Investigate what the average of dying is in America.

64. Do you believe you will die around that age? If not, do you believe you will live longer or shorter?

65. Bristol states that *"repetition is the fundamental rhythm of all progress."* He continues by stating that *"it's the repeated auto or heterosuggestion that makes you and others believe."* What kind of repetition currently exists in your life? Do you repeat the same transportation to work? The same practices at the office? The same rituals at dinner? Make a list of the repetitive practices you have in your life.

66. Do you believe these practices are more firmly implanted into your psyche because of the repetition? Why or why not? Please explain.

67. An example of positive affirmation that the author shared was of mothers who fed their children positive affirmations while they were sleeping. Reflect on your childhood. Did you receive positive affirmations, or fear-based messages, such as *"Be careful not to..."* or *"Don't do that— you'll hurt yourself."* What were the messages that you heard, and how do you believe they impacted your confidence?

68. The author asserts that *"many people become confused and frustrated because they allow themselves to be influenced by negative thoughts of others."* On a scale from one to ten (one being "very little" and ten being "a great deal"), rate how much you believe your thoughts are negatively influenced by others.

1——2——3——4——5——6——7——8——9——10

69. According to the author, *"faith without action is dead."* The author cites Nicola Tesla as an example of a man who coupled his *"faith with action"*. Can you think of other such individuals who have been unwavering in their faith, and committed in their actions? Write about them and why you believe they were so successful. What makes them different that you or I, or are they?

Chapter 6

The Mirror Technique for Releasing the Subconscious

The toughest problem that confronts most people is the lack of money, and while I have read and heard of people finding bundles of $1000 bills by using this Mind Stuff, I think that money comes as a result of combining Mind Stuff and energized action. Money certainly can be attracted by your thought, and once it appears on the horizon your thought will lead you to ways and means of acquiring it. While I was in the investment banking business I knew many people of large means, and I found that every one of them had a "money consciousness." They thought wealth and their coming to possess it was quite similar to my own experience related earlier in this book.

It is always the same technique, no matter what your desires. Get the picture of what you want and keep telling yourself that you're going to get it. But don't think it is going to come to you if you merely indulge in a period of watchful waiting. Go to work, always keeping your goal in mind, and start saving. Every dollar you save out of your weekly pay check is a step nearer to the fortune that is going to be yours. Consider it as such and save as many dollars as you can. The more you save, the faster you will build that fortune. Then put your savings out at interest, invest them where they will work advantageously for you, not by gambling or playing the market, but in securities of proven worth, in real estate, or in a business of your own. As your investment grows under your money consciousness, you'll be agreeably surprised to find that the more you have, the more you accumulate. Furthermore, you'll find it exciting and stimulating. Opportunities for profitable investments will come to you from many unexpected and unknown sources, but don't make the mistake that many do and follow will-o'-the-wisps; get sound advice before you invest a cent.

I recall one woman and her daughter who in twenty-five years accumulated more than half a million dollars, which today is largely represented by apartment houses and store buildings. The woman's husband died shortly after World War I, and she was left with a fairly large-sized house. She was at her wits' end how to support herself and her daughter who had just finished high school. She had had no previous experience in holding a job or carrying on a business, but she could cook and keep house. One morning the idea came to her to take in roomers and boarders. That was the start, and success came rapidly. Within two years she sold the house and the business, realizing a handsome profit, and then bought a much larger house directly across the street from a well-known men's club, believing that with her high-grade cooking she could get much of the club's overflow business. She did—and prospered; even though she employed plenty of help, no task was too lowly for her in a rush period.

A retired elderly businessman who had taken up his home at her place one day suggested that she open a tea room. He said he would provide the necessary funds to fix up a place. The top floor of an office building in the business section was found and the tea room opened. With herself as hostess and her daughter as cashier during the rush hours, and at other times helping in the kitchen and directing her employees, she soon made the tea room a favorite eating-place for business men. That led to the purchase of a beach hotel through a mortgage company, and also to the profit-able sale of the tea room. All of this time she was investing in securities and it wasn't long before she had accumulated a nest egg of $25,000, which went as the first payment on a run-down apartment house. Remodeling under her di-rection made the building remarkably attractive, and it be-came very popular under her management. With the great results achieved her reputation came to the attention of an insurance company that owned other apartment houses in those days, and she was offered the management of a number of them on a salary and a percentage basis. As her capital grew, her opportunities to buy apartment houses followed, and the last time I heard of this woman with the "money-consciousness" she not only owned apartment houses in this particular city, but she had also purchased an apartment house at a near-by beach resort which previously had operated only during the summer months, but which she now operates all the year round.

It has long been my observation that a person with a workable idea seldom has any difficulty in getting money to finance himself. However, he must be thoroughly "sold" on the idea himself before he can convince others to lend him money. If you contemplate having your own business, think about this and use the science of belief, for you'll find someone with money who will help you.

Great fortunes are not built in a day but come as a result of dollars adding themselves to those you already have or to those you earn and save. But if you want a fortune, you must put your mind and energies to work. It will come—just use the magic of believing.

Here's another case where by using this science success followed in rapid order—in fewer than ten years. A corner druggist had gone into bankruptcy. The fixtures were owned by the owner of the building and most of the stock by a wholesale druggist. A young pharmacist heard about the location, but had no funds with which to proceed. Finally the wholesaler and the landlord got together, and the young fellow "sold himself" to both of them. The landlord, anxious to keep the place occupied, agreed to finance the young fellow for several months, and with necessary guarantees to the wholesaler the place was reopened. His wife helped behind the counter and at the fountain and the business began to grow. For a long time the young druggist had been interested in a preparation which he thought would help people, but he had never had the funds to finance himself. One day he decided to talk with the owner of the building, a man of considerable wealth. So thoroughly did he believe in his plan that he had no trouble in convincing the owner, who organized a company for the young fellow and put up $5000 to start. For months the preparation was bottled in the basement of the rented home of the druggist during evenings after the store was closed. People began to buy it in increasing quantities and the business began to expand. It spread all over the country, and within a few years not only was the landlord paid off, but he told me that his profit was better than $50,000 and that the young fellow's income was now more than

$100,000 a year. He and his company now own the building where he started.

Another remarkable story came to my attention a few years back in the midst of the so-called depression. The story is from the man's own lips. He had been in clerical positions most of his life but one day found himself on the WPA payroll. His wife in an endeavor to get help for some of her troubles had taken up "religion." The religious organization was one that insists upon tithing—that is, upon the payment by each member of 10 per cent of his income.

(By the way, there are thousands of people who are firm believers in tithing, and, as a matter of fact, one of our greatest industrialists, who preaches religion in his own organization and to outsiders, attributes much of his success to his practice of tithing. Another man who is very successful in the selling of baking machines and equipment, credits his success entirely to his tithing. Whether this giving of one-tenth of their income to the church or to some religious or charitable organization has anything to do with the success of these individuals, is, of course, something that the writer cannot answer; but surely these tithers believe thoroughly in the efficacy of their practices, and who is there to say that it doesn't work for them?)

One night the husband on WPA was prevailed upon to accompany his wife to church and then "the light hit me," as he told me. Upon arriving at his home, "something" led him to search for an old formula which his father had used in preparing a lotion or a tonic that could be used in all barber and beauty shops. With the finding of the formula, he began to gather old bottles from junk-shops and scrap piles, which he took home and washed—and they became the first containers. This man went personally from barbershop to barbershop, from beauty parlor to beauty parlor, and so convincing were his stories that it wasn't long before he gave up his WPA job and opened up a plant of his own. He believed thoroughly that the tithing principle was responsible for his good fortune and for all of the ideas that came to him. His product became widely known throughout the country, but the trade was no longer supplied by the man personally—wholesalers pushed it and he had his own sales organization as well. Another illustration of the magic of believing.

Everything on the material plane is first an idea, a thought in someone's mind. A person selling a commodity is actually selling an idea—if it's a machine, what the machine will do—if building material, how it can be used—if food, how nutritious and tasty it will be, and so on endlessly. All businesses, all fortunes are the outgrowth of an idea, the workings of someone's imagination followed by action.

For years I have watched the progress of the Jantzen Knitting Mills, makers of the famous Jantzen swimming suits. I have seen this manufacturing concern grow from practically nothing but an idea to an organization that circles the globe, and the success story of those behind it rivals any told by Horatio Alger. Several times I've discussed this science with J. A. Zentbauer, president of the company and chairman of its board, and with his permission I quote a letter he wrote to me:

As you say, some people seem to possess an indefinable something which spurs them on to a successful and happy life, while others apparently work hard but without that something in their characters which brings them satis-

faction and success. I have never tried systematically to develop this indefinable spirit but believe it has been developed in me by my parents, and especially by my mother, who promptly fought our inclination as youngsters to say, "I can't do this or I can't do that," by saying to us that we should not say we can't do it, but that, of course, we can do anything anyone else can do, and all that was necessary was to tackle the job and keep on trying until it was mastered; and that we would then be ready to tackle a bigger job, and to shrink from no job because it was great or unimportant. Then she was constantly resisting our inclination as youngsters to complain or growl about anything. When we were in a complaining disposition, she would say, "Don't grumble but think what a privilege it is to live in such a wonderful world and instead of complaining, brace right up and keep smiling and enjoy the blessings at hand." There were four youngsters in our family, three boys and one girl. We have always been exceptionally happy and I attribute it to the training of our parents; mother, with her constant training and father corroborating her often by saying: "Always look on the bright side, never on the dark side of things." If one has not been fortunate enough to have the advantages of such influences, I can see where it would take a great amount of self-discipline and training to bring one up to the point of view which you clearly point out is necessary to get the most out of life. Regardless of one's present circumstances, I am sure the application of your science would be valuable to him.

In a postwar world, the competition is unusually keen and naturally the person best prepared for a certain position is in a far better situation to get it than one who is not. I say this because I do not wish to give the idea to any of my readers that a man who has had neither the education nor the experience can step out of the army, or out of a job in an industrial plant, and immediately take over the reins of a large industrial corporation simply by using this science of belief. There may be exceptional cases of men doing this, but they are few and far between.

First things come first, always, and if a man feels and believes he is entitled to a better job and has prepared himself for it, then with the use of this science he can get that job or some other as good or better.

A well-known executive once said to me, "The difficulty I see with most people seeking employment is that they are so wrapped up in themselves that they make no effort to impress their prospective employer with what they can do to help him, overlooking the fact that the other fellow is only interested in you to the extent that you can help him."

To some of my readers this may appear a cold-blooded attitude, but in the world of competition, self-interest is a reality that all prospective employees must face.

There is an old saying that "If you do not follow your own thoughts, then you will follow the thoughts of the fellow who followed his," and it means exactly what it says—it marks the difference between a leader and a follower. You who do not think or use your creative ability are always being given orders by those who do. Unless you are willing to think, you will have to labor physically, and this means you will receive less for your work.

Therefore, visualize the kind of job you want, and use your cards and your constant affirmations until belief in your goal becomes a vital part of you and you feel it in your blood, your bones, and in every tissue of your body. See yourself actually doing the things you visualize and it will all work out, because every thought held constantly and persistently sooner or later materializes after its kind. All of you sometime in your life have taken vacation trips. Did you ever stop to analyze the mental processes involved? First you got the idea of the trip, then you decided where you would go, and shortly you began to visualize yourself in the mountains, at the seashore, or visiting some new city, and the vacation turned out as planned because you saw yourself doing it—actually before the vacation trip became a reality. Could anything be clearer? Whatever you want to do, just apply the same principles and you will get the same successful results.

You will remember the card device, which I explained in detail. There is another device, which I call the mirror technique. Before explaining it, I want to tell you how I happened to discover what a truly wonderful thing it is, and how it can be used to bring quicker and more effective results.

Many years ago I was the dinner guest of a very wealthy man who owned many patents covering logging and sawmill machinery. He had invited a number of newspaper publishers, bankers, and industrial leaders to his suite in a prominent hotel, in order to explain a new method he had devised for mill operations. Liquor flowed freely and it wasn't long before the host himself was very much intoxicated. Just before dinner was served, I noticed him staggering into his bedroom and pulling himself up abruptly before his dresser. Thinking that I might help him, I followed him to the door of his room. As I stood there, I saw him grab the edge of the dresser top with both hands and stare into the mirror, all the time mumbling as a drunken man sometimes does. Then his words began to make sense and I moved back a little to watch the performance. I heard him say: "John, you old _____, they tried to get you drunk, but you're going to fool them. You're sober, you're sober, cold sober, this is your party and you've got to be sober."

As he kept repeating these words, while continuing to stare at the reflection of his eyes in the mirror, I noticed that a transfiguration was taking place. His body was becoming more erect, the muscles of his face were tightening, and his drunken look was disappearing. The whole performance was over in perhaps five minutes, but in all my experience as a newspaper man and more especially as a police reporter where I had opportunity to observe many drunken people, I had never seen such a rapid change. Not wanting him to know that I had observed him, I made for the bathroom. When I got back to the dining room I found the host at the head of the table, and while his face was still a little flushed, to all appearances he was sober. At the end of the dinner he presented a very dramatic and convincing picture of his new plans. It wasn't until long afterward when I got a better understanding of the power of the subconscious mind, that I understood the science involved in transforming the obviously drunken man into a cold-sober host.

I have for many years given the mirror technique to thousands of people, with some very unusual results. During these years a large number of people came to me for help with their problems. There were a surprising number of women, and practically all of them started their stories with weeping spells. The first thing I did was to stand them before a full-length mirror and have them take a good look at themselves; I made them look into their eyes and tell me what they saw there—crybabies or fighters? Their crying soon ceased, and those cases convinced me that a woman cannot weep while looking at herself in a mirror. Whether it be pride, shame, or the repudiated idea that they are weaklings that stops them short, is of no moment. The fact remains that the tears cease flowing.

Many great orators, preachers, actors, and statesmen have used this mirror technique for years. Winston Churchill, according to Drew Pearson, never made a speech of importance unless he made it before a mirror first. Pearson also declared that Woodrow Wilson employed the same technique. It's what I call a supercharging method of stepping up the subconscious forces of the speaker so that when he appears before an audience those forces flow out to and affect his listeners. By using the mirror in rehearsing the speech as you are going to deliver it, you are creating at that moment a picture of yourself, your words, the sound of your voice, and your sight of the audience, to which the immediate future is to bring reality. By looking into the mirror, you increase the mental vibrations by which the force and meaning of your words will quickly penetrate to the subconscious minds of your audience.

This mirror technique gives a clue to the power and the personal magnetism of Billy Sunday, the evangelist. I knew Bill Sunday in his heyday and often heard him preach, but in those days, knowing little or nothing about this Mind Stuff, I was puzzled as to how he, as well as Gypsy Smith and other great evangelists, was able to influence people to such a remarkable degree.

However, we now have proof that Billy Sunday was versed in the use of the mirror technique; it is given by Eric Sevareid, Columbia Broadcasting System commentator, in his book *Not So Wild a Dream*, published in 1946. Mr. Sevareid tells how he as a young newspaper reporter secured an interview with Billy Sunday.

> *"He bounded about the hotel room, now peering intently out of the window, with one foot on the sill, now grasping the dressing table firmly in both hands while lecturing his reflection in the mirror."*

One of the most outstanding insurance salesmen in America who early accepted the science of belief told me that he never called upon an important prospect without first giving his sales presentation in front of a mirror. His sales were phenomenal.

Every salesman has heard the statement, "If you can convince yourself, you can convince the other fellow," which is basically true. Every great mass movement in history from religious to military has come about through one individual, whose flaming belief in his own cause gave him the power to convert thousands of others. A man need not be a student of psychology to know that enthusiasm is very contagious and can readily be transmitted to others if one is bursting with it. The mirror technique is a simple and effective method by which a person can strengthen his belief in his own sales ability and thus intensify the power of his enthusiasm.

When the mirror technique is considered in the light of the science given in this book, it becomes a master method by which the mighty forces of the subconscious mind can be employed to influence those with whom you are dealing.

Whether we know it or not, we're all engaged in selling something—if not our wares, then our personalities, our services, our ideas. As a matter of fact, all human relationships are based upon selling of one kind or another, and we all engage in it whenever we undertake to persuade others to our way of thinking. Legally a contract or an agreement is based upon a "meeting of the minds," and unless you can get the other person to think your way, you do not get very far. But once the minds meet on the major issues, the rest is easy, and the name on the dotted line is but a matter of a few more moments.

During the "depression" days when I was working with many business and sales organizations to increase their business, I introduced this mirror method with some startling results. In one concern, a pie-making organization, I had mirrors fastened to the inside of the back doors of all the trucks, so that when the driver-salesmen opened the doors to get their goods for delivery, the first thing to be seen were the mirrors. I always admonished each man to determine before calling upon a customer how many pies he was going to sell him, and then to tell himself in the mirror that pies to that number would be left on the customers' counters. One driver told me that for many months he had been trying to sell one woman restaurant owner, but she had always refused to purchase. Then he decided to try the mirror technique. That day he sold her ten pies. At the time he related his story to me he was selling her an average of fifteen pies daily.

The mirror technique was used with great effectiveness in insurance companies, financial houses, rubber mills, automobile agencies, cookie manufacturing plants, and many other organizations where there were salesmen or where there was a combination of salesmen and production operators. In my own old organization where a complete about-face movement had to be made to avert disaster, I first used this technique by placing a mirror in a back room of the office where the employees left their hats and overcoats. It was so placed that everyone had to see it when entering or leaving the room. At first I pasted strips of paper with such slogans as "We're going to win," "Nothing is impossible to an indefatigable mind," "We've got the guts, let's prove it," "Let's show the world we're not licked and then go to town," "How many are you going to sell today?" and a great many others. We then took to using soap to write the slogans directly on the face of the mirror. Every morning a new slogan appeared, with the sole purpose of convincing our employees that they could get business even though other firms in the same line were having a struggle to keep their doors open. Later this setup was augmented by a second mirror placed alongside the door-frame of the main door to the office, which would always be the last thing seen by the salesmen as they left the office. Subsequently I had mirrors placed alongside calendar frames on the desks of all salesmen and executives, and the startling thing about it all was that during the worst of the "depression" days the salesmen—and I mean all of them—trebled and quadrupled their incomes, and they have maintained their progress ever since. There are a number of men whose monthly income probably never exceeded in the best of times $300 who now and for several years have averaged better than $1000 a month. This may sound incredible to some of my readers, but it's true. In my files are many letters from executives, salesmen, and others who have testified to the effectiveness of the mirror idea.

Now to outline the technique. Stand in front of a mirror. It need not be a full-length mirror, but it should be of sufficient size so that you may at least see your body from the waist up.

Those of you who have been in the army know what it means to come to attention—stand fully erect, bring your heels together, pull in your stomach, keep your chest out and your head up. Now breathe deeply three or four times until you feel a sense of power, strength, and determination. Next, look into the very depths of your eyes, tell yourself that you are going to get what you want—name it aloud so you can see your lips move and you can hear the words uttered. Make a regular ritual of it, practice doing it at least twice a day, mornings and evenings—and you will be surprised at the results. You can augment this by writing with soap on the face of the mirror any slogans or key words you wish, so long as they are the key to what you have previously visualized and want to see in reality. Within a few days you will have developed a sense of confidence that you never realized you could build within yourself.

If you are planning to call on an exceptionally tough prospect or are proposing to interview the boss whom you may have previously feared, use the mirror technique, and keep it up until you are convinced that you can make the proper presentation without any trepidation. And of course, if you are called upon to make a speech, by all means practice before a mirror. Gesticulate—pound your fist on the palm of your other hand to drive home the arguments—use any other gestures that come naturally to you.

As you stand before the mirror, keep telling yourself that you are going to be an outstanding success and that nothing in this world is going to stop you. Does this sound silly? Don't forget that every idea presented to the subconscious mind is going to be produced in its exact counterpart in objective life, and the quicker your subconscious gets the idea, the sooner your wish becomes a picture of power. Certainly it is not good business for you to tell anyone of the devices you employ, because you might be ridiculed by scoffers and your confidence shaken, especially if you are just beginning to learn the science.

If you are an executive or sales manager and you want to put more push into your entire organization, teach your employees the mirror technique and see that they use it, just as many organizations now do.

Much has been written about the power of the eyes. The eyes are said to be the windows of the soul; they reveal your thoughts. They express you far more than you imagine. They permit others to "get your number," as the saying goes. However, you will find that once you start this mirror practice your eyes will take on a power that you never realized you could develop (something that writers have referred to as a dynamic or fascinating power); this power will give you that penetrating gaze that causes others to think you are looking into their very souls. Sooner or later there will come an intensity that will bespeak the intensity of your thought, which people will begin to recognize. It will be recalled that Emerson wrote that every man carries in his eye the exact indication of his rank. Remember that your own gradation or position in life is marked by what you carry in your eyes. So develop eyes that bespeak confidence. The mirror will help you.

This mirror technique may be used in many different ways and with very gratifying results. If you have a poor posture, or are slovenly in your walk, you will find that practice before a full-length mirror will work wonders for you. Your mirror shows you the person others see when they look at you, and you can fashion yourself into any kind of person you would like them to see.

It is said that if you act the part you will become that part, and here again there is no better way than rehearsing your acting before the mirror. Vanity has no part in this science. Consequently, don't use the mirror in a supercilious manner, but use it to build yourself into the person you wish to be. Surely, if some of the world's most outstanding men and women use this mirror technique to build themselves and increase their influence over other people, you can use it for your own special requirements.

Much has been written about intuition, hunches, and the like. Some psychologists claim that ideas which come to us intuitively are not something "out of the blue," but come as a result of our accumulated knowledge or because of something we may have seen or heard in earlier times. That may be true to some extent with chemists, inventors, and others who work by the "trial and error" method of using their knowledge and the results of previous experiments, but it's the writer's belief that by far the greatest number of discoveries, illuminations, and inspired works come from the subconscious mind, without previous knowledge having been planted in the mind. Every custom we follow, everything we utilize was first an idea in someone's mind, and those ideas came first in the way of "hunches," intuitive flashes, or call them what you will. So it is wise to heed your intuitions and to trust them to the end.

Many great leaders, industrialists, and inventors have openly declared that they have followed the hunches which have come to them in odd moments of relaxation or in periods when they were engaged in some other task than trying to solve their problems. A good way to let your subconscious mind solve a problem is for you to tackle it from all angles consciously; then some night just before dropping off to sleep, order the subconscious mind to bring you the answer. You may awaken in the middle of the night with the answer, or it may come to you upon awakening in the morning or at some odd moment of the day when you are engaged in something quite different. Be quick to grasp it when it comes and waste no time in following through with it.

You may have a hunch to call on or telephone a certain man. He may be the head of some concern and in a position to be of great help to you. However, because of his position you may fear to make the move and you struggle with your "hunch" on one hand and your fear on the other. The fear too often wins. The next time fear or doubt enters your mind, ask yourself this question: "What have I got to lose if I do see him or call him? What harm can I do?" Your fears and doubts can't answer that question. So obey your hunch without delay.

A word of warning should be given here, however. Many people like to gamble. Some play cards, others bet on the horse or dog races, and many play the market. Undoubtedly there are those who say that they follow their hunches and now and then make a "killing," but the writer urges you not to use your hunches in an endeavor to get something for nothing. There is something fundamentally wrong about it, because most gamblers die broke. Also, beware of hunches that would lead you into untried fields. They may not be hunches at all, but just sudden fanciful longings. The true kind of hunch is always concerned with something that is related to you directly or indirectly, and it gives you the idea to do a certain thing, followed by the momentum to carry out the necessary action.

The writer takes it for granted that none of his readers will assume that this book is an open-sesame to riches and fame overnight. It is intended only as a key to unlock the door that opens on the roadway which will lead to the goal of your desire. Certainly it wouldn't be wise to rush into undertakings far beyond your capabilities or your development. If you would be the head of a great utility concern, you would naturally have to know the business, just as you would if you aspired to become head of a huge transportation system. But by using this science, you could learn the various steps which would take you to the top. However, you must have a plan of action before any program is undertaken. You wouldn't go to the corner drugstore and ask just for drugs. You would be specific and name the drugs desired. And so it is with this science. You must have a plan of action—you've got to know what you want and be specific about it.

If you have definitely determined what you want and have fixed a goal for yourself, then consider yourself extremely fortunate, for you have taken the first step that will lead to success. As long as you hold on to the mental picture of your idea and begin to develop it with action, nothing can stop you from succeeding, for the subconscious mind never fails to obey any order given to it clearly and emphatically.

STUDY GUIDE

Chapter 6

The author opens this chapter asserting that many people have issues with lack of money, and states that money comes as a result of combining energized action and Mind Stuff. He takes you through one of his most powerful techniques that assist you in learning how to gain abundance in your life. He then shares poignant situations where individuals were able to use this technique to draw to themselves circumstances that supported their wishes and desires. He emphasizes that everything on the material plane is first an idea, and outlines an exercise in which you write about upcoming goals you would like to see accomplished. He then shares the remarkable mirror technique, providing humorous and potent examples of how it has worked so effectively for many. He ends this chapter, discussing how important it is to follow your hunches. He warns, however, that you should use the gift of intuition for your highest good and for the good of others.

1. Claude Bristol opens this chapter stating that the toughest problem that most people have is the lack of money. He believes that money comes *"as a result of combining Mind Stuff and energized action."* Define what you believe the author means by *"energized"* action.

2. On a scale from one to ten (one being "very little" and ten being "a great deal"), rate how much *"energized action"* you take towards acquiring your financial goals.

1———2———3———4———5———6———7———8———9———10

3. Every one of the people who Bristol knew to be wealthy in the banking business had a *"money consciousness."* In your own words, describe what you believe money consciousness to be.

4. Do you believe you currently have money consciousness? Why or why not? Please explain.

5. Are there steps that you believe you can take to gain more money consciousness? If so, please list them.

6. According to the author, the secret to manifesting success is to *"Get the picture of what you want and keep telling yourself that you're going to get it."* He continues, however by stating *"don't think it's going to come to you if you merely indulge in a period of watchful waiting."* Have you been idly waiting for your desires to come to you? What is one action step you can take right now to get closer to your goals? List it, and then act upon it before you continue with this study guide.

7. You are encouraged to start saving out of your weekly paycheck. Do you have a wealth-building strategy in which some of the funds in your paycheck go directly into savings? By setting up a fund that directly comes out of your paycheck, you can easily keep committed to saving without missing the funds. If you haven't already done so, take some time to set up such a program, even if its only a small amount that is saved each paycheck. Small amounts add up. Write about any actions you take, and describe how you feel after taking them.

8. Many companies offer 401K programs or discounted employee stock purchase options. Are any such programs available to you? If so, do you partake in them? Why or why not?

9. Bristol suggests that you invest in *"securities or proven worth, in real estate, or in a business of your own."* Have you done any investing? If so, what has been the outcome to date? If you have not, what is preventing you from doing so? Could you start by investing a small amount into a fund each month? Consider doing so, and write about any actions you take.

10. According to the author, *"as your investments grow under your money consciousness, you'll be agreeably surprised to find that the more you have, the more you accumulate."* Have you ever experienced this? If so, describe the situation. If not, do you believe this statement to be true? Explain.

11. When you have money consciousness, investment *"opportunities will come to you from many unexpected and unknown sources."* Are there any further steps you can take to align yourself with such surprises? If so, what? If not, list the opportunities that come your way as you make this attitudinal shift.

12. The author urges you to get sound advice before investing. Do you have investment advisors who have proven track records? If so, how have they supported your goals to date? If not, take some time to research and find someone who has a proven track record, to advise you.

13. A story is shared of a resourceful woman who built her wealth by taking in boarders. She grew her business to great success. Do you know of anyone who has amassed great wealth by being so resourceful? If so, describe their experience. If not, take some time to research and write about someone who has.

14. Do you have any such *"workable ideas"*? If so, list them.

15. Are you completely sold on these ideas?

16. Would you be willing to take out a loan to build on these ideas? Why or why not? Please explain.

17. If you haven't taken action on these ideas, why? What is stopping you from doing so? Please explain.

18. What do you believe the author would say in response to the reasons you listed?

19. While the author does not advocate tithing, he asserts that many who do so have amassed success. Do you tithe? What you are beliefs around doing so?

20. If you believe that tithing can help you gain your financial freedom, if you are not tithing, why not? If you are tithing, have you noted any changes in your financial disposition since doing so? Explain.

21. If you don't believe you can currently afford to tithe, is your current attitude that of "lack"? Is there a small amount you could start giving? Please explain, and if you believe tithing would help, stipulate an amount and start to give it. Note any shifts you make after doing so.

22. The author shares remarkable success stories about a young druggist, a man who prepared a lotion based on his father's recipes. When you read these stories what were your thoughts? Did they create excitement in you, or a sense of hopelessness? Please explain.

23. If these stories created a sense of hopelessness, what might you do to gain a more positive and uplifting frame of mind? Write about your options, and then take the necessary steps to act upon them. Write about any changes you note.

24. The author shares a letter given to him by J. A. Zentbauer, president of Jantzen swimming suits. Zentbauer attributes a great deal of his success to the encouragement that his mother gave him as a child. Was there anyone in particular in your childhood that you felt supported you in becoming the person you are today? If so, who and how did they support you? How has their support helped to lead to your current successes?

25. When he and his siblings complained, Zentbauer's mother would tell them not to grumble and to focus on *"enjoying the blessings at hand."* He claimed that his family members were always happy due to the encouragement they received to focus on the bright side of things. There are two schools of thought around this. Some would concur with Zentbauer, while others would say it is healthiest to honor, respect and express your feelings; that suppress-

ing them would only make them more powerful. Which school of thought do you follow, and why?

26. Can both schools of thought be true? Why or why not? Pleases explain.

27. A well-known executive once shared with the author that *"The difficulty I see with most people seeking employment is that they are so wrapped up in themselves that they make no effort to impress their prospective employer with what they can do to help him, overlooking the fact that the other fellow is only interested in you to the extent that you can help him."* Have you ever made this error during a job interview? Please explain.

28. The author asserts that *"those who do not think or use your creative ability are always being given orders by those who do."* Are you currently being creative, or are you being given orders by other? Why are you in this position? What further changes do you need to make to find contentment in your career?

29. If you have not already done so, write a list of affirmations on index cards. Remember to write them in the present tense, and include a sense of gratitude, as if they have already happened. At least once a day for a month, read your affirmations aloud. Then after reading them, feel into your desires as if they are already manifesting in your life. Track and write about your experience in practicing this exercise.

30. Claude Bristol shares the dramatic story of how he watched the host of a party turn himself sober by looking in a mirror and affirming that he was. Have you ever witnessed such profound transformation at work? Please explain.

31. Do you believe one could "will" or "affirm" him or herself sober? Why or why not? Please explain.

32. If you had faith that the right job will appear at the right time, do you believe you would be less interested in yourself, and perhaps more interested in how you can best serve future employers? Please explain.

33. The difference between leaders and followers is that leaders think and use their creativity. How do you put your creativity to use? List the ways in which you do so.

34. What elements of your current job could also be found in the job that you are seeking?

35. What elements of your current job are far from the elements of the job you would like to manifest in your life?

36. The author likens materializing of your desires to taking a trip. You plan, and then you visualize experiencing the destination in ways that inspire and uplift you. Organize your greatest desire as if it were a trip you are planning. Map it out, and then visualize experiencing it fully and deeply. Write about your experience in doing so.

37. Many great orators, preachers, actors, and statesmen have used the mirror technique to help them achieve success. Have you ever done any emotional work in front of a mirror? If so, what was the outcome?

38. Winston Churchill and Woodrow Wilson used the mirror to assist them prior to making public speeches. Set a timer. For the next 5 minutes, get in front of the mirror and have a dialogue with the image you see in the mirror. At first you may attempt to judge your appearance. Make a choice to move beyond self-criticism. Look into your eyes. Write about what you see and experience.

39. The author encourages you to use the mirror in rehearsing your speech as if you were delivering it in that moment. Picture yourself, the words you are speaking, the quality of your voice, and your vision of the audience. By looking into the mirror, you *"increase the mental vibrations by*

which the force and meaning of your words will quickly penetrate to the subconscious minds of your audience." Write a short speech, perhaps in response to an award that you can imagine yourself receiving in response to your future success. Then practice your acceptance speech in the mirror. Imagine your audience—how large it is, who is in the audience, how much they enjoy hearing you speak. Once you complete this exercise, write about any feelings you had while doing it and thereafter.

40. *"If you can convince yourself, you can convince the other fellow"* was the statement that one of America's most outstanding insurance salesmen used. What causes do you believe deeply in? Write a list of them.

41. Enthusiasm is contagious. What are you most enthusiastic about in your life? How can you use your enthusiasm to assist others in their lives?

42. The author asserts that we all engage in selling something—our wares, our personalities, our services, or our ideas. Make a list of what you sell in your life—your wares, aspects of your personality, services you provide, or ideas you have.

43. Do you believe you have blocks around conducting sales calls or promoting yourself?

44. On a scale from one to ten (one being "not at all" and ten being "extremely"), rate how effective you believe you are at self-promotion and sales:

1——2——3——4——5——6——7——8——9——10

45. What steps can you take to better support selling yourself and your wares? List three things you can do to improve yourself.

46. Any legal contract is a meeting of the minds. Do you believe your mind power has an effect on the outcome of contractual agreements that you make? Why or why not?

47. Write a contract to yourself on the commitment that you will make to develop your mind power by practicing the techniques and using the tools outlined in this book. Then be sure to date and sign it.

48. Do you believe that creating and signing a contact makes your commitment more powerful? Why or why not?

49. The author encouraged pie salesmen to use the mirror technique before going out on sales calls. Their sales numbers really grew. Claude Bristol placed mirrors with affirmations in the coatroom of his business. Sales trebled and quadrupled. How might you use mirrors in your business? List the places where you would place them, and be sure to do so.

50. Track your progress as you work with the mirror technique. Gratitude increases your energy and adds fuel to the positive fire. Be sure to voice your gratitude for the shifts, perhaps by keeping a gratitude journal.

51. Here is an outline of the mirror technique *"Stand in front of a mirror. It need not be a full-length mirror, but it should be of sufficient size so that you may at least see your body from the waist up. Those of you who have been in the army know what it means to come to attention—stand fully erect, bring your heels together, pull in your stomach, keep your chest out and you head up. Now breathe deeply three or four times until you feel a sense of power, strength, and determination. Next, look into the very depths of your eyes, tell yourself that you are going to get what you want—name it aloud so you can see your lips move and you can hear the words uttered. Make a regular ritual of it, practice doing it at least twice a day, mornings and evenings—and you will be surprised at the results."* Choose one of the most important desires that you would like to manifest into your life. Practice this mirror exercise at least twice a day, as suggested. Keep a daily journal of your findings.

52. Bristol adds, *"As you stand before the mirror, keep telling yourself that you are going to be an outstanding success and that nothing in this world is going to stop you."* Try doing this now. How do you feel when you first say it in the mirror? How do you feel after repeating it several times? Be sure to repeat this to yourself each time you look in the mirror. Note any changes you see in yourself in relation to doing this exercise.

53. The author encourages you to teach this technique to colleagues, especially if they are in sales. Is this viable for you and your colleagues? Why or why not?

54. If you have blocks in sharing this technique, work on those blocks using the mirror technique itself. Then once you feel confident enough, be sure and share it with your team. Write about your progress.

55. Practicing this technique will also give you *"penetrating gaze that causes others to think you are looking into their very souls."* You are encouraged to *"develop eyes that bespeak confidence."* Look deeply into your eyes. What do you see?

56. Ask three people you trust what they see as they look into your eyes. Do your eyes reveal confidence, or insecurity? Are they penetrating or ineffectual? Write about your findings.

57. Poor posture, or a slovenly walk will also show up in the mirror technique. Take note of your posture. On a scale from one to ten (one being "very poor" and ten being "excellent"), rate your current posture:

1———2———3———4———5———6———7———8———9———10

58. What exercises or steps can you take to improve your posture?

59. Try walking in front of the mirror. On a scale from one to ten (one being "very poor" and ten being "excellent"), rate

effect and confident your walk is (if you don't know, ask a couple of friends to give you honest feedback on it):

60. What steps can you take to improve the way you walk?

Do you dress for success? On a scale from one to ten (one being "very poor" and ten being "excellent"), rate how effectively you dress yourself:

61. Are there any steps you need to take to improve your sense of style and the way you dress? There are stylists that you can hire to assist you, or if you know of someone that you believe has good fashion sense, you could ask them for assistance. Write out your plan on improving your sense of style.

62. How effective are you at listening to any hunches that arise from your subconscious? On a scale from one to ten (one being "very poor" and ten being "excellent"), rate well you hear and follow through on hunches:

63. The author suggests that you call upon your subconscious mind for guidance before drifting off to sleep. He then suggests that you be quick to grasp any messages and be sure to follow through on them. Try this exercise, keeping a notebook by your bed, so that you can write down hunches as they arise. After one month of doing this exercise, review your findings and summarize anything you gained from doing it.

64. When fear to follow your hunches enters your mind, Claude Bristol suggests that you ask yourself *"What have I got to lose? What harm can I do?"* Usually taking action can cause no harm. Next time you struggle with following through, ask yourself these questions, and then be sure to take action thereafter.

65. The author encourages you not to use your hunches in order to *"endeavor to get something for nothing."* In other words, do not use it to gamble, play the market, etc. He asserts that it should not be used, anticipating overnight success. Have you ever used it in such a way? If so, what was the outcome?

66. Using your hunches is an integral part of your growth, as you progress step by step towards your goals. You are encouraged to have a plan of action before undertaking any major endeavor. You need to *"know what you want and be specific about it."* While you have likely already done so, summarize your goal, providing as much specific deal as possible. Who will it serve? How will it serve them? What can it further develop into? What are your short-term goals in relation to it? What are your long-term goals? How will it affect you? How will it affect others? How will it affect the world? Could it be a starting point for other creative endeavors? If so, how?

Chapter 7

How to Project Your Thoughts

Success is a matter of never-ceasing application. You must forever work at it diligently. Otherwise it takes wings and flies away. At no time can you afford to rest on your laurels—a pause for self-admiration—because there are others who may have eyes on your coveted place and who would like nothing better than to push you out of it, especially if they observe that you have a weak hold on it or are doing nothing to strengthen your position.

Despite the great strides that America has made, it is still a country with great resources, many of which have not yet been tapped. Even though the war, with its atomic bombs, radar, rocket guns and ships, amphibious boats, and daring uses of plastics and metals opened up a mighty unexplored field where still greater things will be accomplished by men with imaginations and the spirit-to-do, the writer believes that "we haven't seen anything yet"; those of us who are alive fifty years hence will be looking upon a world which in comparison will make the early postwar years look like the Stone Age.

Already in our laboratories scientists are at work on what many may consider fantastic ideas. These include light and wearable fabrics from wood and other products that will be fire- and water-resistant, materials that will make ships unsinkable, machines that will capture energy from the sun, and even apparatus that will actually record our unspoken thoughts. These are only a few of the things appearing on the horizon, and they are all coming from the imaginations of men, or from their subconscious minds. Perhaps in less than fifty years thought transference or telepathy will be as commonplace as the radio of today. Who knows?

It has been said that man can bring into materialization anything that he can conceive mentally, and the millions of things we use and enjoy today prove it. When man fully comprehends the great power of his mind and earnestly puts it to work, not only will he have dominion over this earth and everything on it, but he may be reaching out to control the near-by planets. You yourself have this inner spark, but it must be fanned until the fire is of white-heat intensity and it must be constantly stoked, which you do by adding fuel—ideas, ideas, more ideas, and action.

One man I know who has many achievements to his credit and who has passed the seventy mark, declared that most people fall by the wayside because they are never starting anything. "I make it a plan, and have for years, to start something new—that is, new for me—at least once a week. It may be only the making of some simple gadget for use in the kitchen or it may be an entirely new sales plan or reading an unfamiliar book. I find in following this plan not only that I keep my body and mind active, but also that I put to use a lot of imaginative qualities that otherwise might fall asleep and atrophy. This idea of a man's retiring when he's sixty is to me a great mistake. As soon as a man retires and quits becoming active mentally and physically, he's on the way to his grave in short order. You have seen what has happened to fire horses when they are retired. You know what happens to your automobile when you leave it outside unused and neglected; it starts to rust and is soon headed for the junk-shop. Humans are the same; they rust out or wither and die when they go on the shelf."

The plan of starting something new at least once a week brings us to the matter of initiative and how valuable an asset individual initiative is for any person who seeks success. Without it a man is stopped almost as soon as he starts. Men and women remain in minor clerical positions all of their lives because they never display initiative in their work, never attempt to find new ways of doing their work, and never suggest improvements. During the war a number of organizations placed suggestion boxes in their plants and offered prizes for those that were considered most practical. Frequently these suggestions led to greatly improved methods in plant operations, as well as rewards in advancement for the employees offering the suggestions. In a number of instances employee suggestions led to patentable devices that brought fame and fortune to those supplying the initial ideas. Bear in mind that no matter how long a piece of work has been done in a certain way, there's always a better way. The war demonstrated that, so give heed to initiative. Even if you are just a clerk behind the counter in some store, you certainly must have some ideas of how goods may be better displayed or how the customers may be better served. Good ideas for lighting, color schemes, arrangement of the counters, display shelves are always acceptable to management, and are rewarded.

Closely linked with this matter of initiative are interest and attention. The more interest you take in your work, naturally the more attention you give it and the greater are the results. We all know that we do best the things in which we are interested, so if you do not find the task before you of interest, look for one that will interest you. The more absorbing the interest, the better—the interest factor alone will give you momentum that will carry you a long way forward.

One woman I know who was employed in a large department store as assistant to the manager of one of its largest departments, although her salary was fixed under the wartime ceiling, for several years received the store's highest Christmas bonus because of her interest and initiative, and her advice, rather than that of the manager of the department, was often sought by the head of the store.

The personnel manager of a huge defense plant employing many thousands of both men and women told me that the greatest fault he had to find with people was that they could not be depended upon. Some fail to keep their word, others are always late for their engagements, still others are forever changing their minds. So if you tell another person that you are going to do a certain thing, even though its fulfillment may cause you some inconvenience, do it no matter what the consequences or the cost in time or energy. You will be amply repaid, for you are building a reputation for reliability, which will be of great value as you proceed up the ladder.

Many employees hold to the idea that their work is given to them merely that they may further the interests of their employers. They never entertain the thought that they are actually working for themselves, the employer merely furnishing the tools and the place for the employee to work. There is an old saying that unless a man has learned to take orders he can never learn to give them. How true this is; but how few, working day after day, ever realize that it is within their own power to sit some day in the executive's place and give orders.

"The only way to have a friend is to be one," said Emerson; but few people ever give thought to this fundamental requirement. You can't cast your bread upon the waters without having it returned, and you can't do a good deed without having a good deed done to you in return; this is true, no matter how Pollyanna-ish it may sound to some people.

Rare indeed is the man who doesn't make an enemy now and then. You get out of tune with a man or perhaps he gets out of tune with you. Naturally, you don't like him; as a result of your thinking he doesn't like you. Fortunate is he who is able to make a friend of that enemy—and it's so easily done.

Several men who had taken a violent dislike to me, perhaps because of something I may have said in an unguarded moment, and would have liked figuratively to cut my throat, have become my staunchest friends merely by my thinking and believing that they were really friendly people.

I don't know where I got the idea of converting enemies into friends, whether it came to me out of the blue, whether I read it, or whether someone told me, but for years it has been part of my creed, and I've always found it to work. In illustration, let me tell the story of an executive who had taken a dislike to me for something I said critically about the operations of his company. For months, he was profanely "knocking me" at every opportunity. Naturally, my first impulse was to fight back and "knock" him in return. But the day came when I realized that his enmity had resulted from something I had said about him rather than the company, and I said to myself: "He's not a bad guy. I'm wrong. I started the feud, and I'm sorry. The next time I get near him I am going to tell him that mentally." One night I met him in a club of which we were both members. He would have avoided me, but we met nearly face to face, and I spoke first, saying, "How are you, Charlie?" He immediately responded and in the friendliest of manners. He caught "something" from my voice which meant a gesture of friendliness on my part, and today we're the closest of friends.

So remember this: some of our enemies may be of our own making. Those friends or enemies are merely a reflection of our own thoughts—the other fellow will consider us an enemy or friend according entirely to the picture which we ourselves conjure up.

Only today, as this is written, I had an example of this thought projection. The waste pipe of the laundry sink in my home had been clogged, and I had to call a plumber. A few blocks from our home was a plumbing shop, the proprietor of which was an unfriendly person and offensive in his treatment of customers. Several times I had tried to get him to do work for us, but he was always too busy.

The last time I had called him he had told me that I would have to wait my turn. Probably he could get around to fix up the water heater in a couple of weeks. I had asked him if he could give me the names of other plumbers who might help me, but he had been entirely uncooperative. Naturally, his unfriendly treatment had given me a bad impression of plumbers in general and I found myself damning all of them.

However, I had to get the heater repaired and I quickly realized that the angry attitude toward plumbers which had been engendered by this experience would cause me to have difficulty in obtaining the services of any one of them. I simply changed my thought, saying something like this to myself: "All plumbers are good fellows—the old guy you called is just an old grouch—forget it."

I had a friend, the manager of a wholesale plumbing house, and I called him to learn if he couldn't suggest a plumber who would help me. He did, and I telephoned him at once. He said he was busy, but if an imperative job had to be done he would be out immediately. His promise pleased me and my gratitude for service was immediately felt by the plumber when he entered our home fifteen minutes after my call. In less than two hours—he worked swiftly, thus differing from some plumbers I had employed—the heater had been replaced. I was genuinely delighted by his service and told him so. That naturally pleased him.

Today it was a little before 8 A.M. when I called for help. I told the plumber who I was and reminded him that he had been the one who had fixed my water heater. He remembered me immediately and said that he'd be out just as soon as possible— probably around noon. Within five minutes after I had hung up the telephone receiver, a man appeared at the front door asking if I had called a plumber.

I asked him how it happened that he was on the job so soon when I had been told by his boss that he couldn't send a man before noon, and he replied, "Mr. _____ had just received your call as I came into the shop and he told me to come up to your home and do what was necessary before I went out on my all day job."

I was elated with this treatment and told the plumber, which, of course, pleased him. With my help the necessary repairs on the waste pipe were made in less than half an hour. I told him of my previous experience with the old plumber and his own boss, and he replied:

"My boss is a fine fellow. He's always putting himself out to help people and he's building a huge business as a result. Never have I found a better boss."

You wager, think and believe that the other fellow is a fine chap, and that's what he'll turn out to be—for never forget that the thing we get back is a reflection of what we project mentally.

Do not reject this great truth. Just apply it and you'll be amazed at the startling results. Watch the bus driver respond, the elevator operator beam, and the clerk behind the counter hurry to oblige you when you send out friendly thoughts. It can be used in every encounter in life, and if you're wholly sincere about it, you will never have to worry about making enemies.

"And as ye would that men should do to you, do ye also to them likewise," says the Bible. As a matter of fact, many successful men and women, irrespective of any motive that may actuate them, work on the assumption that when they do something for the other person, something will be done for them. That may sound rather calculating, but the basic law of reciprocity remains, regardless of the situation or circumstances. It is simply that there must be a logical effect from every cause.

It isn't a matter of boot-licking when you try to please the boss. It's just common sense to make him a friend, for in any organization the people who get ahead are those who do their work well and try to please the boss. The boss is the man who does the promoting, and the more he is pleased with you and your work, the faster is your own progress. No matter how great your self-esteem, if you expect progress in any large organization, you must not only do your work well, but you must have the good will of the boss. Look around you a bit and you'll see this principle at work everywhere. You saw it work in the schoolroom when you were young, you saw it at work in the army, you see it in American politics, and if you have studied animal life you have recognized it working among the highest and the lowest types.

Take the initiative. Always try to do something for the other fellow and you will be agreeably surprised how things come your way—how many pleasant things are done for you. Doing something for others always pays dividends in one form or another.

You can experiment for yourself with your dog. Pet him and be kind to him, and his tail will wag in grateful appreciation and he will try to lick your hand or your face if you'll give him a chance. Scold him or strike him and he may cringe, snarl, or even attempt to bite you. The reactions of people are similar, and no matter what the motive may be that actuates you to do something for the other person, whether it be merely a friendly impulse or your own knowledge of the law, of cause and effect, the results will be the same. Sincere compliments will always gain you friends, for most people are extremely susceptible to compliments. Compliments gratify their ego, and up you go in their friendly estimation. Successful politicians learn early in their careers the art of making friends by doing things for other people, and by speaking in praise of them. The corner newsboy you befriend today may some day be the judge before whom you stand when you have violated some traffic rule, and then you will discover what it means to have "a friend at court." The same principle applies in all walks of life, yet many people overlook the fact.

I sat in the office of the merchandise manager of one of the largest department stores in the country not long ago when a woman employee came in to thank him for some advice given her regarding the accepting of a better position with a firm in another city. When she left, he said:

"You know, one thing I like about this job is the number of people who come to me for advice. While you are aware that the job here keeps me on the jump, I always take time off for employees who come to me for advice. It flatters me and makes me feel as though I'm quite a fellow, and naturally I feel like doing everything I can for the people who so compliment me."

This brings me to another point—a person who desires riches must go where riches are. Alone on a desert island, a man would probably have a tough time eking out an existence, to say nothing of trying to amass a fortune. So it is in everyday pursuits. Therefore if you want money, you've got to associate yourself with people who have it or who know how to make it. This may sound rather gross. But the truth is that if it is money you are after, you must go where it is and where it is being spent, and also you must become personally acquainted with those who have the authority to spend it. If you are a salesman selling advertising and you know the head of the firm is the man with the final say, it's a waste of time trying to convince minor clerks and junior executives. The same holds true if you are trying to sell other commodities, or, what is more important, trying to sell yourself.

"If you work for a man, for goodness' sake work for him," said Elbert Hubbard, which brings me to a failing of many people with whom I have worked over a period of years—lack of interest in their jobs. They make no effort to learn anything outside the small sphere in which their jobs place them. Once I made a wager with the executive of a large concern whose name was frequently in the newspapers that I could find at least twenty people in his own local organization who had never heard of him, to say nothing of the position he occupied. He was nettled when he got the proof. Not only did he lose the bet, but his pride was hurt. Curiosity prompted me to check with other organizations that were nationwide in their operations, and not a single employee could tell me the name of the head of the company or the street address of its main office.

This may sound unbelievable and even ridiculous to many readers. But if you have friends working in a minor capacity with some large institution, ask them the name of the treasurer or the senior vice-president of the concern. Unless the employee is an exception, the ignorance will surprise you. If you are a salesman for a major oil company or even a telephone operator, surely you should make some endeavor within a short time after your employment to learn the names of the men who head the company and something of their history. Yet it is surprising how many people accept positions and make no attempt to ascertain what the adjacent department manufactures or to learn anything about the company's general operations. Perhaps the heads of big organizations err in not carrying on educational campaigns for the benefit of employees.

Of course, there are large corporations that have house organs containing the names of the executives, main office locations, and the like, and giving details about their method of operation. I talked with a woman employed by a large manufacturing plant who had been with the concern for many months, and outside of the name of the personnel manager who had employed her, she did not know the name of a single executive of the company in spite of the fact that the company's publication with articles written by various department heads went into her hands monthly.

The job you now hold is the stepping-stone to the job above. How much do you know about it before you start moving toward it—just how much do you know about your company and its policies both inside and out? Many firms carry group insurance for their employees, with the employees paying a small part of the premiums. How many employees have ever read their policies? Few do, and, further, few know anything about their social security rights or what the various amounts taken from their payroll checks actually represent.

"Man is heir to the wisdom of the ages found within the covers of great books," remarked one of our great wise men, and yet it is surprising how many people never read a book, although the war did cause more people to seek the companionship of books. Strange as it may sound, few business men read anything besides the newspapers and a few trade journals, and when a check is made among professional men you find that they more or less limit themselves to books and literature dealing with their respective fields. I mention books, for no matter what the book may be—biography, fiction, history, or a scientific text— it is a rare book that doesn't contain an idea or two useful in your own work.

No one has a monopoly of knowledge, and yet we all know that knowledge is power when put to use. The greater the reader, the more his thinking is stimulated, and if he is a man of action, the more his efforts are accelerated.

Now is the right time to mention the highly interesting phenomenon of association of ideas and how one idea quickly links itself with another. This is of great value and should be cultivated by everyone, especially by a person engaged in creative work such as advertising, writing, selling, or kindred lines.

For example, you see an automobile on a country road. Consider for a moment how many ideas can be derived from the mental picture of the automobile. It's made of steel, alloys and plastics—each furnishing major ideas that can be broken up into many others. Then we consider the wheels and tires—casings, the inner tubes, the valves—all bringing further association of ideas. We think of the roads over which they have traveled, and this suggests roads and their construction. Then we think of oil and gasoline, which brings further ideas through association, and before we know it we have started with an association of ideas that is seemingly endless.

Let's take a single idea in business. Suppose you are interested in the growth and sale of a new kind of nut. The first question naturally is: Can it be grown and sold at a profit? Naturally, by association of ideas you will be led to determine all matters dealing with the growth of the nut, the soil, location, climatic conditions, costs, labor problems; these will lead on to marketing programs, packaging, dealers who would be interested, brokers, shippers, and, finally, the ultimate consumer. The field of ideas becomes enormous although association started with the thought of a single little nut.

A word should be said about packaging and eye-appeal, because here again we deal with the power of suggestion. Dealers in groceries, fruits, and garden vegetables know that even if there is no improvement in the products themselves, artistic, attractive-looking packages will bring a better price for the goods. You have only to stroll through a grocery store and note the articles which attract your attention to discover this fact for yourself. Excellence in packaging distinguishes the skilled chef from the ordinary restaurant cook. The expert chef knows the value of eye-appeal and accordingly arranges the food on the platters or plates to give it a more appetizing appeal, while the average cook, probably neither knowing nor caring, piles it on in any old fashion.

For several years I was interested in a celery farm. Prior to the interning of many Japanese during the war, my renter, an Italian, was always complaining that he could not compete with the Japanese and gave this as an excuse for his inability to fulfill his rent contracts. Intuitively, the Japanese knew the value of proper packaging. Their celery would be thoroughly washed, placed in new crates, and frequently, if sold in the form of hearts, would be attractively wrapped in paper carrying a boastful little message about the quality of the celery. My renter, a slovenly fellow, never, in my memory, washed a single bunch of celery. He placed it in second-hand crates and then he complained that his Japanese competitors were getting all the business.

Anyone who has traveled through the great farming belts of our country and Canada can tell by a glance at the house or barn whether the farmer is alive or whether he is dying on his feet. I think of some of the great orchardists of the Pacific Northwest who twenty or thirty years ago couldn't sell a whole wagonload of pears or apples for twenty dollars; and yet men who had the idea of attractive packaging and marketing in recent years have made large fortunes. It's nothing to get people to pay two dollars or more for a dozen apples or pears carefully wrapped in tissue, waxed paper, or tinfoil; some of these alert orchardists sell their products by mail to thousands of buyers throughout the world. I happen to know personally a number of these operators and their success in each instance has been predicated upon an idea that came to them in a flash and which developed as a result of their believing.

Now consider this matter of packaging in connection with yourself. Do you have eye-appeal? Do you wear clothes to give yourself the best appearance? Do you know the effect of colors and study those which best suit your form and temperament? Does your whole appearance set you apart from many who pass unnoticed in the crowd? If not, give thoughtful attention to personal packaging, for the world accepts you as you appear to be. Take a tip from the automobile manufacturers, the Hollywood make-up artists, or any of the great show producers, who know the value of eye-appeal and package their goods accordingly. When you have a combination of proper packaging and highest quality goods within the package, you have an unbeatable combination. The you within can do the same thing for the you outside—and you, too, have the unbeatable combination.

To satisfy yourself on what the right appearance will do for you, just pass by where there is construction under way.

If you are well-dressed and have an air of prosperity and importance, workmen who may be in your path will step aside as you pass. Or you might try stepping into an outer office where others may be waiting to see a certain executive. Notice that the important-looking individual with the air and voice of authority gets first attention not only from the office attendants but from the executive.

No better example of the impressiveness of a good appearance can be given than the distinction made between individuals by attendants at a police station or jail. The stylishly dressed, well-poised business man is seldom ill-treated, while the man who has the appearance of a bum lands almost immediately in a cell.

As a police reporter on metropolitan newspapers for a number of years, I saw this happen times without number. The fellow who looked as though he might be "somebody" and who had been arrested for a minor law infraction, often got a chair in the captain's office until he could telephone the judge or some friend to obtain his release, while the bum was carted off to jail, to get his release when and if he could.

The head of a huge automobile distributing agency told me that he was frequently called upon to close a sale with wealthy men who always bought the most expensive cars. "Not only do I take a shower," he said, "and change all my clothes, but I go to a barbershop and get everything from a shave to a shampoo and manicure. Obviously, it has some thing to do with my appearance, but further than that it does something to me inside. It makes me feel like a new man who could lick his weight in wildcats."

If you are properly attired when you are starting out on some important undertaking, you will feel within yourself that sense of power, which will cause people to give way before you and will even stir others to help you on your way. The right mental attitude, keeping your eyes straight ahead and fixed on your goal, throwing around you the proper aura, which is done by an act of your imagination or an extension of your personal magnetism, will work wonders, as Theos Bernard, in his Penthouse of the Gods, learned when he was cornered and stoned by a crowd of natives in Tibet. In his book he says that his first reaction was to fight, but the thought was immediately dismissed when he recalled that he had been taught to assume and maintain his own aura. Thus he straightened his shoulders, lifted high his head, directed his eyes straight ahead, and moved forward with a firm and rapid stride. Not only did the crowd give way, but others came forward and made a path for him.

A number of years ago I was on intimate terms with the chief of a large metropolitan fire department, a middle-aged man who seemed to fear nothing. His associates declared that the chief bore a charmed life. Once, in getting material for a personal story, I asked him if he thought he had a charmed life, and he laughed: "I don't know as you'd call it that. Maybe I'm somewhat of a fatalist, but I have never believed that I would be killed as long as I am chief. When I go into a place of danger, I always throw a white circle about myself, and nothing can come through that circle. It was a trick I learned from the Indians who lived near us when I was a kid. Maybe it's the worst kind of superstition, but that white aura has saved my life more times than I like to think about." He lived to be retired and died in his seventies from natural causes.

We all know the story of Babe Ruth, the great baseball player, and how "he called his shots." If he wanted to make a home run by batting the ball into right or left field, that's where he batted the ball. How he did this is perhaps known only to that great hero of all American boys, but surely it was uncanny. Against the mightiest pitchers he was able to bat the ball where he wanted, and his home-run record is something that will stand for a long time to come.

The name Ernie Pyle immediately brings to mind the premonition of death this famous war correspondent experienced before shipping out to the Pacific war. It will be poignantly recalled that the beloved Ernie had the feeling that when he left for the Pacific Theater of War, he would not return. On the contrary, there are many of the stories told by ex-servicemen who had the "feeling or belief" that even though frequently under intense fire, they were going to come through without being wounded—and come through they did.

You will find that many people subjected to great danger believe in the efficacy of this white-circle aura. Perhaps here again it is the result of the magic of believing. There are millions of automobile owners in this world who have a small disc in their automobiles which they believe will save them from accidents. But why stop with discs in automobiles?

The vibrations set up by others affect us much more than we realize, for we take on the characteristics of those with whom we are more or less constantly associated. It is well known that a man and wife frequently after long years of association grow to resemble one another and acquire many of the habits of one another. A baby will take on the emotional characteristics of the mother or the person who habitually cares for it, becoming susceptible to the fears, the likes and dislikes of the mother or the nurse, and frequently these emotional qualities remain for life. And the lovers of pets, especially of dogs, declare that the animals will take on some of the emotional characteristics of their owners—they will be ugly, friendly, happy, or quarrelsome, depending upon the emotional pattern of the person with whom they are most closely associated.

It is always important to remember that a negative person can raise havoc in an organization or a home. The same amount of damage can be done by a strong negative personality as good can be done by a positive personality, and when the two are pitted against one another, the negative frequently becomes the more powerful. We all know what occasionally happens to a man living among uncivilized people—he goes native. Englishmen employed as plantation or mine operators in jungle outposts guard against this by shaving and meticulously dressing each evening for dinner.

An extremely nervous person in a position of authority can put nearly every person associated with him into a nervous state. You can see this happen in almost any office or shop where the executive is of a nervous type. Sometimes this emotional pattern will extend throughout an entire organization. After all, as has been said, an organization is only the extended shadow of the man who heads it. Thus, to have a smoothly running organization, all its members must be attuned to the thinking of the principal executive. A strong negative personality in such an organization, who is out of tune with the ideas of the management, can extend his negative vibrations to others and do great damage, just as one rotten apple in a box will soon cause all the others to rot. Likewise, one woman weeping can cause others in the same room to weep, one person laughing can cause others to laugh, and the yawn of a single person can cause an epidemic of yawns. We seldom realize how much our emotional vibrations affect others and how much we are affected by theirs.

If you would remain a positive type, avoid associating too much with anyone who has a negative or pessimistic personality. Many clergymen and personnel counselors often become victims of prolonged association with people who come to them with their troubles. The impact of the steady stream of woe and sorrow vibrations eventually reverses their positive polarity and reduces them to a negative state.

To get a better understanding of the effect of these suggestive vibrations, you need only remember your varying feelings upon entering different offices or homes. The atmosphere, which is the creation of the people habitually frequenting the office or home, can be instantly detected as being upsetting, disturbing, tranquil, or harmonious.

You can tell almost instantly whether the atmosphere is cold or warm—the arrangement of the furniture, the color scheme, the very walls themselves, all vibrate to the thinking of the persons occupying the place, and bespeak the type to which their thoughts belong. Whether the home be a mansion or a shack, the vibrations are always a key to the personality of those who occupy it.

Are you afraid to take on responsibilities, afraid to make decisions, afraid to step out alone? Most people are—that's why there are so few leaders and so many followers. If you are confronted with a problem, the longer you put it off, the greater it becomes and the more fearful you become of your ability to solve it. Therefore, learn to make decisions, because in not deciding you fail to act, and in failing to act you invite failure. Experience will soon teach you that once a decision is made, the problems and troubles begin to disappear. Even though the decision you make may not be the best one, the mere deciding gives you strength and raises your morale. It's the fear of doing the wrong thing that attracts the wrong thing. Decide and act, and the chances are that your troubles will fade into thin air— whether you make a mistake or not. All great men are men of quick decision which flows from their intuition, their accumulated knowledge, and previous experience. So learn to be quick in making decisions and audacious in your actions.

The writer makes no claim to being a faith-healer, but anyone who knows anything about the power of mind knows of the effects that emotionalized thinking has upon the condition of the body and knows also what suggestion can do toward bringing disease, as well as curing it. In some faith-healing movements, cures are effected by denying that the disease exists, and there are thousands who attest to the validity of this method of healing. Followers of other schools of healing make no attempt to deny the existence of disease, but instead ignore it, affirming that they are well and happy and getting better every day. Members of the various schools of thought are the best judges of the methods that work best for them; but it must be remembered that in all cases it is the individual's belief that determines the success of the individual method of cure. However, it is interesting to note that the movement which advocates denial has a tremendous following, and its membership continues to increase by leaps and bounds.

Just how far suggestion can be used to cure disease or physical ailments is still a matter of great controversy among the various schools of mental healing and members of the medical profession, but the fact remains that there are many thousands in our country alone—and the number increases daily—who are of the firm belief that a cure of their ailments came as result of mental-healing.

It has long been known that the emotions developed by fear, hate, and worry can lead to many bodily ills, even to fatal illnesses, although there are still some members of the medical profession who refuse to acknowledge this fact. However, Life magazine (February 19, 1945), in an article entitled "Psychosomatic Medicine," declared that during the war period it was found that 40 per cent of all army disability cases originated from psychosomatic causes. ("Psychosomatic" refers to a combination of mind and body ailments brought on by the emotions, and the prescribed treatment is a combination of psychotherapy and medical treatment.) The article pointed out that many cases of hay fever, bronchial asthma, heart disease, high blood pressure, rheumatic disease, arthritis, diabetes mellitus, the common cold, and various skin conditions such as warts, hives, and allergic reactions, were caused either by emotional upsets directly or by physical disturbances in which the emotions were an aggravating factor. The treatment consists of locating the source of the emotional disturbances and endeavoring to eradicate it.

Because of the experiments of the psychiatrists and psychoanalysts during the war, the whole subject of both medical and mental treatment is probably due for a complete revision, with resulting mind-cures which may prove astounding.

However, those who understand the science of psychotherapeutics are fairly well agreed that a cure does not come through treatment on the part of the healer nearly so much as it does from the patient himself. In other words, the suggestion, no matter in what form it is given by the healer (whether in accordance with the principles of psychotherapeutics or in conjunction with some special religious belief), is in turn transmitted by autosuggestion to the patient's own subconscious mind where it becomes effective. The writer realizes that the following statement may invite criticism, but the fact remains that if a patient refuses to believe in the suggestive appeals of the healer, the purpose is never accomplished. The two, the healer and the patient, have to be en rapport to get results, and it is the writer's theory that any person who possesses an understanding of the use of the power of suggestion could get the same results without the aid of a healer, provided he were sufficiently strong and constant in his own convictions and suggestions. The same technique, the cards and the mirror, with suitable affirmations, can be used to great advantage.

In recent years there has been a renewed interest in telepathy or thought-transference, arising out of the experiments and investigations carried on in many colleges and universities, particularly those conducted under the direction of Dr. J. B. Rhine of Duke University. Of course, Joseph Dunninger, radio's self-styled mentalist, with his so-called feats of thought-projection as well as mind-reading, has done much to widen popular discussion of the subject.

The records of both the American and British Societies for Psychical Research are filled with case reports of telepathy, clairvoyance, and similar phenomena, but many people, despite the published reports of scientific findings, are prone to scoff at the idea that telepathy exists.

It has always struck the writer as odd that many people who profess to believe in the Bible, in which there are countless stories of visions, clairvoyance, and telepathy, declare that today telepathy and kindred phenomena are not possible.

Notwithstanding the general skepticism, some of the world's greatest scientific thinkers have declared that telepathy is not only possible but that it is a faculty that can be used by most people when they understand it. In addition to the findings of both the American and British Societies for Psychical Research and the results made public by Dr. Rhine, there are numerous old and new books on the subject. A few of the better known ones are *Mental Radio*, by Upton Sinclair; *Beyond the Senses*, by Dr. Charles Francis Potter, well-known New York preacher; *Thoughts Through Space*, by Harold Sherman and Sir Hubert Wilkins, famous explorer; *Telepathy*, by Eileen Garrett, editor and publisher; and *Experimental Telepathy*, by René Warcollier, Director of The Institute Metaphysique International, in Paris.

When the results of Dr. Rhine's experiments at Duke University were first made public, there were many men who rushed into print to declare that the results could be laid to chance, and considerable time and money were spent in an endeavor to prove that telepathy was non-existent. Yet the experiments continue at Duke and at other leading universities. The writer has often wondered why many opposing so-called scientific investigators do not try to prove that the phenomena exist instead of trying to prove the contrary; but here again the writer has a theory that belief is the miracle worker, and this is partly substantiated by what Dr. Rhine himself says in his book on extrasensory perception. He declares that satisfactory results were secured when the experimenters caught the "spirit of the thing," and that the ability to transmit and receive became weakened when the original novelty wore off. In other words, while there was enthusiasm there was spontaneous interest and the belief that it could be done. But when students were called back at later dates to continue their experiments in the course of their studies, enthusiasm was lacking, and the results were not satisfactory.

Perhaps many of my readers will recall an article which appeared in the *American Weekly* magazine, August 25, 1946, captioned "Scientific Evidence Man Has a Soul," written by Dr. J. B. Rhine. In view of the fact that his explanations deal directly with the subject matter of this book, I quote the article almost in full.*

What has science to say about the soul? For the answer to this question we would naturally turn to psychology because it is literally "the science of the soul." But here we have a surprise coming to us, for we find that the soul theory of man has been practically dropped from psychology books and lectures.

Most psychologists will even smile tolerantly if one speaks of the mind itself as if there were such a thing apart from the brain. Everything has to be physical to be real, according to the prevailing view; anything non-physical or spiritual, as the soul is supposed to be, therefore simply cannot be. Such an idea has to be dismissed as pure superstition.

The principles of physics are expected to explain everything that we call "mental," if they continue to expand as they have been doing. However, some things occur now and then that just do not fit in at all with this physical

---

* Reprinted by courtesy of the author, Dr. J. B. Rhine, and with the permission of *The American Weekly*.

view of man. For example, a person may awaken from a horrible dream in which a friend or relative is dying.

The shocking picture turns out to be essentially true and the timing about right, although the friend may be a thousand miles away.

The oddest feature of all this is that in some cases the event perceived may not occur until hours or days after the dream; yet it may have been accurately pictured and even experienced in considerable detail.

The first thought is, of course, that such experiences are mere coincidences. Not many people get beyond this first easy explanation, but fortunately a few have done so; and when one studies great numbers of these experiences, they lose all appearance of being accidental. The scientific thing to do, of course, was to set to work to discover what might lie behind these happenings.

Obviously if any of these "psychic" experiences showed that the mind has the power to reach out beyond space and time, they would plainly be transcending physical law. The mind would then be demonstrated to be a spiritual rather than a physical system. Here was a clue to the soul. Just a clue—nothing more; but it provided the necessary lead to reliable evidence.

It was from these "psychic" experiences that the ESP tests were derived. ESP is the abbreviation of extrasensory perception, which includes telepathy and clairvoyance. In other words, telepathy and clairvoyance are two different modes of acquiring knowledge without the use of the recognized sense organs such as the eyes and ears. In a typical telepathy test the person being tested tries to identify which card or number or other symbol is being held in mind by another person—who is, let us say, located in an adjoining room. In a clairvoyance test, on the other hand, it is the object itself, commonly a card, instead of the thought of it, which the percipient tries to perceive. In a word, telepathy is the ESP of the state of mind of another person; clairvoyance, the ESP of an object.

At Duke University in 1930 a small group of psychologists began a series of ESP experiments of both types, telepathy and clairvoyance. This work was sponsored by the great British psychologist, William McDougall, Fellow of the Royal Society, who was at the time the head of the Department of Psychology at Duke. This work which was carried out in what came to be called the Parapsychology Laboratory ("para" meaning the unusual, the exceptional, the unorthodox) was by no means the first of its kind. Experiments had been done here and there, some of them even in universities, for as much as fifty years before, but there had been no systematic, consecutive experimentation following up the problems through the years, such as took place at Duke. That university was the first to offer a permanent haven to active research on "psychic" problems.

The experimenters in the Parapsychology Laboratory found fresh confirmatory evidence of both types of ESP, telepathic and clairvoyant. They developed and standardized new tests, making it easier to repeat the experiments. This had the effect of starting a movement of ESP experimentation which spread to many other institutions here and abroad. Elaborate precautions were taken to insure that no sensory cues were possible and that no other type of error could affect the test results. The tests were of such a nature that the scores could be evaluated by standard and long-approved statistical methods. It could be shown clearly that the scores made in the tests could not reason-

ably be accounted for, either by chance or by experimental weakness of any kind.

Once the experimenters were satisfied that the occurrence of ESP was soundly established, they set to work on the vitally important question as to what relation that capacity had to the physical world. Do telepathy and clairvoyance operate strictly under physical law? Or do they reach beyond the limits of physics as the spontaneous "psychic" experiences seem to do?

Fortunately it was a simple matter to test ESP in relation to space. For example, we needed only to conduct tests with long distance between the cards and the person trying to identify them by ESP, and compare the results with short-distance tests. Both telepathy and clairvoyance tests gave as good results at great distances as they did with small. Distance measured in yards, miles, or hundreds of miles simply did not matter in the operation of ESP, as far as the experiments went. For that matter, angles, barriers, and other physical conditions seemed likewise to have no effect on success in the ESP tests.

What, then, about time? We argued that if space does not influence ESP, time should not be expected to affect it either. The tests for ESP of the future, or precognition (prophecy is a more familiar word), were easily derived from the regular ESP tests. People who could successfully identify cards extrasensorially at a distance were then asked to try to predict what the order of cards was going to be after the deck was shuffled. We found that they scored as well on decks of cards that were mechanically shuffled before checking as they did trying to identify the cards as they were in the deck at the time. Moreover, they did as well at predicting the order of the deck of cards ten days ahead as for a two-day period. Length of time beyond the prediction and the check-up following the shuffling made no more difference than had the length of distance in the earlier experiments.

There was only one interpretation of these experiments possible—namely, that the mind of man somehow transcends the space-time limitations of the physical world in these capacities we are calling "extrasensory perception." As the experiments were confirmed by other research men and women in other laboratories, the conclusion became firmly established that the mind does indeed possess properties not belonging to physics as we know it. Since space and time are the surest indications of what is physical, the mind must, therefore, be extraphysical or spiritual in nature. And all we mean by the "soul" in man is that the mind is non-physical—or spiritual—in character. The ESP experiments, then, have yielded evidence of the soul in man.

To some people this will seem a very small beginning on the problem of the soul. Certainly we must not exaggerate the extent of the findings. Actually we have done little more than produce evidence for an elemental sort of soul theory. There is, of course, a great deal more to the religious concept of the soul than has been found in these researches. There are many great problems remaining. Is the soul capable of separation from the body? Can it survive bodily death? If it can and does, can discarnate souls have any contact with the living, or in any way influence them? What about the idea of a world-soul, or God? What about communication between souls, especially the soul of man and God? These and many other fundamental questions of religious doctrine remain untouched by anything thus far discussed in this article.

All we have a right to conclude is that the physical concept of man which has increasingly prevailed in intellectual circles since the rise of materialism is now thoroughly disproved.

There is something—how much, we do not know—definitely extraphysical about humans.

There is an order of reality in human life not subject to the laws of time and space.

But it is just as important, I think, to recognize, too, the tremendous possibilities we can now see. The soul-theory of man gives us much to build on in our further thinking on religious problems. We have now verified the essential foundation upon which the spiritual philosophy of man was originally erected. It remains for scientific inquiry to go on further to find out by the same methods all we can about human personality, its nature and destiny—in short, to take up the other great questions of religion.

There was a time when experimental inquiry into the problems of religion would have met with vigorous opposition from orthodox religious leaders. There are still many conservatives that would resent the intrusion of science into the domain of what they think should be pure faith. But a great many of the most deeply religious men and women of today are eagerly reaching out for a more tangible sort of knowledge regarding the human mind and all of its potentialities that lie far beyond our present knowledge.

Surprisingly enough, it has been from orthodox science that we have met with the main opposition. The scientific conservative especially fears any division in nature, any such dualism as that of soul and body—so much so that he is likely to refuse to look at any evidence which suggests such a duality. Such anxiety is quite groundless, for if, as we may now claim to know, man does have a soul as well as a body, both fundamentally different, the two are still in some sense unified.

They do interact; therefore they have something in common. Two things cannot affect each other if they differ in every single point. We see, therefore, that there must be a world of hidden realities, probably neither physical nor mental as we know them, from which the manifestations of mind and body, the psychical and physical, originally stem. This realm beyond mind and matter lies there almost as unknown as the American continents were to Columbus, silently awaiting some fortunate explorer of the future. But he will have to be someone who, like the great Genoese sailor, was daring enough to question existing charts of knowledge and belief—and put them to experimental test.

The writer has frequently attended séances at which the medium has refused to perform, declaring that someone in the audience was a scoffer, a nonbeliever, whose vibrations were creating a hostile atmosphere. The materialistic skeptic may laugh at this, but the writer has been present at large meetings where one lone heckler in the audience with his persistent hostility has not only disrupted the meeting, but completely defeated the efforts of the speaker.

I think that anyone who understands the vibratory theory of thought power can also understand why unsympathetic vibrations can be "monkey wrenches thrown into the machinery." Verification of this is found in the experiments by Dr. Rhine, who discovered in his psychokinesis tests that when a subject operated in the presence of an observer who tried to distract him and depress his scoring, the results were always below expectancy. And, contrariwise, when the same subject performed alone or in the presence of neutral or sympathetic observers, his score of successes was correspondingly high.

You have only to read the history of witchcraft, the story of voodoo medicine men and "hexers," and even the achievements of present-day mental-healers to realize that there is undoubtedly some force at work which influences others even at a distance. True, the suggestion first planted in the mind of the patient or victim, as the case may be, has for its purpose either good or evil; but that doesn't account for the results, especially in the absent-treatment method where the patient may have no knowledge that the healer is "working" on him. Whether telepathy is involved here is something that has not yet been established.

It is to be noted that practically all of the great electrical scientists, including Edison, Steinmetz, Tesla, and Marconi, were greatly interested in telepathy. Dr. Alexis Carrel not only believed in telepathy but declared that a study of it should be made by scientific men, just as physiological phenomena are studied.

Despite the fact that the secretary of the London Society for Psychical Research after twenty years of investigation by its members stated that telepathy is an actuality, and the further fact that experiments at the various colleges continue to pile up amazing evidence of its existence, there are many scientific men who refuse to accept the findings. Moreover, the number of people who are carrying on investigations of their own is constantly growing, even though they are regarded in certain quarters as being eccentric and somewhat gullible. I have often wondered if those who belittle this research work are really being fair, both to themselves and those interested in the phenomena, especially when the research work may lead to greater discoveries than hitherto dreamed possible.

Many horse and dog fanciers, especially those who have kept horses and dogs as pets over a long period of years, stoutly maintain the existence of telepathy between the animals and themselves, and there have been countless stories told regarding telepathic phenomena among primitive people in all parts of the world.

Long years ago a business executive told me that he got rid of people who were taking up his time by simply repeating mentally to his visitor: "It's time for you to go, leave now, leave now." The visitor would shortly get fidgety, look at his watch or get up from his chair, reach for his hat, and soon be on his way out.

You can get the same results when visitors overstay their time in your home. When you feel it is time for them to go, simply say to yourself, "Go home now, go home now, go home now," and you will find that they glance around the room looking for the clock and say, "Guess it's about time we were leaving."

I recognize that some skeptics will say that telepathy has nothing to do with this, that your facial expressions, your bodily movements, signs of nervousness or weariness are what warn the visitor that it is time for him to leave. However, experiment for yourself; but take care that you give the visitor no outward sign, either by word or facial expression, that it is time for his departure. You will find that there are times, especially if the visitor is intent upon putting over a point or winning an argument, that this procedure will not work. But the moment there is a lull in the conversation, try it and the results will astonish you.

A number of years ago I had my office on the second floor of a large office building. In later years the firm with which I had been associated moved to the tenth floor. Often upon entering the elevator I would say, "Ten, please," to the operator, and then immediately begin thinking about the second floor and of its various associations in connection with my work. Time after time I found the elevator operator, who didn't know me or my earlier association, stopping at the second floor and then turning around to look at me.

A well-known Pacific Coast clergyman who was a deep student of Mind Stuff told me that every time he wanted flowers in his church, he simply sent his thoughts out to members of his congregation and someone would send flowers. He also told me that every memorial window in his church came as a result of the mental suggestions which he gave whenever he felt the time was propitious for another window.

Dr. Roy Chapman Andrews, in a radio program in April, 1945, told of one of the most unusual "coincidences" on record. He related the story of an American song writer who just after the publication of one of his songs discovered that the same piece of music, note for note, had been composed and published in Germany only a short time previously. The fact that the compositions to the last note were identical makes the story more unusual than the many cases that have been reported of widely separated people who have had the same idea at the same time. The writer, living on the West Coast, submitted a short time before this book was written an article to an eastern publication only to receive a note from the editor saying an article embracing the same material had just been accepted from another writer living in the East. Elisha Gray claimed that he had the idea of the telephone at the same time as Alexander Graham Bell. Independent simultaneous discovery of ideas often happens among writers, inventors, chemists, engineers, and composers.

Even during the preparation of this book, when suggestions were being made for changes and additions, both my agent adviser and myself were often surprised to learn that we both received ideas at almost identical times. Not only did we get similar ideas, but the suggestive use of identical names of people came to us almost simultaneously. Early when my publishers suggested additional matter, I had been engaged in research work for a week when I received a letter from my adviser stating that he had suggested to the publisher the identical subject matter on which I had been working. Checking disclosed that the same thoughts had come to us at approximately the same time. Naturally, there is no way of knowing whether my adviser in New York caught my thoughts or whether I caught his. I merely report the facts.

STUDY GUIDE

Chapter 7

In order to be successful at anything, you must be diligent and consistent in your efforts. Claude Bristol claims that man can bring anything that he can conceive mentally into materialization. He asserts, however, that you need to act on your hunches when you get them, as ideas without action is futile. He also emphasizes how important it is to be reliable. In this chapter, he introduces the technique of thought projection, and discusses how important it is to support others as you seek your own fame and fortune. He emphasized how imperative it is to have knowledge of your field of endeavor, and complete commitment to its evolution. He ends the chapter emphasizing the importance of effective packaging, and how mental imaging is key to maintaining overall health and well-being.

1. The author opens this chapter with the following statement, *"Success is a matter of never-ceasing application. You must forever work at it diligently. At no time can you rest on your laurels . . ."* He was accurate in anticipating great changes in America's future. What do you think is the most outstanding creation in America since the 1930's? Why?

2. Do you believe that the creator of this innovation used the "mind power" that Bristol references to manifest their creation into existence?

3. Of the many inventions the author references are *"machines that capture energy from the sun."* In order to maintain the "fuel" that sparks this kind of imagination, he insists that you need to constantly stoke it with *"ideas,*

ideas, more ideas, and action." Do you find yourself constantly generating ideas? If so, do you ever get them to the "action" phase? Why or why not?

4. Do you believe anything happens energetically when you do not act upon your creative ideas? In other words, if your imagination keeps generating ideas, but you do not take action on them, what do you believe is the message that you are giving to the subconscious from which those ideas come from?

5. One of Claude's wise contemporaries insists on starting something new at least once each week. This may be as simple as reading a new book, or creating a basic kitchen gadget. He believes that one's imagination may atrophy without ongoing use. Do you concur? Why or why not?

6. The author asserts that retiring at age sixty is a bad idea, as once you become inactive mentally and physically, you are on your way to your grave. What are your beliefs about this?

7. Do you have any active life plans for when you retire? If so, what are they?

8. List three retirees that you know or know of. Are each of them thriving? Of those thriving, do they live an active or sedentary life?

9. The author emphasizes that many remain in minor clerical positions because they never display initiative in their work. What are your thoughts on this point?

10. During the war, several organizations offered rewards for employee innovations, bringing about great inventions. Have you ever worked for a company that encouraged imagination and innovation among its workers? If so, what was the outcome? If not, do you believe more of such initiatives would benefit companies? Why or why not? Please explain.

11. The author also links success with your interest in the work that you do. *"The more attention you give it, the greater are the results."* On a scale from one to ten (one being "very little" and ten being "a great deal"), rate how interested you are in the work that you do:

12. If your current job tasks do not interest you, you are encouraged to look for tasks within your organization that do. Write a list of tasks that you would find interesting. Then write a plan for taking action towards adding them to your job functions.

13. The author shared an example of a staff member, who through her initiative, commitment and interest in the work that she had done, received the highest possible Christmas bonus at the store in which she worked. He encourages, *"If you tell another person that you are going to do a certain thing, even though its fulfillment may cause you some inconvenience, do it no matter what the consequences or the cost in time or energy. You will be amply repaid, for you are building a reputation for reliability, which will be of great value as you proceed up the ladder."* On a scale from one to ten (one being "very little" and ten being "a great deal"), rate how reliable you believe yourself to be:

14. Write a list of those individuals that you can most rely on. Now go through that list. On a scale from one to ten, rate how much you trust each of the individuals on the list. Do you see a correlation between reliability and trust? Please explain.

15. There is an old saying, *"Unless a man has learned to take orders, he can never learn to give them."* Do you believe this statement to be true? Have you seen experienced it in your life? Please explain.

16. The author also asserts, *"You can't do a good deed without having a good deed done to you in return."* Similarly, the only way to have a good friend is to be one. Do you believe these sayings to be true? Please explain, using specific examples in your life to support your theory.

17. Claude Bristol was of a mindset that he could convert enemies into friends merely by thinking and believing that they were really friendly people. He asserts that our enemies are a reflection of our own thoughts; they are based on the picture we conjure up of them.

18. The author shares the story of how he changed his mind about plumbers, and because of this, his experience in finding a friendly, responsive plumber changed. Perhaps you make similar blanket judgments, like, *"All rich people are cheats"* or *"All bankers are just out to make money."* Write a list of individuals or career groups that you struggle with.

19. Write a positive, more affirmative statement about each of the individuals or groups you listed in #18. Take time to read each aloud, and make a point of truly changing your mind. Then note the exchange you have when you next meet with them. Did your experience change? If so, how?

20. You are encouraged to honor the law of reciprocity—there must be a logical effect from every cause. Write a list of the ways in which this law has proven itself in your life.

21. The author asserts that doing for others always pays dividends in one form or another. We often get caught up in thinking, *"What is this company doing for me? What is my boss doing for me?"* Consider what you can do for your company and for your boss; how you could best support them, and see how this flip in perspective shifts your experiences. Make note of any changes you see.

22. Bristol instructs that *"A person who desires riches must go where riches are."* He goes on to share *"You must become personally acquainted with those who have the authority to spend it."* On a scale from one to ten (one being "very little" and ten being "a great deal"), rate how important wealth is to you:

1———2———3———4———5———6———7———8———9———10

23. If you wish to become rich, do you have many friends or acquaintances that are rich? Write a list of rich people that you have befriended.

24. Do you believe you surround yourself enough with wealth and wealthy individuals? If not, what steps can you take to bring more successful, wealthy people into your life? List at least three action steps you can take, and set goals with each. Then be sure to follow through on them. Write about your findings.

25. The author cites several examples in which staff did not know who managed the company with whom they were employed. Are you knowledgeable about the executives who own and run the business you are working for? If not, make a point to know who they are. If you are self-employed, are you acutely aware of your competition in the industry? If not, take time to get to know who they are and how they have attained their success.

26. Effectively packaging your products or services can have a massive effect on their successful outcome. On a scale from one to ten (one being "not very good" and ten being "excellent"), rate how effective the packaging of your products or services is:

1———2———3———4———5———6———7———8———9———10

27. What steps can you take to improve the packaging?

28. Do you have a highly professional and effective website? On a scale from one to ten (one being "not very good"

and ten being "excellent"), rate how effective your website is:

29. List at least three specific steps you can take to improve upon your website. Then be sure to take them.

30. How effective is your personal packaging? On a scale from one to ten (one being "very little" and ten being "a great deal"), rate how much eye-appeal you have:

31. On a scale from one to ten (one being "very little" and ten being "a great deal"), rate how well you dress:

32. Are you familiar with the colors and styles that best suit you? If so, what are they? If not, be sure to learn more about what suits you best, or even book an appointment with a personal stylist.

33. The author asserts that, as a reporter he has seen many well-dressed men treated with dignity at the jail, while other disheveled and poorly dressed men were thrown into a cell. Have you experience such varied treatment depending upon your looks? Please explain.

34. You are encouraged to maintain the right attitude while keeping your eyes fixed on your goal. Doing so will provide you with a powerful aura, which will extend your personal magnetism. Do you feel good about your overall appearance? Do you believe you are magnetic? What might you do to enhance your overall magnetism?

35. Bristol shares the story of a fire chief he knew who always envisioned a white circle around himself that protected him from harm. Do you believe this is a silly superstition, or do you believe this technique worked for him? Please explain.

36. Have you ever used such a technique in your life? Please explain.

37. The author asserts that we seldom realize how much our emotional vibrations affect others. He maintains that one bad apple can spoil the energy of all others around him or her. Do you believe this to be true? Have you experienced this in your life? Please explain.

38. The author claims that many clergymen and personnel counselors are reduced to a negative state after spending so much time with pessimistic people. Write a list of the individuals in your life that you believe are generally pessimistic people.

39. Reflect on each person that you listed in the question above. Take note when you are around them. Do you find that your energy is depleted after spending time with them? If so, what steps can you take to protect yourself?

40. The author asserts that you can almost instantly get a feeling about the people who have inhabited offices and homes, whether warm and inviting or cold and negative. Next time you walk into your office, stop and note the feeling you get. Do this exercise with your home as well. If you are unable to detect anything, start paying more attention to the energy around you, and see if you can eventually get a feeling about the energy of these places.

41. By failing to act on your decisions, you invite failure. What decisions are you avoiding making in your life? List them, big or small.

42. Merely making a decision, whether the right one or not, will move you forward in your life. According to the author, your fear of doing the wrong thing attracts the wrong thing. Have you ever experienced this in your life (you waited too long to make a decision and because of your negative thoughts, you manifested a negative resolution? Please explain.

43. All great men and women are quick in their decision-making abilities, and audacious in following through on them. On a scale from one to ten (one being "very slow" and ten being "extremely fast"), rate how fast you are at making decisions:

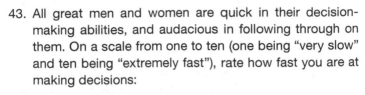

1———2———3———4———5———6———7———8———9———10

44. The author asserts that the condition of your emotions affects your physical health. Do you believe this to be true?

45. On a scale from one to ten (one being "very little" and ten being "a great deal"), rate how much tension you believe you hold in your body:

1———2———3———4———5———6———7———8———9———10

46. The author asserted that movements that proclaimed denial of illness or disease were growing at the time that he wrote this book. Do such movements continue to grow in the world? Please explain.

47. Why do you believe denial is so rampant?

48. The author references an article in *Life* magazine (February 19, 1945) entitled "Psychosomatic Medicine." It claimed that 40% of all army disability cases originated from psychosomatic causes. Since then, post-traumatic stress disorder is widely known as an emotion-based condition. What percentage of disease do you believe is rooted in emotional upset?

49. The article pointed out that *"Many cases of hay fever, bronchial asthma, heart disease, high blood pressure, rheumatic disease, arthritis, diabetes mellitus, the common cold, and various skin conditions such as warts, hives, and allergic reactions, were caused either by emotional upsets directly or by physical disturbances in which the emotions were an aggravating factor."* Do you suffer from any of these ailments? If so, list them.

50. If you suffer from any of the disorders listed in the previous question, do you believe there is an emotional component to the condition? Please explain.

51. Since this book, Louise Hay wrote the NY Times best-selling book, *Heal Your Mind, Heal Your Body*. In this book she provided a list of disorders, along with the emotion that is connected with that ailment or part of the body, and then a positive affirmation to offset and eventually heal the condition. For example, it is believed that respiratory conditions are often rooted in emotional grief. If you are not familiar with this book, take some time to investigate it. Write about your findings.

52. Do you believe that healing your emotions can affect your physical condition? Why or why not?

53. Claude Bristol states that, *"the suggestion, no matter in what form it is given by the healer (whether in accordance with the principles of psychotherapeutics or in conjunction with some special religious belief), is in turn transmitted by autosuggestion to the patient's own subconscious mind where it becomes effective."* While he anticipated a great deal of criticism when making this remark, because of pioneering individuals like himself, such theories are now widely known and accepted by many. Reflect on your life. Write about at least one autosuggestion that you experienced and integrated, consciously or not, into your life.

54. The author points out that it strikes him as odd that while many people believe in the many instances of telepathy, clairvoyance and similar phenomenon in the bible, they do not believe that such powers exist beyond it. Do you believe this to be true? If so, why?

55. Why do you believe masters like Christ had such powers?

56. Do you believe there is a correlation between spiritual enlightenment and mind power? Please explain.

57. In Dr. Rhine's experiments at Duke University, the findings showed a correlation between the subject's enthusiasm and the power of their extrasensory abilities. As their original enthusiasm wore off, their abilities weakened. On a scale from one to ten (one being "very low" and ten being "extremely high"), rate how much enthusiasm you have in tapping into your mind power:

1——2——3——4——5——6——7——8——9——10

58. Dr. Rhine describes psychology as *"the science of the soul."* What are your thoughts and feelings around this assertion?

59. Bristol shares the phenomenon in which one dreams of an event that ends up actually happening either at the same time as the dream, or at a later time. Have you ever experience premonition or a psychic "knowing" in your dreams? Please explain.

60. Do you believe that one can have such experiences in their dreams? Why or why not?

61. ESP (extrasensory perception) tests determine one's ability to experience mental telepathy or clairvoyance. Bristol describes telepathy as the ESP of the state of mind of another person, while clairvoyance is the ESP of an object. Have you or has anyone you know had telepathic experience(s)? If so, please describe them.

62. Have you, or has anyone you known had clairvoyant experience(s)? If so, please provide detail(s).

63. If you haven't had such experiences, do you believe that you possibly could someday?

64. The 1930 Duke University ESP experiments indicated *"the mind of man somehow transcends the space-time limitations of the physical world in these capacities."* Do you believe your mind transcends space-time limitations? If so, where do you find evidence of this? Please explain.

65. It was further concluded that space and time are indications of the physical, thus the mind must, therefore, be *"extraphysical or spiritual in nature."* Could one re-phrase the mind as non-physical, as opposed to *"spiritual"*? Why or why not?

66. The question arises, *"Is the soul capable of separating from the body? Can it survive bodily death?"* What are your current beliefs on this subject?

67. Do you believe that discarnate souls can have contact with the living (in other words, do you believe in ghosts)? Why or why not?

68. Have you, or has anyone you have known had first-hand experiences with discarnate beings? If so, please write about the experience.

69. The author references the concept of God as a *"world-soul."* What are your thoughts and feelings about a *"world-soul"*?

70. List the kind of images the term, *"world soul"* conjures in your mind.

71. Do you believe in communications between God and the soul of man?

72. Do you believe you communicate with God? Why or why not? Do you have evidence of such communication? If so, please describe it.

73. According to the author, scientific conservatives fear division in nature, or any such dualism as that of soul and body. Do you believe that present day scientists still hold such fear? Please explain.

74. Claude Bristol asserts that hecklers can negatively influence the energy of someone who possesses ESP, and is attempting to use it. Their negative energy can disturb the vibrations. List the naysayers that you currently engage with in your life.

75. Do these naysayers in your life affect your intuitive or extrasensory abilities? Why or why not?

76. According to the author, practically all of the great electrical scientists were greatly interested in telepathy. What do you think the correlation or bridge is between the study of electricity and the study of mind power?

77. The author writes about telepathy between horse and dog owners, and their pets. Do you believe this exists?

78. Do you have a pet(s), and if so, do you believe you share in telepathic communication? Please explain.

79. The author asserts that when you have a visitor who has overstayed his or her welcome, you can mentally focus on phrases like, *"Go home now, go home now, go home now"* and, in response, they will get agitated and will leave. Have you ever tried this strategy? If so, did it work? If not, make a point of trying it sometime in the next couple of weeks, being sure not to indicate your desire with bodily gestures. Write about your findings.

80. The author shares examples of how his editor received the same messages about potential changes in his book at the same time that he did. Have you ever experience such synchronicity? If so, how? If not, why not? Please explain.

Chapter 8

Women and the Science of Belief

As ideas for this book occurred to me, I frequently thought of the many famous women who had used the power of belief, and once in discussion with Ben Hur Lampman, nationally known author and naturalist, he suggested that I specifically cover its use by women, saying:

"Many women, perhaps, may not realize that they can use your science just as advantageously as men, and you should be specific in your message to them. Once they understand and apply what you give, they'll find themselves in a position figuratively to turn the world upside down. If there were some way for women of all nationalities to unite and use this science, there would be no future wars.

"Women are supreme egotists—in the sense that when they get the idea they can do something, and that idea becomes thoroughly imbedded in their consciousness, they will stop at nothing to achieve their purpose. You know the old saying, 'The female of the species is more deadly than the male.' That is true, and once women understand their power—and you can give them the clue—nothing will stop them. If they wish, they may actually run this old world. 'Heaven has no rage like love to hatred turned, nor hell a fury like a woman scorned,' and once they are aroused and understand what they can accomplish there will be no stopping them. Women are more versatile, more adaptable. Even though Napoleon declared that he made circumstances, most men are its victims, while women by their very nature of thinking make circumstances serve them."

Then when I read an article by a woman complaining that American women "don't get a break," it dawned on me that if women of today "don't get a break," it is the fault of no one but themselves. The only thing they have to do is to follow the examples of their sisters who have preceded them and have made their own "breaks."

Therefore, I want to emphasize the importance of the adoption of this science by women for their own special needs, and in the following pages I shall give examples of women in the past and present who have used it with great effectiveness. Let us realize that when woman awakens, she is going to play a more vital part than ever in the affairs of the world.

As a matter of fact, even today American women, although they may not be aware of it, are potentially in a position to have things pretty much their own way, for they actually control the wealth of this country! Statistics prepared shortly before World War II showed that of the country's total wealth of approximately 300 billion dollars, about 70 percent, or the huge sum of 210 billions, was in the possession of women.

During the war, we had women welders, women riveters, the Wacs, Waves, and Spars, and they all had a taste of actually performing tasks heretofore handled only by men. To thousands of single girls and housewives who had never had an opportunity to do anything outside the home, those experiences should have pointed out their own potential opportunities for taking a more active part in the work of this world.

In our own country today there are thousands of outstanding women—from great educators to bankers and industrialists, to say nothing of the numerous writers, editors, and other professional women. Many of the greatest reforms in America have been the ideas of women; if the facts could be assembled, it could easily be proven that not only did the ideas for these great reforms originate with women, but the women were the driving force behind the ideas. Some male readers may resent these statements, but there is no escaping the facts.

As a former newspaper man, naturally I had to follow the feminist movement, and for nearly forty years I have seen and felt the power of outstanding women.

When it was first suggested that I emphasize the use of this science for women, I immediately thought of Mrs. R. E. Bondurant, who has been active in women's work, charities, the inauguration of child labor laws, the building of homes and hospitals for delinquent girls, numerous legislative measures to further the interest of women and children, and public movements to aid the blind and other handicapped people. Her nationally known record of nearly forty years is an outstanding one, and today at seventy-one, even though perhaps a partial cripple for the rest of her life, she is just as enthusiastic as ever and is seeking new worlds to conquer.

Of late years, Mrs. Bondurant has been an ardent worker in the cause of the Chin-Uppers, an organization consisting of blind, crippled, and otherwise partly disabled men and women. Now she is planning to open a store where articles made by these people may be sold. In this she has the cooperation of a number of business men. Mrs. Bondurant told me that if necessary she was going to pay the rent out of her own pocket, but that all the profit would go to the Chin-Uppers. I spent a Sunday afternoon with her in her sitting-room among her books and flowers. A pair of crutches stood in a corner near the door. (For months Mrs. Bondurant has had to use them, but even at her advanced age she gets around on trolley cars, buses, and in and out of automobiles without help.) Although today she uses a cane when she leaves her home, in my presence she moved around the room without limping. We discussed at length this matter of believing. Mrs. Bondurant said:

> *There is no question about it, and I can speak from a pretty full life of seventy-one years, during which time I not only raised a family but have taken part in the various movements and activities with which you have long been familiar. There is certainly something, call it a power, God, or anything you wish, which is always there to sustain us in time of need. I have never seen it fail. We've just got to believe and when I look back through the years and recall the fine women with whom I was associated when we were working for legislation to bring about better working conditions for women and children, I realized that it was the "indomitable spirit" of these women, who thoroughly believed in the righteousness of their cause, that made the legislation possible and effective.*
>
> *I am astounded at the fact that the average woman doesn't realize her tremendous power. I don't call it stupidity because I would never admit that women are stupid, but rather they lack interest. I am amazed, in talking*

to women's groups, to realize that many of them never knew that these great reform movements to help them and their children were initiated by women, and it is my opinion that once women become aware of their strength and power, they can do more to bring about lasting peace and make this world a better place in which to live than all the famous male warriors and would-be peacemakers. All the great forward movements, as a matter of fact, I might say, all the great things in this world, have been done by men and women who were dreamers and believers in their dreams coming true. They could not have accomplished things otherwise. It's like the old story about climbing to the top of the mountain in search of that indefinable something. It makes no difference from which side the approach is made, those who steadfastly climb reach the top, and so it is with this matter of believing. It isn't so much what the real or imaginary object of our belief may be, it's the belief and following through that makes the thing possible.

I don't want to appear critical, but it has been my observation that people don't have sufficient action or driving force behind their beliefs. For example, some women's organizations will pass resolutions in favor of or against this and that, and think that settles the matter. The resolutions are no good unless the sentiments expressed are actually brought to the attention of the powers that be. I don't know of any greater thing in life than the satisfaction that comes through serving. During the many years I spent in sponsoring the various causes and getting legislation adopted, I never received a penny in pay or to cover my expenses. While it may sound like Pollyanna business to many people, bread tossed upon the waters does come back.

In illustration, I might tell you that during the depression my husband lost $80,000. He was sick in bed at home and I would go to the office daily to get the mail and check the routine. Sometimes it looked as if we would not have sufficient money to meet imperative needs, but just about when we had to meet the obligations, checks would appear in the mail from people to whom Mr. Bondurant had lent money or from long overdue accounts. We had some pretty hard times those days, but help always came through just in time and I never lost my belief.

As I watched and listened to Mrs. Bondurant, I realized that I was in the presence of no ordinary woman, but rather of a human dynamo who had the spirit and determination to get things done through her great belief. When I recalled that she had been credited with having had more laws in the interest of women and children passed than any other woman or organization in the state, I realized what it would mean to the world if all women with her vision and driving force undertook to use this science.

In the news not so long ago were found the stories a few weeks apart of the passing of two great women, one of whom was Grace Moore, she with the beautiful singing voice, and the other, that fiery British woman leader, Miss Ellen Wilkinson. Both women knew early in life what they wanted.

In common with a great many men and women who have reached great heights, Grace Moore won her success in the face of difficulties that would have stopped even some of the strongest of men. As a child, she dreamed of becoming a great opera singer. The little girl went out to win the hearts of people everywhere. Even as a penniless runaway in New York, where often she had to sing for her supper in small Greenwich Village cafés, Grace Moore never lost her courage. She made her debut at seventeen and was close to the zenith of her career at forty-five. Again and again when it appeared that she was hopelessly defeated, she, with unquenchable courage, emerged victorious. When she lost her voice and was told by a throat specialist she would never sing again, she put up a tremendous battle, and emerged from a year of retirement and rest, singing more beautifully than ever before. Her glorious voice brought her great fame, and up to the time of her unfortunate death in the airplane crash at Copenhagen early in 1947, Grace Moore continued to believe in her dreams.

She was one of the few stars who believed in helping other talented people to achieve their objectives and her timely aid assisted many unknown aspiring singers. When one of her protégées who had achieved success became temperamental about her part in a performance, it is said that Miss Moore told her that a famous singer had once advised her that to great artists there was no such thing as a small part and to small artists there were no big parts.

Ellen Wilkinson, who was the British Minister of Education, was a tiny, red-haired woman who drove her way upward through her persistence. Less than five feet tall, she was never cowed by the biggest of the British leaders. It is said that she made a career of annoyance, first as a school teacher, than as a suffragist, a novelist, newspaper writer, and finally cabinet minister. She was pleased when someone said of her that no woman in the whole of Britain had been more active, more persistent, or more annoying. Probably her greatest contribution in the interest of the people was her campaign to raise the age of leaving school from fourteen to fifteen. She won this fight in the face of stiff opposition of fellow ministers and the great demand for youths in British industry.

From the time of Cleopatra to the present, there have been thousands of women who, relying on their inmost convictions, have had a direct hand in shaping the lives of millions. It has been said that behind every great ruler was a woman. This may not be historically correct, but certainly we have enough evidence to know that women have had very much of a guiding hand in history-making. The names of several women who achieved success through their beliefs come to mind.

One was Empress Eugénie who married Napoleon the Third.

When a small child she had fallen against a bannister and bruised her body. Her gypsy nurse told her not to cry, that she would be a queen and live to be a hundred. She believed in gypsies and her fortune materialized nearly as prophesied. She became Empress Eugénie and lived until she was ninety-four, just six years less than the age fixed by her gypsy nurse.

Madame Marie Curie, the famous co-discoverer of radium was told when a child in Warsaw by an old gypsy woman that she would be famous. The story is that Marja Sklodowska, later to be known as Madame Curie, was running to join a group of playmates when the old gypsy woman stopped her, demanding that the girl show her hand. The other children did not want Marja to listen to the gypsy, but the gypsy woman held on to the little hand, excitedly commenting on the remarkable lines in her palm and telling the child she would be famous. As we all know, Madame Curie became one of the most famous women of modern times.

The desire to discover what lay behind that strange element all around us known as radioactivity, literally drove Professor Pierre Curie and Marie, his wife, to the epochal discovery of radium. Whether or not the words of the old gypsy fortuneteller inspired Madame Curie and influenced her career, perhaps history will never know. But as one reads about her life, that conclusion would appear to be an obvious one, for early in her girlhood Madame Curie made up her mind to become a scientist. When she was refused permission to study science at the University of Cracow (the secretary told her that women should not concern themselves with science, and suggested that she enter cookery classes), she went to Paris and entered the Sorbonne, supporting herself by teaching and working in the laboratories. It was there she met Pierre Curie and, once embarked with him on the task of tracking down at least one source of radioactivity, nothing stopped her. She had two daughters, a household to manage, as well as the problem of combatting ill health, but she refused to give up her laboratory work even when her husband begged her to. Few women have been so greatly honored as Madame Curie, the woman who was told by an old gypsy that some day she would be famous. Madame Curie certainly made those childhood prophecies come true.

An amazing story, perhaps one of the strangest on record and one proving further that there is great power in believing, is found in that of Opal Whiteley. This astounding historical case clearly shows that, as pointed out by William James, belief creates its verification in fact; it affords unmistakable proof that often events are influenced by our very great desires.

This is the story of a girl who, according to those who knew her in her childhood, was the daughter of an American family named Whiteley, the head of which was an Oregon logger. She, however, believed herself to be the daughter of Henri d'Orléans, heir to the Bourbon claim to the Crown of France. She was credited with having written a diary supposed to have been compiled when she was six or seven years of age, which told about her "angel" father and "angel" mother of royal blood; this was printed in 1920 under the auspices of the Atlantic Monthly. It created a sensation and precipitated a big literary controversy. Drawn into the controversy were psychologists, scientists, astrologers, psychics, editors, clergymen, literary critics, and almost every person who had at any time known Opal.

In Alfred Powers' History of Oregon Literature, there is a chapter by Elbert Bede, in which Mr. Bede says: "I haven't the least doubt that a large part of Opal's diary is a hoax and a large part plagiarism, and I have presented facts that show the foster parentage claim impossible."

The diary was printed when Opal was about twenty-two years of age, and even though Opal Whiteley may not have been born of Indian royalty, she was actually accepted as such in later years.

In 1933, some thirteen years after her diary had been printed, the newspapers carried a story about an American woman traveling in India. While she was in the state of Udaipur, she had a remarkable experience. She was sitting in her carriage, when she was astounded to see another carriage led by a half troop of cavalry coming toward her. In the other carriage was Opal Whiteley, the girl from the logging camp of Oregon, and later investigators disclosed that Opal Whiteley was actually residing in the household of the Maharaja of Udaipur, the ruling Indian prince. The same newspaper stories told how Ellery Sedgwick, editor of the *Atlantic Monthly* when her diary was printed, verified the story that the girl was actually residing in the royal household. They further related that Mr. Sedgwick had received from the secretaries of two maharaja's courts, substantiation of this story and in his book, *The Happy Profession*, Mr. Sedgwick has a chapter devoted to this strange tale.

I have had several talks with Mr. Bede, who for many years was a well-known Oregon newspaper man, and is now editor of the *Oregon Mason*, regarding the remarkable way in which Opal molded her destiny, and Mr. Bede said to me: *"It was uncanny, almost supernatural, the manner in which circumstances suited themselves to her plans."*

Mr. Bede, like most people who knew the girl in her childhood, is absolutely convinced that Opal was born of American parents, the Whiteleys. He told me that he had known her quite well and that she had frequently been in his home in Cottage Grove. "My first knowledge of Opal came when I was reporting a Junior Christian Endeavor convention in Cottage Grove, and I was informed that a seventeen-year-old girl from a nearby logging camp had been elected president. My first impression of Opal was that of a vibrant, fluttery, exotic, whimsical person, informed strangely beyond her years, eager, deeply earnest, and seriously religious. She later became to me an inexplicable enigma.

"She was always planning, always planning well in advance anything she would undertake. It was most amazing how, in preparation of a nature book, *The Fairyland Around Us*, which she was writing, she could solicit contributions from such persons as Andrew Carnegie and John D. Rockefeller, and actually got money from some of them. A leaflet advertising the book carried expressions of wondering admiration from such persons as Queen Elizabeth of Belgium, Theodore Roosevelt, Nicholas Murray Butler, Gene Stratton Porter, and others of equal prominence."

I was struck by this paragraph in Mr. Bede's story: "With all these plans so well laid so long before the jaunt of Opal to Massachusetts' center of culture, I have often wondered what plans she had made to give the diary to the publishers. And then how Ellery Sedgwick should accidentally ask for this diary."

As I studied these words, I wondered if it was really an accident that Mr. Sedgwick should ask for the diary and if this strange girl had not "telepathically" given the thought to Mr. Sedgwick. I did not discuss this point with Mr. Bede, but if Opal Whiteley knew how mentally to transmit her thoughts to others in advance, then it explains how Mr. Sedgwick happened to ask if she had kept a diary.

For years I have carried the conviction that people close to nature and those intimately associated with both wild and domesticated animals have an understanding or an insight that enables them to see far beyond the horizons of most ordinary folks who live in the cities and never get nearer to a cow than a milk bottle. I have always believed that to these people nature reveals many of her secrets which are withheld from those who live in penthouses in our modern cities. Whether or not telepathy, or the ability to transmit our thoughts silently so that others catch them, is one of the secrets which nature reveals to those close to her, is something I cannot answer, although it is common knowledge that jungle dwellers and savages in all quarters of the world know the secret of telepathy and have used it for centuries. There are numerous books on telepathy among primitives; as a famous editor once said to me, "To accept the idea that these natives don't use it would put us in the class of the uninformed."

Now let's review what Mr. Bede had to say about Opal and her closeness to nature.

"A volume would hardly suffice to summarize the personality of the nature-tutored child, who had at the age of six, so her diary would have us believe, confided her most intimate secrets to Michael Angelo Sanzio Raphael (a fir tree), and whose associates instead of people were Lars Porsena of Clusium (a crow), Thomas Chatterton Jupiter Zeus (a most dear wood rat), Brave Horatius (a shepherd dog), Peter Paul Rubens (a pet pig), and other characters with equally classical appellations.

"In her adolescent years, Opal gathered geological specimens, and bugs and worms by the thousands, by the barrel. She garnered chrysalises by the bucketful and watched how God brought life to his fairies of the great outdoors. Somewhere, somehow, she gained a prodigious amount of knowledge about these things. Without having completed a high school course, this little maid of mystery presented herself at the University of Oregon, where entrance requirements were waived because of her knowledge of geology, astronomy, and biology."

According to Mr. Bede and others who knew Opal as a girl, no one was ever heard to mention anything that would cause others to believe that she was an adopted daughter of the Whiteleys, and Mr. Bede says it was only with the publication of the diary by the *Atlantic Monthly* that relatives and friends received the first intimation that Opal claimed foster-parentage.

I asked Mr. Bede what Mr. Whiteley (Opal's real or foster father) thought about her claim to royal blood and he told me that the father thought "his daughter" had been caught in the meshes of some wily promoters.

Shortly after her diary was printed, Opal Whiteley left the United States very secretly, traveling with a confidential document—not an ordinary passport—signed by our Secretary of State and Sir Edward Grey of England of the British Foreign Office. Just how she was able to do this is amazing to Mr. Bede and others who knew the girl in her childhood; but obviously, if she was the bona fide daughter of American parents and not of Indian royal blood, we certainly have here evidences of the workings of the strange powers of the human mind, of which, I repeat, we know little.

At this writing, Opal Whiteley is reported to be living in England. But when Mr. Bede wrote his article a number of years ago he said: "When last definitely heard of, she had been accepted as a princess of India, through an alleged marriage of Henri d'Orléans, the 'angel' father of the diary." I asked him to explain how Opal had been accepted as a princess of India, if she was not in fact born one, and he said he couldn't. Then I asked him if he thought her constant thinking so, her very deep belief, had anything to do with it.

He replied: "Frankly, I do not know. It may be, for we haven't probed to the depths of the mind and don't know the extent of its powers."

Reading Mr. Sedgwick's own story of this strange girl, it would appear that he is also convinced that Opal's real parents were the Whiteleys and that her belief that she had been born of royal blood was pure fantasy. It may have been fantasy, but she was accepted by royalty, because Opal obviously knew a lot of secrets unknown to the average person. Here in his own words is Mr. Sedgwick's theory of how this nature child from Oregon made her vision come true.

I have a theory and hold to it. Among an infinitude of letters came one written by an American of French parentage, whose father, so he told me, was a sergeant in the Franco-Prussian War of 1870. Of this sergeant's regiment, the colonel or perhaps the general of his division was Prince Henry of Bourbon, and toward the close of his life the prince, traveling across America, stopped in Oregon to have a chat with his old soldier. Whether or not this is fact, I cannot say, but my correspondent had no doubt of it since, chief among his childhood memories, was the arrival of the prince at the cottage door of his father. "I sat on his knee," he told me, and I believed him.

Now, according to my theory, the visit of a prince of the blood to an Oregon hamlet was an event. The truth and the legend of it spread through the lumber camps and what is more likely than that such a tale captivated the mind of a lonely and imaginative child and that her daydreams centered about it. At the heart of every little girl, Cinderella sits enthroned, and with Opal, the legend grew to be true, and the truth magnified with the years, and finally permeated her entire mind, her fancy, and her life.

Such is my theory of Opal's childhood, but in after years the story becomes an attested record of fact and yet, to my thinking, loses nothing of its wonder thereby. Opal, who had come to know many notable people in New York and Washington, and who had been petted and patronized by them, grew sick of it all. She went to England, always making friends, took up the faith of her "father," and established herself in a Catholic community at Oxford. Then one day I had startling news of her. A friend of my youth, Mrs. Rosina Emmet Sherwood, mother of a playwright long since grown famous, wrote me asking whether it was possible to believe a correspondent of hers who stated that with her own eyes she had seen Opal sitting like the princess in the story in an open barouche driving in state down the streets of Allahabad, royal outriders clearing the way for H.R.H. Mlle. Francoise de Bourbon! The story was credible for it was true. I verified it beyond conjecture. First I wrote to Opal, who sent me a collection of photographs of her Indian tour. There she was perched in a howdah on an elephant's back, ready for a tiger hunt (Henri de Bourbon, be it noted, was famous for his bag of thirty-six tigers, and I laughed as I recalled Opal chanting French verses in honor of his victory), and there she stood the center of many another turbaned group. Photographs, as I have remarked frequently in the narrative, can be liars and many of them stem from Hollywood which hardly contradicts the term. I was not satisfied, and since Opal's narrative identified two of the greatest maharajas who had been her hosts, I wrote to both their courts. In due time two letters returned, emblazoned with regal crests, each informing me the writer's royal master bade the secretary reply that it had been his high privilege to entertain H.R.H. Mlle. Francoise de Bourbon, and that a series of fêtes had been given to do her honor. And the wonder of all this had not subsided when an unsolicited letter arrived from a lieutenant colonel of His Majesty's forces occupied at the moment with maneuvers at Aldershot, informing the editor with some asperity that the colonel himself had been honored by an order to attend Her Royal Highness at an official garden party given for her entertainment, and further he begged to ask who it was that had questioned the authenticity of the lady who had graced the occasion.

"I close this account on a melancholy note. In the journal which Opal sent to accompany her photographs, no vestige remained of the contagious fascination of an earlier day. She described things as they are. The dew of the morning had vanished. The hard sunlight of middle age beat down upon a world that everybody sees only too clearly. The fairy kingdom was now the playground of other children. Its gates were closed, and Opal stood without. But while she was still the Opal of the Journal of an Understanding Heart, she had had her vision, and the vision was true. There is no truth more certain than that which makes bright the heart of childhood."*

Some readers may question this weird story, but the facts are as related and obviously, as Mr. Sedgwick states, "The child who wrote Opal's diary believed in it. She knew it for her own."

No greater verification of the fact that there is genuine magic in believing can be offered than this strange story of Opal Whiteley, who believed she was born a princess of India and later was accepted as one.

From early Biblical times to the present, there have been prophets, oracles, soothsayers, astrologers, and fortune-tellers. As a newspaper man (and I had the reputation of being a hardboiled one), I have investigated a number of these so-called seers and while some were obviously charlatans of the first water, there were others who mystified me. Certainly there are many of these fortune-tellers who believe in their ability to foretell the future. Materialists will

---

* From *The Happy Profession* by Ellery Sedgwick. Copyright, 1946. Reprinted by courtesy of Little, Brown & Company and the Atlantic Monthly Press.

say that that is impossible. For myself, having spent years in research work, I am not so positive, for actually some of the great prophecy of the past have certainly been fulfilled.

Even though there are many who deride the ability of astrologers, fortune-tellers, and the like, there are millions of people in this world, including at the present day some of our greatest financiers, statesmen, and even according to reports in recent years, members of our own cabinet, actors and actresses, and people in all walks of life, who believe in prophecies. No matter what my views are about the ability of anyone to foretell the future, I have long held the thought that it wasn't so much what the prophets foretold as it was the reliance of the subjects upon what the astrologer or soothsayer predicted for them that brought certain things to pass. In other words, a suggestion in the form of a prophecy was planted by the seer in the mind or the subconscious mind of the individual, which immediately went to work to make it come true. It was the power of suggestion working in the individual to make the prophecy a reality that finally produced the outcome. I believe that is what happened in the cases which I have cited.

I think of that great trouper, Marie Dressler, who probably evoked more laughter from a greater number of people than any other actress of modern times. Those who saw her in *Tillie's Nightmare*, *Tugboat Annie*, and various stage and screen appearances, will never forget that great personality; those of my readers familiar with her story know that Marie Dressler had a very hard time, suffering many privations before she became the great screen star known to millions. Whether true or not, I have read and heard that it was the advice and prediction of astrologers that landed Marie Dressler at the top.

In this connection, I relate the story of a strange experience I had shortly before Miss Dressler's death. In explanation let me say that I firmly believe that when people get on a certain plane of thinking or are attuned with their subconscious minds, they automatically become en rapport with one another.

Shortly after I had written my little book, *T.N.T.: It Rocks the Earth*, it hit me in a flash that all great men and women had been using what I had outlined, and I set out to verify this by writing numerous outstanding men and women for their views and comments.

Marie Dressler, probably because I was her ardent admirer, was one of the first women selected. I heard her on the radio one night and knew instantly that she had a grip on "that something" which many people seek and seldom find, and I "knew" that if I wrote Miss Dressler, I would get a reply. My secretary, when I dictated the letter, volunteered the statement that Marie Dressler would never acknowledge receipt of it or my book. We even made a small wager, as I did later with several others. (It is common knowledge that very few great screen stars personally acknowledge letters from unknowns and it was upon this premise that those who wagered against me based their judgment.)

While I felt that Miss Dressler would immediately respond, I was astounded at her answer and comment, and especially at the sight of her enclosure, a check for twenty copies of my brochure. In her letter she said:

"Thank you so much. Oh! what a book, if used rightly. As I read through it and look back, which I very seldom do, and check up on my own life—it looks as though I had been going down the right path."

Naturally, now that this great woman has left us, her letter is among my cherished possessions, because I never had personal correspondence with a woman who had put so much of her great heart and soul into her work to cheer up humanity and yet who had had more personal trouble or who had put up a greater fight to reach the pinnacle of success.

Incidentally, there are two fine thoughts in her letter.

First, it is futile to dwell on or think about the past. It is apparent Miss Dressler discovered this a number of years before her death, realizing that she couldn't give full play to thoughts of future accomplishments if she cluttered up her mind with thoughts of the past.

Second, as she indicated in ordering extra copies of my brochure, she was always trying to help people, which may be a forlorn gesture in many instances; but she must have realized that the extending of such help did bring its own reward, even though it might have meant only personal satisfaction in knowing that a helping had been extended.

The name of Helen Keller is known to millions. This famous woman was a marvel to me. As the world knows, she was deprived of her sight, hearing, and speech when she was twenty months old, and yet she became an inspiration, through her talks and her many articles and books, to thousands who were less handicapped than she. The story of her life is fascinating, because when Helen Keller, through stupendous effort, learned to speak, she gave to the world a new vision of what handicapped people could do when once they believed in their ability to achieve. It is interesting to know that Helen Keller was a confirmed Swedenborgian. As many readers may know, Swedenborg lived in the early days of the eighteenth century and was perhaps one of the world's greatest mystics. He was a very unusual man, as he, too, could foresee the future, having anticipated the submarine, the machine gun, flying machines, and the horseless carriage that would go twenty miles an hour.

I don't know whether Swedenborg could be called a spiritualist, as we know the meaning of the word today, but he certainly had something far beyond the ken of the average person. He believed greatly in the power of the mind and had trances, visions, and strange dreams, which must have come from his subconscious mind.

Another outstanding woman of our time, who has been the subject of much controversy and whose name is known to millions because a motion picture depicting her life has been shown throughout the world, is Sister Elizabeth Kenny, who brought from Australia in 1940 an idea for treating polio victims. As a nurse in Australia, she discovered what is known as the "hot pack system," a method of applying hot-water packs to the afflicted portions of the polio victim's body. Despite the fact that she was ridiculed by many people professional and unprofessional, Sister Kenny, with her vision, persistently through what may even be said to be forceful methods, brought herself and her principles of treatment to the attention of the American public, and through her efforts established the Sister Kenny Institute at Minneapolis.

One has only to study the photograph of Sister Kenny's face to see in her rugged features the reflection of a powerful mind, which, once in action and aided by a ready tongue, would ultimately help her force her way to victory. In her native land she was fought at every turn, and it was only through the woman's sheer persistence that the medical profession of America finally gave her recognition. Few women of our day have been the subject of more controversy.

From what one reads and hears about Sister Kenny, she is convinced to the nth degree that her methods are right and practicable, and even though the whole world might attempt to discredit her, she could go marching bravely on. Here is an example of a woman with an idea, a singleness of purpose, and the utmost belief in the efficacy of her methods of treatment who has brought new hope for many polio sufferers throughout the world. Now we come to a story which shows how the dynamic power in some women continues into their late years. The story concerns Captain Mary Converse, whose exploits were given in newspaper articles early in 1947. Mrs. Converse at seventy-five, a veteran of nearly 34,000 seafaring miles, wants to go to sea again. Born in Boston, she learned seafaring from her late husband, Harry E. Converse, owner of a steam yacht. As a junior navigator, she sailed the seven seas, obtained her second pilot's license in 1935, and her captain's license in 1940. Approximately 2,600 navy officers learned navigation from Mrs. Converse. She taught them in the dining room of her Denver home. Captain Mary Converse sails again!

While today a *Who's Who* of American women lists 10,222 biographical sketches selected from some 33,000 suggested names of outstanding women in business and the professions, including a number who are executives making more than $50,000 a year, our history recognizes no greater business woman than Lydia E. Pinkham. Her name may not be so well known to the women of today as to those of fifty years ago, but the business which she established and its product, Lydia Pinkham's Vegetable compound, still go merrily on. From a single idea, she built a huge business, which brought a return of millions and established a career the likes of which, for a woman, the world has perhaps never known.

Being a man, I know nothing about the efficacy of Mrs. Pinkham's vegetable compound, but I can remember as a boy often seeing a bottle of it in the family medicine chest. It was Mrs. Pinkham and her business associates who really modernized advertising, for she was one of the greatest of all advertisers. Ideas used in many advertisements today were originally voiced by Mrs. Pinkham. She tied in with much of her advertising a sort of homely philosophy embodying emotional appeals which seemed to have a way of penetrating to the hearts of her fellowwomen and which resulted in not only millions of dollars in sales of her vegetable compound but also brought for more than half a century tons of enthusiastic testimonials to the laboratory at Lynn, Massachusetts.

Once more, in this extremely remarkable woman, is demonstrated what belief in personal achievement can and does accomplish. During Lydia Pinkham's early life, many people were interested in the manufacture of home remedies, and she, too, became interested in the idea. She started making her compound in her kitchen and for some time gave the mixture away to ailing women neighbors, only to awaken later to the fact that it could be sold. She then began promoting it. Like most people who start with an idea, she had many discouragements—lack of finances, the opposition of others, and manufacturing and sales difficulties. But nothing daunted this New England woman, for her tremendous driving force and enthusiasm reached and engulfed every member of her family. Especially was this true after her business really got going.

No book documenting the great power of believing would be complete without mention of Mrs. Mary Baker Eddy, also a New England woman, who built up that huge religious organization known as Christian Science. As almost everyone knows, Mrs. Eddy was faced with discouragement, strife, and the bitterest ridicule. But after she had caught the flash which gave to the world her *Science and Health with Key to the Scriptures*, she began to develop powerful leadership, a tremendous and unshaken belief in her teachings, and a dynamic personality which has left its imprint upon millions of people throughout the world. It has been said that few writings have done so much to influence the sciences of medicine and theology as hers. Christian Science is another practical demonstration of the power of believing.

The world will always be indebted to Florence Nightingale, who was greatly instrumental in saving the lives of thousands, and brought the nursing profession to the high standard now recognized by the entire world. Here again is an example of a woman who knew early in life what she wanted and who set out to realize her ambition. She had been born with a passion to nurse the wounded and the sick; at the time she undertook her great work, nursing was not even recognized as a profession.

She came from one of the richest families in England, but that meant nothing to this great woman. She started in by scrubbing the corridor floor at the Fliedner Nursing School in Germany and she soon showed that she could not only scrub floors but bind wounds, and with her encouraging talk, revive hopes. She, too, was fought at every turn, but being inspired with the vision of the destiny which she thought was hers, obstacles meant nothing to her. She hated bigots, believing that all should be cared for, irrespective of faith, color, or creed, and she had a quick tongue when aroused.

During the Crimean War, the males of the British War Office scoffed, saying that Florence Nightingale's work would only result in failure. Reluctantly they let the "madcap" have her own way. She organized, at her own expense, a private expedition of nurses and took them to Scutari, and even though the officers in charge of the hospital there wanted no woman to interfere with their work, interfere she did. Under the leadership of this originator of modern nursing, the women took over the handling of the hospital. Throughout her stay in the Crimea, her iron will constantly fought against a stone wall of opposition. Something had to give way, and this time it was the stone wall.

Some of the most powerful statesmen of Great Britain ridiculed this astonishing woman's work and did everything possible to stop her in her reforms; but her letters, "filled with dynamite," awakened her countrymen until she was adored everywhere. The story is told that when at the age of eighty-two, she became sick, her nurse tucked her into bed, only to have Florence Nightingale get out of her own bed and tuck in her nurse. At the age of ninety, just before she died, a friend asked her if she knew where she was and she replied, "I am watching at the altar of murdered men and I shall be fighting their cause."

When we think of martyrs, most people have in mind men who have died or been crucified or jailed for espousing causes in which they believed. Let us always remember there are many outstanding women of history who have suffered martyrdom as much as men, from Joan of Arc who was burned at the stake to women of modern times who fought and were jailed because of their efforts in furthering women's rights.

The name of Carrie Nation is probably becoming dim to the younger generation and perhaps is fading in the memory of many of the older generation. But during the years around the turn of the century, Carrie Nation was one of the greatest of women martyrs. Like many people imbued with an idea, Carrie Nation was convinced that she was "divinely" appointed to destroy the saloons and she set out to end the illegal sale of liquor in her own state of Kansas. Aided by some of her followers, Mrs. Nation succeeded by public prayer and denunciation in closing many illicit barrooms. When she saw this method was slow in its effectiveness, she took to wielding a hatchet, smashing bottles and beer kegs, and demolishing bar fixtures. She was constantly ridiculed and frequently jailed, but so thoroughly was she convinced of the righteousness of her cause that she accepted martyrdom gladly.

Surely everyone knows the story of Sarah Bernhardt. She had the temper of a tigress and yet history records her as one of the greatest emotional actresses of all times. She suffered innumerable failures in her early days on the stage, but she had a passion to make good, and make good she did; by the time she was twenty-four she was famous. She, a woman who smoked cigars and drank strong drinks, was a creature of extraordinary moods. She would visit cemeteries and sit on tombstones as if in grief for the departed. Sarah Bernhardt never appeared to be concerned with what people thought about her, and, as a matter of fact, she reveled in their comment. She was an individualist in the highest sense. The memory of her dramatic acting will probably go on forever. Even though she had to have an artificial leg toward the end of her life, she continued her stage work, for nothing could change her lifelong belief that she was a supremely great actress—and she was to the end of her life in 1923.

Then there was that dynamic person, Madame Schumann-Heink, who was equally an exemplification of what belief can do, once the mind that carries it gets into action. She was inspired early in life, giving to the world her beautiful voice at the age of fifteen when she became an opera singer. She, too, became famous in the Old World, but when she came to America, it was the fulfillment of a dream that had burned fiercely within her for many years. Her heart was torn many times, but even in the face of overwhelming odds, Madame Schumann-Heink always came smiling through.

Here was a woman whose oldest son had gone off in World War I to fight for the Kaiser while her other four boys were in the opposite trenches, but among those of us who heard her sing "The Star-Spangled Banner" in her quaint, foreign accent, there were many who took off their hats and wept. Over a national radio hookup, her voice became known to millions. She was beloved by everyone and she had that basic thing, born in most people but seldom aroused, the spirit of never quitting. It was at the age of seventy-two, when she was signed up as a successor to Marie Dressler, that the curtain rang down on this great performer.

No matter of what race, creed, or color, who has heard the wonderful contralto voice of Marian Anderson without being deeply moved and charmed by it! Yet few realize the very humble background of this great artist. I recall the story that as a child of six she wanted a violin; it was at the time she was learning that she could earn five or ten cents by scrubbing doorsteps in Philadelphia. If there ever was a woman who believed in her dreams, and who made them come true, it was Marian Anderson; she climbed to world fame and yet had to overcome, especially in our country, many handicaps and prejudices. Her triumph is one of the most dramatic in musical history. It was in Washington, D. C., on Easter Sunday of 1939, that this Negro girl of humble origin, standing before the Lincoln Memorial, thrilled an audience of 75,000 people, studded with cabinet members, senators, congressmen, and famous people in business and society. As we read the story of Marian Anderson, we must become convinced that she, too, succeeded through her belief, and that the great source of her inspiration came from her subconscious mind.

In this book are to be found numerous examples of men using the subconscious mind to achieve, but it is rather unusual to run across any written records of its use by women. Let me introduce here the story of a young woman who tells how her subconscious mind was directly responsible for her success. She is Angela Lansbury, the well-known young movie actress, who was interviewed by Mildred Mesirow for *Reach* magazine. The interviewer tells us:

> *Angela Lansbury, the brilliant young screen star, aside from having beauty and dramatic ability, was also a girl with an exceptionally good brain. Angela's blond beauty has become familiar to millions of movie-goers through her masterly interpretation of the maid in Gaslight, her charming adolescent buoyancy in National Velvet, and her poignant interpretation of the tragic café singer in The Picture of Dorian Gray.*

So varied a range of character-interpretation requires brains as well as beauty. Angela has both.

It was during a rest interval here [Hollywood] that she launched forth upon one of her favorite themes—her faith in her own destiny. "Ah," she amended quickly, "I think perhaps I've phrased that badly. I don't mean anything magical or occult. Perhaps faith in the power of the subconscious mind would be a better way of saying it."

"In the manner of Tennyson, perhaps, or Stevenson?" was suggested.

"Exactly! Not that I think my abilities in any way resemble their genius, you understand. But I think I've learned how to tap the resources of the subconscious. Everyone knows that the subconscious mind stores all sorts of abilities, memories, and aptitudes we don't ordinarily utilize . . . What I'm trying to say is that, when you've learned how to draw on your subconscious powers, there's really no limit to what you can accomplish."

Angela has schooled herself in the technique of this self-suggestion. Since first she chose acting as a career, she has constantly held in her mind a picture of what she aspires to achieve. She has even, she confessed, written down from time to time the goals she wants to reach. Obviously, she has tapped the reservoirs of creative material which few of us know how to use. Within the subconscious lie the materials of genius itself; of powers which, when properly recognized, may burst into the mental field of activity in patterns which surpass our conscious abilities.

"And how do you go about tapping your subconscious mind?" I asked.

"Heavens! I don't want to sound stuffy and highbrow, but it's really awfully simple. If you tell yourself over

and over again that there's no limit to the creative power within you, that's about all there is to it. Honestly, I believe that's true. Whatever intelligence or creative force, or whatever it is, that resides in the world is like . . ." she waved a strong, beautiful hand expressively . . . "oh, like light or air, or something of that sort. It doesn't belong to me, especially. It's there, to be tapped and expressed by anyone who knows how to get at it.

"This isn't a cut-and-dried formula for success by any means," she continued. "It doesn't let you off hard work. You've got to keep plugging like mad, perfecting whatever kind of expression you've got; adding constantly to your skill, whether it's in acting or painting, or even making a dress. So that, when the chance for self-expression does come, when the time arrives for you to call on your subconscious power to express itself, you have a good set of tools for it to work with; a proper medium through which your creative urge can be portrayed. . . . Catch on?" she added with typical humor.

"About the suggestibility of the subconscious?" I prompted.

"Oh that! Well, when you're about to drop off to sleep, just tell yourself that tomorrow's the day you've got to surpass anything you did today. That, whatever demands are made upon you, all your abilities, all you've learned, perhaps things you've forgotten you ever knew—all these will be available to you . . .

"Bearing in mind an actual mental picture of the situation is even better. If you're scheduled to do a screen test, for example, you see yourself acting-out that test better than anyone's ever done it before. Act it like mad in your mind! Be Duse; be Bernhardt! In your mental picture, be

*the best there is! And when the actual test comes off you
find, often to your surprise, that you're acting better than
you know how.*

*"The subconscious is a pretty dramatic factor in per-
sonality, I believe. It likes to act and sing and paint and
express itself. It likes to surpass in anything it's called on to
do. Your responsibility is to equip it with tools for expression, to give it a chance, and then make it an ally behind
the scenes . . ."*

Another example, and one of the most outstanding, is
the story of how *Uncle Tom's Cabin* came into existence. It
will be recalled that it was written by a wisp of a woman,
Harriet Beecher Stowe, whose name will be remembered
as long as there is American history. In 1850 Mrs. Stowe
swore a solemn oath that she would write something "that
would make the whole nation feel what an accursed thing
slavery is." For two months she tried in vain to think of the
story which was later to shake the world. In February, 1851,
while she was attending communion service at the college
church, there came to her mind the picture of Uncle Tom
and of his death. According to the story, Mrs. Stowe went
home in tears and when she had written out the scene of
Uncle Tom's death and read it to her family, they, too, were
in tears.

She did a great deal of research work in trying to secure factual material, but when she actually sat down to
write, she needed none of it. The story obsessed her and
literally wrote itself. Out of her subconscious mind surged
long-forgotten memories and photographic impressions,
which arranged themselves almost automatically in proper
sequence on paper. Mrs. Stowe didn't think out these in-

cidents and their background, she actually saw them; and while in her time little was known of the subconscious mind, it is obvious that it was the source of this story, which many claim brought on the War Between the States. Mrs. Stowe to her dying day insisted that it was God and not she who had written this book.

There are many famous women, including the Brontë sisters, Elizabeth Browning, Susan B. Anthony, Evangeline Booth, Jane Addams, who attained niches in the hall of fame. And today, while it is too early to tell the complete story, there are three women whose names will go down in history as having influenced and shaped the destinies of millions of Chinese. These are the famous Soong sisters, perhaps the best known of whom is Madame Chiang Kai-shek; the others married respectively Dr. H. Kung and Dr. Sun Yat-sen, both Chinese leaders.

As we come down to the present day and read the stories of women who have big ideas, we run across such people as Mrs. Matthew Astor Wilks, one of the richest women in the world and the daughter of the late Hetty Green, who, herself, amassed a fortune of over $67,000,000. Mrs. Wilks is following in the footsteps of her famous mother.

Then we have the account of Vera Nyman, which is literally another story of rags to riches. An idea, fifteen dollars, and a bathtub put her into a business for which Mrs. Nyman recently refused a million dollars. When she married her husband, Bernard, in 1920, she had the belief that she and her husband were going to make a million dollars. It took her twenty-seven years to achieve her objective of the million, but she had it within her grasp when a drug concern offered her that sum for her plant. Mrs. Nyman rang doorbells selling a liquid cleaner and later, by cooking chemical stews night after night in her own home, hit upon a combination of ingredients that would clean 90 per cent of painted surfaces. Her product today is known to millions of housewives and last year her sales topped $2,500,000. Mrs. Nyman, who day after day of making personal calls encountered more than 50,000 housewives, knows what it means to face discouragement, but her belief that she would ultimately make a million dollars never faltered.

Who's Who in America gives the stories of dozens of women who, as top-flight executives, writers, and professional women, receive from $25,000 to $100,000 a year. For example, here's the case of Mrs. George T. Gilmer of New Orleans, better known under the name of Dorothy Dix, the famous adviser to the lovelorn, who is reported to have received better than $75,000 a year. Then there is Mary A. Bair, president of the Oliver H. Bair Company of Philadelphia, with a salary of $50,000. And by no means is Helena Rubenstein, who owns the famous cosmetic manufacturing company and whose income must be tremendous, to be overlooked.

Success stories could embrace dozens of women, such as Mary Dillon, president of the Brooklyn Borough Gas Company, who started in as a six-dollar-a-week office helper in the $5,000,000 corporation which she now heads; and Mrs. Ora H. Snyder of Chicago, who, about thirty-five years ago and with a capital of only five cents, began building up a candy business which centers around several shops and which was, at one time, worth more than a million dollars.

Add the story of Alice Foote MacDougall, president of the Emceedee Corporation Cortile, Inc., and many others like her who have built up huge businesses which have been managed as well as those headed by male executives.

An entire book could be written about women who have achieved fame and fortune in the field of radio and motion pictures as artists, writers, and executives. The name of Mary Pickford is known to millions, not only as a screen favorite but also as a motion picture corporation executive.

For a number of years Bertha Brainard was program director of the National Broadcasting System, with a salary that ran into five figures; she was said to be one of the highest paid women radio executives. It all came about through her getting an idea for feature radio programs. That was in 1922 and her first effort brought her a return of $50.

The whole world knows the story of Amelia Earhart, famous American aviatrix, who was lost with her plane in the South Pacific. While a teacher and a social worker, she became interested in aviation and became one of the world's greatest flyers. She was the first woman to cross the Atlantic in an airplane. In 1931 she made a solo flight across the Atlantic and four years later flew the Pacific alone from Honolulu to California.

One writer has said that the vast majority of American men do not believe that women are ever their equals. But when we stop to examine the record, the list of women who have achieved success in every line of endeavor is an impressive one.

Here is the story of a great American woman who scored a double success—as a homemaker and a career woman. She is Mary Roberts Rinehart, who for more than forty years has thrilled the mystery-story fans of the world. Necessity forced her to make some money to retrieve the family fortunes which she and her doctor-husband had lost in a stock-market crash. With one hand, she wrote those great stories of fiction which gained her more than ten million readers, while with the other hand, she tended her babies and handled the details of housekeeping.

There are many women who have remained single simply because they feel deeply about marriage and are not willing to marry "just any man." But surely if this science of creative thinking can work for men, it can work also for women—even to the point of woman's actually creating an image of the man of her desires and literally bringing him into reality. In other words, if a single woman could visualize the kind of man she wanted and steadfastly held to the thought, in accordance with the principles of this science, she could bring the object of her mental picture into her presence. This may sound silly to some of my women readers, but it has been my good fortune to have given this science to many women who have used it most effectively. Therefore, if you are single and with your whole heart and soul you desire a certain type of man to walk into your life as a husband, merely picture him, not necessarily in physical form but in the abstract, setting forth in your thought projection the attributes that you would like to have in your man, and the day will surely come when you will meet him.

It seems to me that the women of today have the means of getting about everything they set their minds to. Certainly, opportunities are all around them. In fact, there never was a time in history when the world was so open to women as it is today. There are comparatively few fields among those which were formerly restricted to men in which women are not now represented. Today you'll find women in science, the fine arts, journalism, publicity, government, and various other branches, all working intelligently and with full knowledge of their duties and aware of their new opportunities and responsibilities.

There can hardly be any doubt that all of this is largely because modern women are receiving the same education as men, with the result that they are not alone becoming acquainted with subjects hitherto regarded as essentially for men, but that their conscious or reasoning mind is being developed. In a way, it is perhaps superfluous for me to call women's attention to the importance and advantage of using their subconscious mind, for they have always used it. As a matter of fact, they are experts in the use of it— only they have always thought of it as woman's intuition. My point is that the subconscious is much more than intuition and that it possesses great forces which can be set in motion for the benefit not only of men but of women also, through the application of the power of dynamic believing. As I pointed out earlier, wonderful results are brought about by the conscious mind's conveying the will-to-do through believing to the subconscious, and this immediately sets the subconscious in action to carry out the desires of the individual.

Now the women of modern times have a unique advantage, I might say, a twofold mental advantage: to their subconscious mind the skilled use of which is characteristic of their sex and which has been highly developed and been their unconscious, though intuitive, guide through the ages, there has been added their conscious mind which has been specially developed by the scientific method of modern education. In my opinion, it is this combination which accounts for the speed with which women have acquired such rapid proficiency in so many of the so-called masculine subjects; and it is largely responsible not only for women's emerging from the traditional life within the home, but also for their entrance into the world where their view of people and practical affairs is broadened, made more objective and more understanding. Furthermore, it enables women in the home to have a better comprehension of the work of their men, as well as a deeper interest in the school studies and future lifework of their children.

My fundamental aim is to show how each person can develop his plus-powers, the seeds of which lie within his subconscious mind. It is these plus-powers which will enable you to obtain the things you want and the things you would like to be in addition to what you have and what you are already. By this new co-operation of the conscious and subconscious minds, you can gain those things which you feel deeply are necessary to your life and happiness, and also keep alive the feeling that no matter how long you live, you are undergoing personal development, are, in a word, progressing.

Always remember that the subconscious mind, in addition to being the seat of intuition, is a repository of great power and has inexhaustible resources. The more you call upon these resources, the more there are placed at your disposal. Remember also: the subconscious is ageless; it can never grow old or tired, and you can draw upon it all your life. The only thing you need is the power of believing—sincerely, strongly, and completely; once the subconscious has received your message and understands your desires and ambitions, it will be only a short time when your desire will be fulfilled and your ambition achieved. This book tells of the many men who have used this science and succeeded, but I would like to impress upon my woman readers that they have the same two minds, conscious and subconscious, and that through them they can succeed just as men have. It is all a matter of believing and of co-operation of the two minds, according to the principles here set forth. The magic which comes from believing is real, for it has been demonstrated in the lives of some of the most successful. It can be demonstrated in your life—by your own personal believing.

Chapter 8

Noting how women were treated at the time that this book was being written, this chapter of the book really was revolutionary. In it, Claude Bristol addressed women specifically on their abilities and shared ways in which they could incorporate the magic of believing into their lives. While some may find the references offensive at times, in reality the author believed in the innate power of women have and the influence that they can have in the world. He cites character traits, values, perspectives and the ethics that women possess in general. He shares that, once women completely embrace their power, they can become highly effective and powerful world leaders.

1. Renowned author and naturalist, Ben Hur Lampman, stated to the author, *"Once they [women] understand and apply what you give them, they'll find themselves in a position figuratively to turn the world upside down. If there were some way for women of all nationalities to unite and use this science, there would be no future wars."* This is an extremely powerful statement. Do you believe it to be true? Why or why not?

2. Lampman went on to state that women are unstoppable when they set their mind to something. Do you believe this to be true?

3. Consider the most focused and unstoppable woman you know. On a scale from one to ten (one being "very little" and ten being "very much so"), rate how unstoppable you believe her to be:

1——2——3——4——5——6——7——8——9——10

4. The author claims that women are more versatile and adaptable. Do you believe this to be true? Why or why not?

5. Bristol claims that *"Women are supreme egoists."* Do you find this statement offensive? Why or why not? Please explain.

6. Napoleon declared that most men are victims, while women, by their nature of thinking make circumstances serve them. This statement covers a broad spectrum of individuals. Do you believe that there is merit to it? Why or why not? Please explain.

7. The author asserts, *"If women of today 'don't get a break,' it is the fault of no one but themselves."* If you follow his theory that our minds have extraordinary power, then you might concur with him. What are your thoughts on this statement?

8. While the author may appear a chauvinist as he opens this chapter, you must remember that this book was written in the 1930's. It is likely that including women in it actually moves beyond the norms of the day. Research the treatment of women in the 1930's. Do you believe this position to be accurate? Please explain.

9. According to Bristol, after WWII, 70% of America's total wealth was in the possession of women. As a newspaper man during that time, he met some outstanding women. Research and write about at least two women who exhibited great power in that era.

10. Mrs. Bondurant was a powerhouse woman that Claude Bristol interviewed. He claimed that the *"indomitable spirit"* of these women (who believed in and were deeply committed to their cause) made legislation possible and effective. List at least three women that you know who have an indomitable spirit, and explain why.

11. Mrs. Bondurant claimed that the women of her time lacked the interest in their power. Do you believe this to be true, or might it have been lack of knowledge of the options that were available to them? Please explain your point of view on this.

12. According to Mrs. Bondurant, women were dreamers and all of the great movements in the world originated by men. Do you consider yourself a dreamer? Why or why not?

13. Mrs. Bondurant asserts that *"People don't have sufficient action or driving force behind their beliefs."* On a scale from one to ten (one being "very little" and ten being "a great deal"), rate how much driving force you have behind manifesting your dreams:

1———2———3———4———5———6———7———8———9———10

14. As you consider your drive, what might you do to carve out more time and energy towards manifesting your dreams? List at lease three things you can do to focus more on them, and then take the time to follow through on these initiatives.

15. Mrs. Bondurant makes a key observation when she states, *"I don't know of any greater thing in life than the satisfaction that comes through serving."* Studies have shown that people are much happier when they focus their energy on serving others over themselves. What activities do you do to serve others? If you don't, do some research and find at least one activity that you could do to support others. Then start to do it!

16. Mrs. Bondurant claimed that whenever she and her husband struggled financially, checks would appear from overdue loans. Why do you think this occurred?

17. Have you ever experienced such miracles, where, just when you most needed it, money came your way? Please explain.

18. The author references the famous singer, Grace Moore and how powerful she was. She once said to a protégé, *"To great artists there was no such thing as a small part and to small artists, there were no big parts."* Do you ever struggle with feeling that you are not really being seen and honored for your contributions? Please explain.

19. How do you handle feeling unnoticed? Please explain.

20. Ellen Wilkinson was the British Minister of Education. She was a powerful woman in the political world. Which woman in the field of politics do you most respect and why? If you are not aware of anyone, research your female political leaders and seek at least one that you respect. Write about them and why you do.

21. The author cites several instances where women believed they would become famous and did. Empress Eugenie, Madame Curie, and Opal Whiteley. Both Empress Eugenie and Madame Curie were told by gypsies that they would become famous, and they did. Have you ever received a message from a psychic or channelor that actually came to pass? If so, please explain.

22. Do you believe in psychics and channels? Why or why not? Please explain.

23. Opal Whiteley showed a great wisdom and foresight that was well beyond her youthful age. She knew how to mentally transmit her thoughts to others in advance. Have you ever experienced a situation where you were able to transmit a message to others without actually speaking with them? If not, do you believe you are capable of doing so? Please explain.

24. Claude Bristol states that one is better equipped to transmit thoughts when they have silence. Do you believe you can effectively do so without being in the quiet of nature? Why or why not? Please explain.

25. In reference Opal's mind power and her closeness to nature, with little prior formal education she was waived the entrance requirements into the University of Oregon because of her knowledge of geology, astronomy and biology. How do you believe she acquired such knowledge?

26. Do you believe she tapped into something beyond what she saw and felt to gain such knowledge? If so, how and what? Please explain.

27. Mr. Sedgwick ends his description of Opal's rise to prestige and honor in India with the statement, *"Here is no truth more certain than that which makes bright the heart of childhood."* What does this phrase mean to you? Please explain.

28. The author asserts that there is no greater story that supports the power of the mind than that of Opal Whiteley. She believed she was born a princess of India and later was accepted as one. Do you know of anyone who has so strongly set their beliefs in themselves, that they have manifested exactly the position they have wanted in their life? If so, please explain.

29. Bristol states that *"it wasn't so much what the prophets foretold as it was the reliance of the subjects upon what the astrologer or soothsayer predicted for them that brought certain things to pass. In other words, a suggestion in the form of a prophecy was planted by the seer in the mind or the subconscious mind of the individual, which immediately went to work to make it come true."* So, the power lies not so much in the prophecy itself, but in the seed that the prophet planted in the mind of the individual they shared the information with. Do you believe you have ever been swayed by the power of suggestion in your life? If so, how? Please explain.

30. Before sharing the story of Marie Dressler, the author states that he firmly believes that *"when people get on a certain plane of thinking or are attuned with their subcon-*

scious minds, they automatically become en rapport with one another." Do you believe you have ever experienced being *"en rapport"* or deeply in tune with someone? If so, describe your experience. If not, why do you think you have yet to experience this phenomenon?

31. In Ms. Dressler's letter, she shared two things. The first was that one has to let go of the past; that it clutters up the mind. On a scale from one to ten (one being "very little" and ten being "a great deal"), rate how much you believe you focus on the past:

1———2———3———4———5———6———7———8———9———10

32. For a week, keep a journal, noting how many times you find yourself reflecting on the past. Simply mark each time every day with an "X". Then reflect. Did you focus more or less than you anticipated?

33. The fact that Dressler wanted to share this information with others, indicated that she got personal satisfaction from doing so. What efforts do you make to assist others? Write a list.

34. Do you find that helping others the way that you do drains you or fills you energetically? If it drains you, investigate why and consider a different course. If it energetically fills you, write about why.

35. According to the author, Helen Keller was a Swedenborgian. Have you previously heard of this term?

36. Swedenborg anticipated many inventions prior to their manifesting in the world. Imagine yourself as having the power to project into the future. Allow yourself to imagine experiences and inventions that will eventually come to fruition. Describe your visions.

37. The author shares the story of the controversial figure, Sister Elizabeth Kenny and the hot-water packs she administered to polio victims as another example of

vision at work. He stated that one could see in her *"rugged features the reflection of a powerful mind."* When you consider individuals that you believe to have mind power, do you see *"rugged features"* in their physicality?

38. Despite adversity, Sister Elizabeth Kenney so believed in her technique that she fought hard to gain it the respect she thought it deserved. Have you ever believed in something that was contrary to public norms? If so, what was it, and how did you handle the scrutiny? If not, do you believe you have not allowed yourself to follow the road less travelled in fear of public criticism? Please explain.

39. As respected sea farer and an expert in navigation, Captain Mary Converse was a pioneering woman of great power in the 1940s. What types of initiative would you consider reflective of Mary's power in today's society?

40. Lydia E. Pinkham's vegetable compound made her extremely wealthy and a mogul of the advertising world. While others attempted the same, they were not as successful as she. What traits do you believe sets some above others as leaders in their field?

41. List the skills or traits that you believe you need to hone in order to become a leader in your field?

42. Which of these traits do you currently possess and which do you need to cultivate?

43. What steps can you take to cultivate the knowledge or skills that you still need to master your craft? Write a plan, and immediately begin to take the required steps towards greater success.

44. The author credits Mrs. Mary Baker Eddy for bringing Christian Science to the world. Are you familiar with Christian Science and how it has influenced the sciences and theology? If so, list how. If not, research Christian Science and write about the impact that it has made in the world.

45. Florence Nightingale became famous for her prowess as a nurse and healer. She had no patience for bigotry and believed that all should be cared for. She was said to have a *"quick tongue."* Is there anything that triggers you into having a *"quick tongue"*? If so, what and why do you feel so strongly about it?

46. Nightingale led an expedition to treat fallen soldiers during the Crimean War. Despite a great deal of backlash, she persevered. What is the most trying experience you have had in fighting for what you believe in? Please explain.

47. When Florence Nightingale died at the age of 90, she was quoted as saying, *'I am watching at the altar of murdered men and I shall be fighting their cause."* Bristol believed her to be a martyr, along with Joan of Arc, and Carrie Nation. Are there any causes for which you believe you would die? Please explain.

48. What was striking about Sarah Bernhardt was her lack of concern around public scrutiny. She acted right up until the end of her life. Is there an endeavor that you are so passionate about, that you would want to continue experiencing it through the end of your life? Please explain.

49. Madame Schumann-Heink and Marian Anderson were adored as beloved musicians through their lives. When you were young, did you have any passion towards creative expression? Do you now? If not, do you have a passion for athletic or other mastery?

50. Have you given up on experiencing anything you were passionate about? If so, why?

51. If you have given up hope, is there a way that you could re-ignite your fire towards your passions? If so, what is the first step you could take to do so?

52. Renowned actress, Angela Lansbury stated that she had faith in the power of the subconscious mind, *"If you tell*

yourself over and over again that there's no limit to the creative power within you, that's about all there is to do." If you are not already familiar with her career, research Angela Lansbury's long and successful career. Summarize your findings.

53. Lansbury asserts that you must continue to hone your skills so that when opportunity knocks, you are at your best. What personal or professional develop initiatives do you currently practice? Are there any additional skills that you should hone? If so, set up instruction and a schedule to do so.

54. Lansbury stated that *"when you're about to drop off to sleep tell yourself that tomorrow's the day you've got to surpass anything you did today. That, whatever demands are made upon you, all your abilities, all you've learned, perhaps things you've forgotten you ever knew—all these will be available to you."* Try repeating this phrase each night before bed for at least one month. Write about any changes you note.

55. Angela goes on to share, *"If you're scheduled to do a screen test, for example, you see yourself acting-out that test better than anyone's ever done it before. Act it like mad in your mind! Be Duse; be Bernhardt! In your mental picture, be the best there is! And when the actual test comes off you find, often to your surprise, that you're acting better than you know how."* Have you ever followed this practice before a job interview, presentation or other endeavor? If so, what was the outcome? If not, why not?

56. The next time you have an important meeting, audition, presentation or event, take some time to practice this technique. Then be sure to write about the outcome.

57. Claude Bristol ends the segment on Angela Lansbury with a final statement from her, *"The subconscious is a pretty dramatic factor in personality, I believe. It likes to act and sing and point and express itself. It likes to sur-*

pass anything it's called on to do. Your responsibility is to equip it with tools for expressions, to give it a chance, and then make it an ally behind the scenes." In this quote, Lansbury seems to give the subconscious human characteristics, a personality. She encourages that it likes to creatively express itself. Viewing your subconscious in this light, by not following it, you are disallowing its voice and expression. Find at least one creative endeavor to pursue. Then take some time to ask your subconscious to express itself. Allow it to do so without judgment or criticism. Whether singing, dancing, painting, photography, writing acting, or any other form of expression, allow it to flow through you. Then write about your experience and any insights or ideas that this exercise provided you.

58. In 1850, Harriet Beecher Stowe swore a solemn oath to write something *"that would make the whole nation feel what an accursed thing slavery is."* Have you ever felt so passionately for a cause that you were inspired to change the world? If so, what transpired thereafter?

59. A year after the seed was planted, while attending a church service, an image of the death of Uncle Tom came to Stowe's mind. In the end, the story of Uncle Tom's Cabin wrote itself. Her subconscious mind *"surged long-forgotten memories and photographic impressions, which arranged themselves almost automatically in proper sequence on paper."* Have you ever had an experience where you were so "in the flow" that inspiration came to you easily and without any effort? If so, describe the experience. If not, perhaps set an intention to experience such phenomenon. Then practice the visualization techniques previously mentioned, and await the experience to manifest in your life. When it does, express gratitude and write about it.

60. To her dying day, Harriet Beecher Stowe insisted that God wrote her book. Do you believe that such a phenomenon can exist? Why or why not?

61. When we attribute ourselves to miracles and manifestations, there is a danger of self-aggrandizement. Is there a danger in such self-adulation? If so, what is it?

62. Have you ever found yourself getting caught up in such self-centered focus? If so, how were you able to control it, or were you?

63. The author cites the Soong sister as being very influential among the lives of millions of Chinese. If you are not familiar with these powerful women, research them and their contributions to their society. Write about your findings.

64. Another powerful woman that Claude Bristol references is Mrs. Matthew Astor Wilks. Research her life story and write about how she amassed great wealth.

65. Vera Nyman made millions creating and marketing a cleaning product. Dorothy Dix, Mary A. Bain, Helen Rubenstein, Mary Dillon, Mrs. Ora H. Snyder, Alice Foote MacDougall all procured great financial and business success. Choose two of the women listed, and research their achievements. Summarize their careers. Then note if they have any common traits, and if either or both of them credited their success to "mind power." Write about your findings.

66. Research a woman who has achieved career success in the media, as an artist, writer or executive. Mary Pickford is a great example of success in the motion picture industry, as is Bertha Brainard who was program director for the National Broadcasting System. Again, note if the woman you research attributed any of her success to mind power.

67. Claude Bristol asserts that you can attract the kind of man (or woman) that you want into your life through visualization and steadfast thought. He encourages you to picture (in the abstract), the type of individual you want

to walk into your life. He then asserts, *"The day will come when you will meet him [her]."* Have you ever practiced this technique? If not, try it. If you have a happy relationship, then perhaps do it with a mentor, friend, co-worker, business partner or other individual that you would like to have support you in your life. Commit to a steadfast practice of visualizing him/her and set the intention to meet him/her in the next three months. Write about your findings.

68. The author claims that women have always practiced the use of the subconscious mind. It has been thought of as *"women's intuition."* He asserts that the mind is, however, more powerful than *"women's intuition"* indicates. Do you believe the women in your life to be naturally intuitive? If so, do you believe they are more so than men? Please explain.

69. The combination of the strength of women's subconscious mind, along with the scientific method of modern education have put women at a two-fold advantage, according to Bristol. They have acquired proficiency in so many "so-called" masculine subjects with great speed. Do you believe this to be true? Why or why not? Please explain.

70. The author explains that his fundamental aim is to *"show how each person can develop his plus-powers which will enable you to obtain the things you want and the things you would like to be."* He likens this to a *"co-operation of the conscious and sub-conscious minds".* Do you feel there is any current co-operation between your two minds? Please explain.

71. Does your conscious mind ever make choices to hear the messages of your subconscious mind? Do you ever ask your subconscious mind to instruct you? If not, consider doing so and write about any ideas or insights you might gain by doing so.

72. Is it important for your well-being to feel that you are always undergoing personal development; that you are progressing? On a scale from one to ten (one being "very little" and ten being "very much"), rate how important life-long constant personal growth is to you:

1——2——3——4——5——6——7——8——9——10

73. Beyond being the seat of intuition, the subconscious mind is also a *"repository or great power and has inexhaustible resources."* If you could call upon any power from within your subconscious mind, and there were no limitations placed upon you, what would you wish for? Please explain.

74. The author ends this chapter asserting that *"the only thing you need is the power of believing—sincerely, strongly, and completely."* He insists that your desire will be manifest in a short time when you are passionate and fully commit. If there were absolutely no limitations whatsoever to what you could do and accomplish in your life, write about what you would do, have, see, hear, experience and live. Describe your life's fulfillments as if you are currently living them, fully and in the present, and do so using as much specific detail as possible.

75. Write an article about yourself, as if you were being highlighted on the front page of your favorite magazine. Write as if you have already manifested the life of your desire, and then take some time to visualize yourself experiencing it. How do you feel after doing so—energized or depleted? Please explain.

Chapter 9

Belief Makes Things Happen

n 1944, a popular digest magazine had a story about a group of scientists in Chicago who were experimenting with moths. A female moth of rare species was placed in a room, and four miles away a male moth of the same species was released. In a few hours the male moth was found beating its wings against the window of the room in which the female was confined. The editor declared that he believed that this experiment showed that ideas fly with the sureness with which the female moth communicated her whereabouts across incredible barriers to the one mind for which they are originally intended.

Here is a simple experiment that will make you wonder whether the birds don't possess telepathic or clairvoyant power. In the off-season, put some scraps of bread in the backyard. There isn't a bird in sight. But hardly have you entered the house before birds begin to congregate. First come sparrows and wrens, then robins, and in two or three minutes the yard is filled with birds. Put out anything but food and not a bird appears. What brings them to your yard? How do they know the bread is food for them?

Science can give no answers. Edwin C. Hill in his broadcast of February 17, 1947, in talking about butterflies, made the statement that the more scientists investigate, the more they are becoming convinced that birds and insects have a wireless of their own or some other invisible manner of communication with one another. This has long been a theory expounded by nature students, and as a matter of fact, many books have been written on the subject, notably one by William J. Long, *How Animals Talk*.

It's interesting to note that during the last war, our Army Signal Corps in experimenting with carrier pigeons and shortwave radio, found that the pigeons were affected by the radio waves and often, when confused, flew in circles and were lost.

When we consider that the swallows of San Juan Capistrano, California, fly away each October 23 and return each March 19 with unfailing punctuality; that tagged salmon released from Columbia River points spend four years in the Pacific Ocean, then consistently return to the spots from which they departed; that cats and dogs taken many miles from their homes have returned; that wild ducks and geese wing their way back to their original localities; that other inexplicable things are too numerous to mention here; are we not faced with the fact that there are wave radiations and telepathic forces also operating in the fish, bird, and animal kingdoms, in fact, in everything around us? Some writers claim that all living things have the means of communicating with each other, and in view of the Yale experiments, this may not be so far fetched after all.

Early in 1945 radio listeners heard the voices of blinded soldiers telling of their experiences in "facial sight," through which they were able to detect objects in their paths through a sixth sense or kind of "mental radar." Dr. Jacob Levine, a Boston psychologist, who had charge of the school at Old Farms, in the Avon district of Connecticut, where war-blinded veterans were taught the use of this sixth sense, declared that he could not explain its mechanics, but he knew that it worked. This "facial sight" is based on the hypothesis that the body radiates definite rays of an unknown variety which, coming into contact with an object in front, assemble or group themselves in such form as to make a picture of it, after which they return, still bearing the picture, to the blinded person, who "sees" it through the sensation of the returning rays as they radiate through his body.

I have long had the conviction that various forms of telepathy or thought-transmission are used every day of our lives, far more than most people suspect. I believe that many great leaders, preachers, orators, executives, and so-called super-salesmen, some unconsciously and others thoroughly conscious of its workings, exercise the power to varying degrees. We meet a person, and before a word is spoken we experience a like or a dislike. What is it that causes the feeling to register but some form of thought-transmission? I have already stated that the only possible explanation of healing and affecting others at a distance is through the medium of this phenomenon, of which we are only now beginning to get a scientific explanation.

As I write, I have a mental picture of a famous lawyer in whose office I have often sat as he dictated letters concerning business affairs in which I was interested. When he dictated he always paced the floor, and his concentration was intense. Once I asked him why he stood while dictating and how it happened that his letters always accomplished the end intended. His reply was:

"In the first place, I think better on my feet. Then before I start dictating and during the whole period that I talk, I actually visualize before me the person to whom I write the letter. If I do not know him, I try to picture him as I think he may look. In both cases, I direct all my thought and words to him in person as though he were actually before me in the flesh and tell him mentally that my premises are right and should be followed by him."

A successful book saleswoman told me that if she was satisfied that a customer had the money and really wanted to purchase a book, but was hesitating between two choices, she would keep repeating to herself, but directing her thought to the customer, the title of the one best suited to that customer. She added that many of her sales were made by thought-directive power. An automobile executive told me that when he had a prospect who had the money to purchase, he always said to himself, "You're going to buy this car, you're going to buy this car"—and the prospect did.

I am aware that few people like to believe they are influenced by the silent thoughts of others when it comes to a matter of purchasing anything or doing something, but the fact remains that all of us are subject to this subtle influence, be it telepathy or anything else you want to call it. The fact remains, too, that this invisible power exists, and a little experimenting on your part will convince you that it is both formidable and active.

I am certain that mothers use it on their children and often children use it on their parents. Not infrequently husbands and wives use it on one another without the knowledge of either one. This is especially true where a man and wife are closely attuned to one another. You who are married and have never used this science, have a new field to explore.

One of the most striking examples of this subtle influence in action came to my attention several years ago. The president of a company that I had been helping was dissatisfied with his sales manager, but because of many years of service did not wish to discharge him. "I was at my wits' end," he told me, "when I suddenly got the idea that I could suggest to him mentally that he ought to resign his job and become a salesman instead of remaining as manager. I thought about it for hours one night, but I nearly fell off my chair when the first thing next morning he came into my office, saying that he would like to resign as manager as he felt that he could make more money by getting out on the street as a salesman. I don't know whether I was guilty of using some sort of magic, but my conscience is clear, because the man today is making twice as much money as he did when sales manager and he's much happier, and we're all going to town."

In this connection, here is another story, that of a man and wife who came to see me. The man told me that until a few months before our meeting he had been one of the largest clothing manufacturers in the Middle West, but had sold out and was now traveling the country. His story, taken from a memorandum transcribed at the time, is briefly as follows:

"For more than thirty years I had been a member of one of the largest and oldest secret organizations in the world which embraces this theme of believing from A to Izzard, but I, like thousands of others, never had my mind opened to it and I never realized the 'truths' contained therein.

However, several years ago I attended a series of lectures on the subject of mind control and my eyes were opened for the first time to what a wonderful power man could make available for himself if he saw fit to do so. I could see how it would work in our business to tremendous advantage and I used it. Needless to say, our business started to increase as soon as I put it to work and it has been increasing ever since. During the depression when firms like ours were having a terrific struggle we consistently made money, and when I sold out my interests I guess I can say, with all modesty, that I was at the top."

At this point his wife entered the conversation, saying: "My husband wouldn't openly scoff at me when I talked this subject and what I had learned at the lectures before he started, but he gave me to understand that he believed I was wasting my time. I just knew there was something to it and I was certain that if my husband could get hold of it—it would mean a great deal more business for him. I talked to him about attending the lectures until I was tired and then one day I realized I was doing the wrong thing. Instead of talking to him I should use the very science which I had been taught. I went at it with a vengeance. Both my daughter and I several times a day kept repeating to ourselves mentally, 'Dad is going to go, Dad is going to go.' It took us nearly three weeks, but Dad did go."

Here the husband broke in, saying: "You speak about your tap-tap idea. Well, she certainly worked it on me. When she first talked about what she had heard at the lectures, I just couldn't believe them to be true. I had been brought up in a very practical business world and I couldn't get myself to believe in many of the so-called abstract things. However, one day 'something' impelled me to make up my mind to go with her. I didn't know at the time that the 'something' was my wife's mental suggestion and I had no idea that she and my daughter had been 'working on me.' However, it was the greatest thing that ever happened to me. After the first lecture I did some experimenting and our business began to improve and continued to improve until the day I sold out.

"Don't get me wrong. I am not religious in an orthodox sense, and what I talk about is not goody-goody stuff, but an exact science. What we think or contemplate develops into reality. We radiate our thoughts, perhaps unconsciously, to others, and we affect them. We give forth vibrations of dislike or hatred which we engender in ourselves—and, bingo, they come right back and floor us. All one needs to do is to study and understand the law of cause and effect, and it all becomes plain. Thought has been referred to as a powerful unseen influence, and so it is. There are so few people you can talk with on this subject. Most people ignorant of the subject look at you askance when you mention something about it, and now I understand why the Master spoke in parables. However, I've reached the conclusion that it will not be many years before people generally are into the subject up to their ears, for there are thousands of enlightened people who are recognizing that we are on the threshold of great developments dealing with thought power, and the number is rapidly increasing. I wonder why more men in the business world don't catch hold of it and apply it in their businesses, but I guess that most of them are like I used to be—they keep their minds closed and no one ever takes the trouble to work on them as my wife did on me. All a person has to do is to believe, earnestly and sincerely, that such a power of mind exists and then conscientiously apply the science. It's all just as you say: when one starts tapping the subconscious mind, your own or others, the bricks fall into place as though by magic. Does it work? And how!"

Alfred F. Parker, a highly respected general insurance agent in the Pacific Northwest, has given me permission to quote a letter he wrote to me in 1937, in connection with the use of this science. I do not know whether Mr. Parker is even interested in the subject of telepathy, but I do know that he thoroughly believes in the efficacy of belief. His letter speaks for itself:

Recently I had opportunity to put into further practice your tap-tap idea, and I thought that you might be interested in knowing the circumstances. I have a small son who is quite naturally the apple of my eye. On December 29, 1936, he picked up some obscure infection and for days he lay desperately ill in the hospital. There was grave doubt that he would live. I was in terrible anguish, but I resolved to meet the situation as best I could. Taking a tip from you, I put his picture on my desk and carried another in my pocket. Every hour of the day I kept looking at them and repeating to myself, "He will recover. He will recover." At first I felt I was lying to myself, as he hardly seemed to have an even chance. However, I kept it up and gradually found myself believing what I kept repeating. At just about that time, thanks to the best medical and nursing attention and some of a friend's blood transfused into him, the boy actually did begin to recover. He is now at home and regaining his strength fast. It may have been a mere coincidence that the time when empty words began to turn into belief was the time when recovery began, but at least such coincidence is worthy of note.

Some people have had the experience of walking into a darkened room and feeling the presence of someone there, even before a word was uttered. Certainly, it couldn't have been anything else but the vibrations of some unseen individual that indicated his presence to the other person. Evidence of telepathy? What do you think? It is maintained that if the first person in the room will, at the entry of the second person, think of something entirely foreign to himself and dismiss from his mind all thought of the possibility of his discovery, the second person will not sense his presence. There are thousands of people who have thought of someone, only to hear from them or see them shortly thereafter, and they have given no heed to the phenomena involved. These experiences are usually considered coincidences; but when we properly consider the power of thought, do we not have the real explanation? I cannot help but feel that anyone with an open mind and willing to read and experiment for himself, will sooner or later come to the conclusion that the phenomena of psychokinesis and telepathy are realities, and, as investigators have pointed out, that these powers are latent in everyone, though developed to varying degrees.

Hudson, in his *Law of Psychic Phenomena*, originally published in 1893, recounted numerous experiments to prove the existence of telepathy, among them being the use of playing cards. One member of a group of people was blindfolded, after which a card was selected by another member upon which the others present were told to concentrate. The blindfolded person was then asked to name it, according to the first mental impression he received. The results were further proof of the validity of telepathy.

Here is a simple experiment that may be carried on by only three people. Cut five colored slips of paper from a magazine, each about half an inch wide and three inches long. The more vivid the colors, such as bright red or electric blue, the better, but be sure to have them quite distinct from one another. One person should then place them fanwise between the thumb and forefinger of his right hand, as you would hold a hand of cards. Let either of the other two people touch any one of the colored slips without being seen by the third person. Immediately after this the first person who holds the slips concentrates his mind on the colored slip selected, with a view of communicating the information to the mind of the third person who is then requested to indicate which slip was touched by the second person. It should be made clear to the third person that his decision must be immediate and spontaneous, and that his mind should either be blank or thinking of something entirely remote from the experiment. That is, he should not attempt to guess, deliberate, or try consciously to think of the color of the slip selected, but should act immediately upon the first mental impulse he receives. The number of times the third person will name the colored slip selected by the second person will astound you. With a little practice, people—who are more or less en rapport, such as husband and wife, the husband holding the slips and the wife acting as the third person after some second person has previously indicated a choice—will make an even higher score of successes. I have seen this done twenty to thirty times without a single miss. Here again belief must come into play. The holder of the slips must possess not alone the ability to maintain an unwavering concentration, but the strong belief that he can transmit the image of the color to the mind of the third person.

Let me interpose a word of caution. This experiment, as well as others outlined in this book, should never be attempted in the presence of scoffers or those who profess a disbelief in psychic phenomena, for, with their negative thoughts, they may confuse and obstruct the free flow of your own, especially if their skepticism is aggressive. Always remember that belief is a power operating destructively or constructively, depending upon the end to which it is employed. Recall Dr. Rhine's discovery of how disbelieving could depress the results in the psychokinesis tests. In addition, note this: Dr. G. R. Schmeidler of the Harvard Psychological Clinic, where extensive experiments in telepathy have been made, has pointed out that subjects who maintain that telepathy is a myth or that the hypothesis is false, invariably show scores far below those of chance. Once more we see in action the magic of believing. Believe that it will work, and it will. On the contrary, believe that it will not work, and it will not!

The great French astronomer and scientist, Camille Flammarion, an early exponent of thought-transmission, held somewhat to the theory later advanced by Professors Eddington and Jeans. He claimed that there was mind not only in human and animal life, but in everything—in plants, minerals, even space—and he declared that mind gleams through every atom.

Early in 1947, Dr. Phillips Thomas, previously referred to, publicly announced that upon retiring he intended to devote his time to research in the field of telepathy. Dr. Thomas said:

"You may think I'm crazy, but I intend to devote my time to research in this field when I retire in two years. We can't conceive scientifically how this [telepathy] could come about, but neither can we explain the apparent success of 'mind readers.'"

This announcement caused the Portland *Oregonian* to comment editorially:

The other day in this newspaper there appeared an interview with a successful professional man who spoke of his impending retirement, and added that he should thereafter devote his time to research in the strange field of telepathy and kindred phenomena, generally aggregated as extrasensory perception. Before you exclaim, "Ha, another crackpot!" pray reflect that Dr. Phillips Thomas is an eminent scientist who for many years has been research engineer with the Westinghouse Company. Now he elects to become an explorer of that last dark continent, the human mind, in which, beyond per-adventure, more marvels and mysteries are hidden than ever were discovered in Africa.

It must be evident to the veriest skeptic that Dr. Thomas, international authority on electronics, is convinced—by evidence not lightly to be dismissed—that in our sedulous application to what may be called conventional science we have rather stupidly neglected those challenging phenomena which in times past bore the stigma of sorcery and witchcraft.

The proper and rational attitude toward the seeming phenomena of the mind—if that is what they are—is one of scientific inquiry which, though rigorously exacting, will not resist conviction when incontestable proof has been obtained. Actually there can be no such thing as a supernatural phenomenon, but only the manifestation of natural law as yet unknown to us. Nor is it without precedent, this decision of a distinguished scientist to attempt penetration of the unknown continent of the mind. Dogmatic disbelief, not infrequently manifested by scientists toward telepathy and similar manifestations, is far from being a scientific attitude.

What profit to mankind is there in the quest to which Dr. Thomas presently shall address himself? This is a question most difficult of reply, for it may be that the inner secrets are, indeed, inviolable. But if of this research comes a better understanding of ourselves, and of the forces which are latent in mind, it might be that the knowledge would liberate more of happiness for the race.

In the last couple of years much has been written about Robert R. Young, the aggressive and energetic chairman of the board of the Chesapeake & Ohio Railway, and his plans for railroad improvement and development. While I have never seen anything in print stating that Mr. Young utilizes the subconscious, I think that anyone knowing anything about the subject would conclude from these articles about him, that Mr. Young relies greatly upon it for his ideas. In an article appearing in *Life* magazine early in 1947, it was stated that Mr. Young believed in "extrasensory perception" and that he could "become almost mystical about getting off by himself and 'feeling a truth.'"

Whether it be mind, as we understand the general usage of the word, or whether it be electrical vibrations of some kind, it is the phenomena themselves with which we deal, call them what you wish. The conclusion is that they embrace and pervade everything.

So when we consider the subconscious mind of a single individual as being only an infinitesimal part of the whole and the vibrations therefrom extending to and embracing everything, we get a better understanding of the workings of psychokinesis, telepathy, and kindred phenomena.

In explaining psychokinesis, Dr. Rhine points out that there must be a mental attitude of expectancy, concentration of thought, and enthusiasm for the desired results if a person is to be successful in the experiments. Again we have the magic of believing at work. The subject must have a prior belief that he can influence the fall of the dice.

That belief is the basic factor in the ability to demonstrate psychokinesis (control of mind over matter) and telepathy was more recently confirmed in experiments at Duke University as reported in the *New York Herald Tribune* by its science editor, John O'Neill. Mr. O'Neill declared that these experiments proved that it was possible to "kid" a person out of his power to demonstrate psychokinesis and telepathy.

He told of how a young woman, by distracting the attention of one of the young men attempting to control the fall of the dice, and by scoffing at his professed ability to demonstrate his power of mind to direct matter, succeeded in injecting such a strong negative factor that she weakened his belief in himself and ruined his score for the day. Mr. O'Neill made an interesting speculation about this when he went on to say: "The converse of this experiment, still to be made, in which a test would be made of the possibilities for improving the score by a confidence-inspiring 'pep' talk offers interesting possibilities."

At this writing, the outcome of such an experiment is not known, but in view of the thousands of experiments previously made at Duke and other universities, it is apparent that scores improve when the experimenters believe and are confident of the results. Also, nothing is more logical than that "pep" talks should be helpful to those who lack confidence or belief, and thus they should improve their scores.

If golf shots can be influenced by mental attitudes or proper visualization, and the "galloping ivories" turn up at the mental command of the players, who is there now to gainsay that events are not influenced by thought and that before us is a field that is gradually yielding to modern man some of the secrets of the ancient mysteries? Do not the experiments at Duke University prove that the so-called luck factor is in reality an influence brought about by powerful thought vibrations, rather than coincidence or chance? Writers, long before the experiments at Duke, declared that the luck factor came about from a determined mind—a combination of visualizing, concentrated thought, willing, and believing. Think about this in connection with yourself and the goals you have set for yourself, for in it is the primary secret of this science.

Anyone who has associated with the garden variety of parlor gamblers knows that the word "hot" is often applied to card players or "crap shooters" when they have a winning streak. When the "hot" period wears off, the gamblers either quit the games or begin to lose. What is this "hot" period? Nothing more than an all-knowing feeling, a deep-rooted belief that they can win. Even in gambling the magic of believing plays a major role.

Of course, this book is not written for professional gamblers but for sincere men and women who wish to succeed in life. The material referring to the games of chance is included only to provide further evidence that with concentrated thought, expectancy, and steadfast belief, we actually set in motion vibratory forces that bring about material manifestations.

As stated previously, charms, amulets, discs, talismans, etc., have no power in themselves, but those who firmly believe in them unquestionably tend to develop the kind of force or power now known as psychokinetic. I have tried to make plain how this power through belief can be developed and to take you up the ladder as far as you wish to go. It is necessary, though, to point out that it is easy to lose one's belief or faith. Thousands have risen to great heights of success, only to stumble, roll, or fall to undreamed-of depths. Others, seeking health, have appeared to be more or less miraculously cured, only to find that in later years or even months there is a recurrence of their ailments. There are many weakening factors and influences—all suggestive in nature—which we, in unguarded moments, allow to slip into our subconscious minds, and which, once there, begin their destructive work and undo all the good accomplished by our constructive forces. So step out in front, head toward the sun. Keep facing it and the dark shadows will not cross your path.

The writer knows that it is difficult for the average person who knows nothing of this subject to accept the idea that all is within; but surely the most materialistic person must realize that as far as he himself is concerned, nothing exists on the outside plane unless he has knowledge of it or unless it becomes fixed in his consciousness. It is the image created in his mind that gives reality to the world outside of him.

Happiness, sought by many and found by few, therefore is a matter entirely within ourselves; our environment and the everyday happenings of life have absolutely no effect on our happiness except as we permit mental images of the outside to enter our consciousnesses. Happiness is wholly independent of position, wealth, or material possessions. It is a state of mind which we ourselves have the power to control—and that control lies with our thinking.

"Consider that everything is opinion, and opinion is in thy power," said the great philosopher, Marcus Aurelius Antoninus. "Take away then, when thou choosest, thy opinion, and like a mariner, who has doubled the promontory, thou wilt find calm, everything stable, and a waveless bay."

A modern version of this is found in the statement of the seventy-eight-year-old man previously quoted, who said:

"Distress ensues only when developed by conscious mental attitudes. Disappointments, suppressions, melancholy, depressions, etc.—all are emotional excitations or suggestions from a mode of thinking those things. If these emotional tendencies are resisted and will-power is asserted to prevent such influences reaching our consciousness, the foundation of the thought disappears and consequently the distress vanishes. It will be noted that this weakness to resist repressing thoughts and imaginations arising from emotional reflex develops from failure of self control and command of the situation as thought presents it. Stop thinking! Refuse to think that idea or way. Assert yourself to be the creator and boss of your own habits of thought—in fact, become unconquerable.

No one ever defeated a resolute will. Even death stands still before such a will."

Emerson said: "What is the hardest task in the world? To think." Obviously this is so, when one considers that most of us are victims of mass thinking and feed upon suggestions from others. We all know that the law of cause and effect is inviolable, yet how many of us ever pause to consider its workings? The entire course of a man's life has many times been changed by a single thought which, coming to him in a flash, became a mighty power that altered the whole current of human events. History is replete with the stories of strong-minded, resolutely willed individuals, who, steadfastly holding to their inner convictions, have been able to inspire their fellow-man, and in the face of tremendous and determined opposition have literally created out of nothing great businesses, huge empires, and new worlds. They had no monopoly of thought-power. You and every man and woman have it. All you have to do is to use it. You will then become the person you envisage in your imagination; for with the working of the law of cause and effect, you bring into your life the new elements which your most dominant thoughts create within and attract from without.

Positive creative thought leads to action and ultimate realization, but the real power, much more than action itself, is the thought. Remember always: "Whatever man can conceive mentally, he can bring into materialization." Health, wealth, and happiness must follow if the proper mental pictures are created and constantly maintained, for the law of cause and effect is immutable.

"Know Thyself." Know your power. Read and reread this book until it becomes a part of your daily life. Faithfully use the cards and the mirror technique and you will get results far beyond your fondest expectations. Just believe that there is genuine creative magic in believing—and magic there will be, for belief will supply the power which will enable you to succeed in everything you undertake. Back your belief with a resolute will and you become unconquerable—a master of men among men—*yourself.*

STUDY GUIDE

Chapter 9

1. Claude Bristol opens this chapter siting an experiment done with moths in Chicago in 1944. The findings suggested that somehow the female moths telepathically communicated their whereabouts to the male moths. The author shared the example of birds and how they too sense when food is put out for them. Science has no definitive answers for these phenomenon. What other examples of telepathic communication can we find in nature? If you are not aware of any, take some time to research and write about your findings.

2. William H. Long wrote a book, *How Animals Talk*. He emphasized that carrier pigeons used by the Army Signal Corps during the second world war were affected by radio waves, and were often confused. Fast forward over 70 years to present day. Radio waves fill the air with computers, cell phones and other media that didn't existing during Mr. Bristol's lifetime. Do you believe these waves have a more adverse affect on our wildlife? If you don't know, perhaps you want to first check in with your own mind power, and then perhaps research this topic. Did your senses of the issue match the findings you uncovered?

3. The author cites examples of the swallows of San Juan Capistrano, tagged salmon, flocks of geese, and cats and dogs who, when lost, find their way back home. These are all examples of nature's beings communicating with one another. If we can see examples of it in nature, why do you believe humankind is so skeptical about humans possessing that same innate ability to communicate using the power of the mind?

4. The "facial sight" of war-blinded veterans was a prime example of individuals successfully using their sixth sense. Experiment with this ability. Have someone blindfold you, and have them place various items in front of you. Then note whether or not you can sense that there is something, and if so, what it might be. Write about your findings.

5. Bristol believes that many great leaders, preachers, orators, executives, and so-called super-salesmen exercise this power to varying degrees. Write a list of leaders, preachers, orators, executives and super-salespersons that you know or know of. Do you believe this to be true in their cases? Why or why not?

6. The writer references a famous lawyer who paces when he dictates his communiques. He imagines the individual with whom he is communicating standing in front of him. He then proceeds to tell that individual mentally how his *"premises are right and should be followed by him."* Why do you believe this method is so effective?

7. Next time you have to communicate a letter or email to someone, go through the same process as the lawyer did. Note how effective or ineffective your communique ultimately is.

8. A book saleswomen shared with the author that she used *"thought-directive power"* when she successfully sold books. She would continuously repeat to herself the title of the appropriate book for the customer to purchase, while directing that thought to the customer. A car salesman did the same. Experiment with this technique, but be sure to only use it if you believe the outcome you project is for the other individual's highest good. Track your progress and write about your findings.

9. The author suggests that we often use this technique, consciously or unconsciously with our children, our spouses, co-workers, etc. A man who was the largest clothing

manufacturer of the Midwest shared that his wife and daughter used this technique to encourage him to attend a seminar on mind power. He stated, *"when one starts tapping the subconscious mind, your own or others, the bricks fall into place as though by magic. Does it work? And how!"* Experiment on individual(s) you think could benefit from learning more about his or her mind power. Tap into the subconscious mind and relay the messages to them that they should pursue this opportunity. Then note any changes you see in them or their behavior.

10. Claude Bristol shares a letter he received from Alfred F. Parker, an insurance agent. His son became gravely ill and in response, he constantly looked at his photo, repeating, *"He will recover." He will recover."* He did recover, and the man really believed that his shifting belief from illness to recovery assisted in the transformation. Have you ever done this exercise when someone you cared for that was ill? If so, was it helpful? If not, perhaps you can try it next time you are in such a predicament. Note any changes.

11. Many of us have experiences where we think of someone and soon after, they contact us. Write about such an experience that you've had.

12. For the next couple of weeks, make a point of thinking of individuals who you haven't had contact with in a long time. Bring them into your mind's eye everyday. Then, if they don't contact you, make an effort to contact them. When you speak with them, see if they mention that you have recently been on their mind. Write about your experiences with this experiment.

13. In Hudson's book *Law of Psychic Phenomena,* he recounts an experiment with playing cards where an individual was blindfolded, and asked to identify a card that had been picked out by the others. Have you ever played such games? If so, what was the outcome? If not, experiment with this exercise and see what results you experience.

14. Claude Bristol suggests that you do the colored cards experiment. Try it with a variety of people (friends, children, siblings, married couples, etc.). Track their progress. Did married couples or others who knew each other really well do better than the individuals who didn't know one another? Once completed, do a comparative analysis, and write about your findings. (Note: Bristol suggests that you only do these experiments with people who are open to the idea. Those we are not could affect the outcome).

15. The great French scientist and astronomer, Camille Flammarion claimed that the mind existed in everything—human, animals, plants, minerals, and even space. Do you believe this to be truth—that everything has a consciousness or mind? Please explain.

16. Prominent and successful individuals like Robert R. Young, the chairman of the board of the Chesapeake & Ohio Railway believed in extrasensory perception and spoke of *"getting off by himself and 'feeling a truth."* Do you ever take time to consciously be away from technology, clutter and the influence of others so that you can go within and *"feel the truth"*? If not, take some time to do so, and make note of the outcome.

17. Dr. Rhine points out that for mind power to fully work, there has to be a mental attitude of expectancy. Do you believe you absolutely expect to experience what you see in your mind's eye, or do you still have some doubt? If there is doubt, what might you do to start cultivating more faith? List at least one step you can take to do so, and write about your findings.

18. John J. O'Neill showed that it was easy to weaken one's belief by injecting strong negative factors. Similarly encouraging the validity of such experiments could also positively affect their outcome. Are there negative nay-sayers in your life who, when you are around them,

tend to weaken your sense of the miraculous? If so, how important is it that you remain friends? Is there a way you can continue to remain connected to them without their negative influence?

19. Charms, amulets, talismans and other "things" apparently have no power unless that power in them is believed This is known as psychokinetic power. Do you ever wear or carry such items? If so, do you believe that they have power? Do you believe that your belief is what gives them their power? Please explain your position on this.

20. We are reminded that it is easy to undo faith. The author suggests that you *"step out in front, head toward the sun. Keep facing it and the dark shadows will not cross your path."* What does *"the sun"* look and feel like to you when you are struggling with your faith?

21. What raises your energy and good feelings when you find yourself doubting that your desires will be manifest? Getting out in nature, spending time with animals, creative visualizing, journaling or listening to your favorite music are all activities that may increase your energy and renew your sense of hope. Write at least three activities you can do when you find yourself feeling discouraged or depleted. Then make an effort to do them when you need to raise your energy and sense of hope.

22. The author asserts that *"happiness is wholly independent of position, wealth, or material possessions. It is a state of mind which we ourselves have the power to control—and that control lies within our thinking."* Contemplate this statement, and be completely honest with yourself. Do you believe that you have complete mind control, or do you fall into victim mode every once in a while, seeing outside circumstances as impediments to your success?

23. If you find yourself feeling victim, is there anything you can do to pull yourself out of that mode of thinking and feeling? If you can't think of a solution, do some research

and find an option that would work for you. Describe it and be sure to follow through on using it.

24. The author shares a quote from a wise man who stated, *"Disappointments, suppressions, melancholy, depressions, etc.—all are emotional excitations or suggestions from a mode of thinking those things. If these emotional tendencies are resisted and will-power is asserted to prevent such influences reaching our consciousness, the foundation of the thought disappears and consequently the distress vanishes."* Based on this statement, you need willpower to win over such emotions. On a scale from one to ten (one being "very little" and ten being "a great deal"), rate how much willpower you believe you have:

1——2——3——4——5——6——7——8——9——10

25. The man goes on to say, *"this weakness to resist repressing thoughts and imaginations arising from emotional reflex develops from failure of self control and command of the situation as thought presents it. Stop thinking! Refuse to think that idea or way. Assert yourself to be the creator and boss of your own habits of thought—in fact, become unconquerable."* He instructs us to simply stop thinking. One of the tricks that is quite widely used is to say to yourself, *"Cancel, cancel"* when you note yourself thinking negative thoughts. Try this for at least 28 days. Note any insights or changes as you practice this technique.

26. When you use your thought power you will *"become the person you envisage in your imagination."* If you have not already done so, imagine your best self. What do you look like, feel like? How would you dress? Who would you befriend? Where would you live? What is your state of health? How charismatic are you? What would you spend your days doing? How much money is in your bank account? How much money do you earn each year and how? What are your creative outlets? Do you travel? If so, where? Do you have a summer home? If so, where? What

are your relationships like? Are you philanthropic? If so, what do you do to support others? Do you have your own business? Are there people working under you? What are your working relationships like? Paint as vivid and broad a picture of yourself as you can. Then feel into experiencing the life that you have created for yourself, imagining it in the here and now.

27. Write a list of all the *"new elements"* your dominant thoughts are attracting into your life.

28. The author urges, *"Know Thyself."* On a scale from one to ten (one being "very little" and ten being "very much"), rate how much you really know yourself:

1———2———3———4———5———6———7———8———9———10

Book 2

T.N.T.:
It Rocks
The Earth

A philosophy for today, tomorrow and thereafter

with some practical suggestions as to how

to get what you want in life.

Claude M. Bristol
Writer and Lecturer

*(formerly Vice-President of a well-known
Pacific Coast Investment Banking firm)*

Mrs. Pat Allen
    [Vice-President, term 1932-1933
Women's Auxilliary, International Fidac]
WHO VALUES IT

"No monetary value can be placed on T. N. T. To have the book in your hands is to feel the detonations. Those who seek to accomplish should read it from cover to cover—foreword and all. Reread it again and again, then prize it through life as a most valued possession."

To
R. C. W.
who located T. N. T. in my pocket

To
M. J. E.
who caused me to find it

To
L. B. E.
who had me use it

To
E. L. B. who added to it

And To
all others who aided me in
assembling my supply of T. N. T.,
this high explosive is affectionately dedicated.

FOR EVERY EXECUTIVE and SALESMAN
"This book should be in the hands of every executive
and salesman, and studied at regular intervals.
When followed, it will bring happiness
and success to anyone."
—Horace Mecklem, well known member,
National Association of Life Underwriters.

Foreword

As previously referenced, Claude Bristol wrote *T.N.T.: It Rocks the Earth* prior to writing *The Magic of Believing*. It reinforces the teachings that he shares in *The Magic of Believing*, offering less stories and supportive research, and more practical tools and applications that you can use. Throughout this booklet, he challenges you to take charge of your life by focusing on using these tools in a way that supports goodness and affirms that you can do anything you set your mind to!

T.N.T.: It Rocks the Earth

"He who does not know what the world is, does not know where he is. And he who does not know for what purpose the world exists, does not know who he is, nor what the world is."

A First Century Message
— Tap — Tap — Tap —

For those of you who seek to learn and make progress, I gently lay this in your laps. I do so without the slightest fear but that it will turn your world entirely upside down—bringing you health, wealth, success and happiness, providing you understand and accept.

Remember T.N.T. is a dangerously high explosive so when you gather it closely, handle it gently. Down through the centuries its power has destroyed those who sought to misuse it, therefore exercise great care that it is used only for good.

Do Not Misuse It
It can be proved by the teachings of the Bible, certain well established laws of physics, and last but not least, just plain

common sense. Read and determine for yourself whether or not the proofs I offer stand by themselves.

Some of you may see only the spiritual side, others recognize the scientific truths, and still others may accept it as just a practical operating device to put you on the road to success. No matter—many know the truth and for you who will open your minds the light will pour in with dazzling white brilliancy.

I'm indebted to an old friend of mine, an expert on X-Ray, and electrical high frequency apparatus, who, when I was a boy experimenting with electricity, called to my attention the first bit of powerful T.N.T. in my pocket. Then I didn't know what it was and didn't understand, but fortunately it has remained there all through the years. As I look back I realize why he didn't Make me understand what it was. He believed in me and knew that when I was ready to accept it I would. It's taken nearly 30 years, during which time I sought up and down the highways, looking, seeking and searching for the SECRET—T.N.T.

Feel in Your Pocket

All of the time there was some in my pocket—mine for the mere reaching. However, I've got a firm grip on it now and I will divide it graciously, knowing if used wisely it will blow away all obstacles and straighten out the road on which you've been wanting to travel all your life.

For many years I was a newspaper man and frequently I was behind the scenes. I met great men and women, interviewed famous people. Naturally I studied them and tried to understand what peculiar qualities they possessed that placed them above the others, but their secret evaded me.

Then came the war and I wondered why others made progress while I seemed to be *"blocked"* in my own ambitions. The war did teach me, however, that I could sleep in the mud, eat moldy bread and live to laugh about it. This is part of my T.N.T. so remember what I learned. It helped me to give old man FEAR a solar plexus blow and I believe it will help you.

Hoping to find a royal road to fortune I read hundreds of the so-called "Success" books and they took me nowhere. I did the same with books on philosophy, psychology and still the great Secret kept just a jump ahead of me. I joined secret fraternal organizations, hoping that I might find that which I sought.

However, just like the bit of T.N.T. in my pocket the Secret was in every book, in the great orders, everywhere, and in fact, right under my very nose but something kept me from it. You will have to determine for yourself what keeps you from it if you don't get it from T.N.T. It's there—if you don't find it in the printed word look between the lines—as I've done my best to present it to you.

Following the war I became a member of a coastwide investment banking organization and during the years I cherished quite a dream—as did thousands of others in all lines of business—only to discover that the air castles which I builded were on an unstable foundation. That something which turned the world upside down financially entirely obliterated my air castles, and I became Afraid. I got lost in the fog. Everywhere I turned something fell in on me.

Are You Afraid?
As an executive of the organization my responsibilities multiplied.

Our business, due to the economic changes which were taking place in the world, faced a crisis, and many people failing to understand the catastrophe which had overtaken business everywhere were critical. All of which brought worry and many sleepless nights. I found myself dreading to go to my work—fearing that each day would bring added misery.

The weeks went on and conditions got worse and worse. I was baffled. Several times I talked about getting out of the business and one day in the latter part of June, 1931, I made up my mind to leave. I mentioned it to one of the women with whom I had been associated for several years and saw nothing but reproach in her eyes.

That night I tried to sleep. Again I found it impossible. I paced the floor for hours—when at about 3:30 in the morning I suddenly stopped and sat down. I was face to face with myself. I could follow the inclination to run and leave the others to carry on by themselves, or I could stay and do my share; a duty which I knew was mine. I caught myself saying almost aloud: *"Right is right. It's always been right. It can't be otherwise;"* something I had been taught since infancy.

Suddenly there appeared to be an unfoldment. Out of the air came a voice saying: *"What have you been seeking all these years? What were you taught? What did you learn? Where have you been? Where are you going?"* I jumped to my feet crying: *"I know it. I've got it now. It's the secret. That's what they tried to teach you. It is the Royal Secret, too."*

Out of the Air

Something told me that I would find those identical words in a book which had many years before been given me and which I had tried to read, failed to understand and put aside. It was written by a great man, Albert Pike, a mystic, a poet and a scholar. Grabbing it from the shelf—feverishly I ran through the pages. The words were there and I understood immediately.

I now had the key. I could see a broad smooth highway and at the end of that highway a perfect flood of gorgeously beautiful radiance. *"That's the road you are on now. What a simpleton you have been! They tried to teach you, they tried to help you and you kept your mind closed—thinking that you alone could find the road and stay on it."*

Open Your Mind

I was nearly overcome with the sheer joy of it all. My fears, my worries had disappeared. I smiled. I knew that I was right and that everything would be right for me from then on. I slept like a baby.

There was a different atmosphere in the office that day. The oppressive black clouds which hung over us began to fade away. I told the woman—she with the reproachful eyes— what had happened, and she smiled a knowing smile. She helped me get back on the track and I can never repay her.

As one learned man said: *"All of us are born with the ability to differentiate between right and wrong, and with the ability to achieve, but some of us must run head-on into a stone wall, smash ourselves to bits before we really know what it's all about."* I hit the wall with a terrific crash and it was the greatest and finest thing that ever happened to me.

Many noting the transformation asked for an explanation. I told some of my closest friends. Knowing it will help I give it to all of you.

— Tap — Tap — Tap —
— Tap — Tap — Tap —

Since I caught this theme the book has been put to use by thousands of individuals, firms and organizations. In addition I have talked and lectured, in person and over the radio, to many additional thousands and I am very happy to say that, without exception, phenomenal results have been obtained by those who have understood and applied the principles and mechanics outlined herein.

— Tap — Tap — Tap —
— Tap — Tap — Tap —

The morale of our whole organization was at its lowest ebb. Everyone was discouraged. Afraid. By the very necessity of things we had to do an about-face.

My job was doing everything I could to help the other fellow because I knew it was right. At first I was perplexed as to the methods I should employ to help them, but I used my own system in calling upon the subconscious, and the inner voice said that I should talk to them.

Right Is Right

Some were skeptical, but I said to myself: *"I can prove that I am right,"* and during the week that followed I spent every waking hour reviewing the books that I had studied through the years. Naturally the Bible came first; then followed studies in Yogiism, the philosophies of the old Greek and Roman masters and of the later day teachers and students. I again deliberated over the Meditations of Marcus Aurelius Antoninus. Reread Hudson's Law of Psychic Phenomena, another book, *The Gist of It*, written by a brilliant physician, Haydon Rochester.

Again I studied my books on physics, electricity and those on the vibrations of light and discovered that not only was I right, as I knew I would be, but that peculiarly the same general basic principles ran through them all. I reread numerous books on psychology and found the same story everywhere. Subsequently I quoted excerpts, and lo and behold, things began to move.

— Tap — Tap — Tap —

It has occurred to me again and again that all men and women who use this POWER are showmen, or to use the words of my newspaper days, headliners—those who hit the front page.

Something causes them to toss away the bushel basket under which they hide their heads and they arise above the commonplace.

Surely you will agree they may have the POWER to the Nth degree, but if they do not become headliners they never get a niche in the hall of fame. It doesn't follow that they are newspaper publicity seekers, because some of them are very reticent—and by their very reticence are showmen. Others adopt certain peculiarities or use certain devices to make them stand out from their fellowmen. Some wear an efficacious smile, others scowl—and still others have a certain charm of manner. Long hair, whiskers and sideburns play their part. Flowing robes and distinctive dress are worn by others. The showmanship of some is evidenced by red neckties, others by spats, affected manners.

Where Is Your Niche?

Many master the art of oratory, the science of warfare, banking, statesmanship, politics, the arts—but all of them stand out in the full glare of the calcium—headliners.

The number is legion. I mention a few of those of history and today: Demosthenes, Nero, Julius Caesar, Christopher Columbus, Cleopatra, Balzac, de Maupassant, Sir Isaac

Newton, Joan of Arc, Cromwell, Edgar Allen Poe, Benjamin Franklin, Alexander Hamilton, Bismark, Graham Bell, General Grant, Cecil Rhodes, P. T. Barnum, Clemenceau, Kitchener, Woodrow Wilson, Joffre, Sir Thomas Lipton, Foch, Mussolini, Winston Churchill, Charles E. Hughes, Lloyd George, Mahatma Gandhi, Ramsey MacDonald, Will Rogers, Douglas Fairbanks, Roosevelt, Henry Ford, Lindbergh, Alfred E. Smith, Lenin and Hitler. They have been and are found in every walk of life.

Gandhi uses this POWER, I am sure, and I think he is the greatest headliner of present times. You can find many pictures showing him in the modern civilized garb of man, but today, and for several years he has kept his hair cropped short, worn a loin cloth and a pair of huge spectacles. I have no right to say that Gandhi affected this attire for any particular purpose, but I believe he has done it to focus the world's attention upon himself for India's cause.

I make no attempt to explain why those who use this POWER are showmen. You'll have to determine that for yourself. But remember—

"A city that is set upon a hill cannot be hid. Neither do men light a candle and place it under a bushel . . ."

Again—

"The great truths of life become known only to those who are prepared to accept them."

I repeat. Thousands who used the POWER for evil brought on their own destruction. We get out of life exactly what we put into it—no more, no less. When we put in good thoughts, constructive efforts and do good then we receive like in return, for—

"Whatsoever a man soweth, that shall he also reap."

Detonating Caps are now set! Caution signals are out. Be Careful!

"A man's true greatness lies in the consciousness of an honest purpose in life, founded on a just estimate of himself and everything else, on frequent self-examinations, and a steady obedience to the rule which he knows to be right, without troubling himself about what others may think or say, or whether they do or do not do that which he thinks and says and does."

MARCUS AURELIUS ANTONINUS

— Tap — Tap — Tap —

There are thousands, yes, millions of people seeking the SECRET—the key to health, riches, happiness, contentment and a solution of their problems. Through the ages many men and women had the SECRET, used the POWER, and I am positive you can acquire it too if you'll think as you read, accept and apply the ideas contained herein.

What do you want? Where are you going?

— Tap — Tap — Tap —

An Old, Old Story

I repeat an old story:

Down on a levee in Mississippi, two negroes were dozing—one of them yawned, stretched his arms and sighed:

"Gee, I wish I had a million watermelons."

The other negro asked: "Rastus, if you had a million watermelons, would you give me half of them?"

"No, sir!"

"Would you give me a quarter of them?"

"No, I wouldn't give you a quarter of them."

"Rastus, if you had a million watermelons wouldn't you give me even ten of them?"

"No, sir! I wouldn't give you ten of them."

"Well, wouldn't you give me one lousy watermelon?"

"Say, Sam, I wouldn't give you even a bite of one if I had a million watermelons."

"Why not, Rastus?"

"Because you're too lazy to wish for yourself."

There's much to be gleaned from that story. You'll understand as I proceed.

I am fully cognizant that some will scoff—there have always been scoffers, but scoffers never succeed. They never get any place in life—simply become envious, while the doer or the person who is moving forward has to jump over or go around them. They have nothing but a nuisance value in life. Some of you may dismiss all of this as you have done before—as you always will—but for those of you who are interested, are still willing to learn, I promise you can learn and make progress for yourself.

Scoffers Do Not Succeed

I take it there isn't an intelligent man or woman who isn't really interested in getting ahead, but I have often wondered if there isn't a negative quality in most of us which precludes us from really starting.

There's a saying I thoroughly believe in: *"If you believe it, it's so."* Simply a cryptic statement or digest of what I give you. All the great teachers, Buddha, Confucius, Mohammed, Jesus and many philosophers taught a great fundamental idea. It is found in all religions, cults, creeds and sects. Everywhere runs the same general theme—the gist of which in my words is—"If you believe it, it's so."

If You Believe It—It's So

I quote from the Bible: "As a man thinketh in his heart—so is he." "As a man thinketh in his heart—so is he"—if you believe it, it's so. Note the similarity? Reduce the whole thing to one word—"FAITH." I have heard many, many people say the day of miracles is past, but never in my life have I heard a thinker, a student or a believer make such a declaration. Surely, the days of Aladdin and his lamp are gone—perhaps they never existed—so with the magic wand, the magic carpet, and all of those thing of fairy tale and legend.

When I refer to miracles, I mean those things which can be accomplished through FAITH. FAITH in your belief; FAITH in Yourself; FAITH in the persons with whom you are associated. FAITH in a Power. FAITH in "THAT SOMETHING" which controls the destinies of everyone—and, if you can get that FAITH and dissipate the negative side, nothing in this world can stop you from acquiring what you desire.

Believe in Yourself

While this may sound facetious, you can have anything obtainable if you really want it.

All of us are prone to calculate and weigh things, permitting the negative side to creep to the fore, and our thoughts evidence themselves in such remarks as *"It can't be done;" "I'm afraid;" "What will happen if I do it?" "People won't understand;" "It isn't worth the effort;" "I haven't the time"* and similar verbal alibis. If you haven't expressed these thoughts to yourself, then others have to you, and, through the power of suggestion, you have accepted them as your own conclusions.

Why the Alibis?

This same message has been written and delivered thousands of times. It runs through the Bible; you find it in the great fraternal orders; it led the three wise men; the crusaders carried it; every outstanding character of history has used it; Moses, Alexander the Great, Napoleon, Shakespeare, Washington, Lincoln, Roosevelt, Wilson, Benjamin Franklin, Edison, Dr. Steinmetz, Barnum, and thousands of others had a grasp of "THAT SOMETHING."

The wise men of all ages, the *"medicine men,"* religious leaders, great teachers, the Maya priests, the Yogis, the *"healers,"* the *"miracle men"*—all of them knew this secret. Some worked it one way, some another.

The Wise Men Knew

They were just human beings. If they knew and could achieve, so can you.

Halt! Think! Ponder! What made Mussolini?

What is it that Aimee has? Gypsy Smith? Billy Sunday? BELIEF, FAITH—only that, and the ability of a staunch believer to pass it on to the other fellow. It's the very keynote of all great religions. All big things are started by one person, one believer. It makes no difference where they got the idea originally. All great inventions are the outgrowth of the whole scheme—FAITH, FAITH—

BELIEF in yourself, your ideas. All supersalesmen know this—they use the POWER—that's why they are super-salesmen. Every community drive, every forward move-ment, everything worth while succeeds because some one person has FAITH and is able to pass it on and on and on. Think about that—then think about it some more, and think of it again. Meditate over it, and you'll realize that every word is true.

Many envy the man or woman getting ahead, who ap-pears to be a financial success, a power, an influence. Did you ever seek the explanation? Everything that anyone has ever done constructively has been done from within himself.

Don't Envy: Do

Every one of us, if put on the right track, can accomplish what he or she is after by keeping before him or her my own expression: "If you believe it, it's so," and adopting the old adage: "Where there's a will there's a way." In other words, get that will power—that FAITH—that BELIEF work-ing every minute of the day—24 hours of the day—7 days a week—365 days a year. And I promise you if it's done you will leave people around you in the progress you make as rapidly as high frequency electrical discharges oscillate through the ether.

Pause and think for a moment. What is organized pro-paganda? Nothing more, nothing less than a well devel-oped plan to make you believe. You saw it work in the war days and if you're wide awake to what is going on around you, you know that it's being worked in every line of human endeavor today—just as it was worked thousands of years ago and as it always works. If you're reading the newspaper, listening to the radio and will keep in mind my theme, you will realize that all these speeches of our leaders, our great executives coming to us with clock-like regularity are being given with a purpose—to make us believe.

Those men know it works.

Stop!   Think!   Meditate!

Mahatma Gandhi upon arriving in England to seek a solution of India's problems said: *"I'm doing this because a voice within me speaks."*

Gandhi referred to "something" from within. Call it a POWER, call it something supernatural, call it anything you wish. Some refer to it as the subjective mind. Others call it the subconscious mind. Some instinct. Some universal thought. Still others to the impulses coming from within as hunches. Divine messages.

Spiritualists refer to it as a voice from beyond. No matter what it is, it gets results, and now I show you how to acquire it.

The Voice Speaks

First, however, permit me to set the stage by calling attention to the effect of repetition or reiteration. For example, take a pneumatic chisel—you have seen one used in breaking up solid concrete or piercing holes through steel. It's the tap, tap, tap, tap of that chisel with a terrific force behind which causes disintegration of the particles and makes a dent or hole in the object on which it is used.

Tap No. 1

All of us have heard of the old torture system of dripping water on the forehead. Perhaps you are familiar with Kipling's *"Boots."* It's the tramp, tramp of boots, boots, that makes men mad. It's the constant never-ending repetition that penetrates.

You are familiar with the first part of the picture and how repetition works on material things, but some of you may not thoroughly understand the second part, but here, too, it's the repetition that ultimately makes its impression upon the human mind.

The fundamental of advertising is its repetition, its appeal by reiteration—*"It floats;" "There's a reason;" "I'd walk a mile;" "They're kind to your throat."* A hundred others all impressed on your consciousness by constant repetition—tap, tap, tap. Through the science of repetition you learned to multiply. Everything you ever memorized was impressed upon your consciousness through repetition. You are constantly (tap, tap, tap) being reminded to reaffirm (more tap, tap) your FAITH in your religious belief. The same science—again and again. Repetition, reiteration. Tap, tap, tap.

Reaffirmation and Repetition

The connection between the conscious and the subconscious or subjective mind is close. Every student of the subject knows what may be accomplished by definitely contacting the subconscious. When you get a definite detailed picture in your conscious mind by using this process of reiteration or repetition and make the subconscious mind click, you have at your command a POWER that astounds.

The Science of Suggestion

We hear much about the power of suggestion. We know how easy it is to make a person ill by constantly suggesting to him that he doesn't look well, etc. It's the constant mental review of his crime that makes a lawbreaker confess. As a newspaper man I have been in on many "third degree" sessions. I have seen detectives and prosecutors corner a single individual and shoot questions at that individual until his face was bathed in perspiration. It is the deadly repetition, the reiteration, the tap, tap, tap, through the power of suggestion which brings confession.

Skilled prosecutors, clever defenders appeal to the emotions of jurors, never to the conscious reason. And how do they do it? Simply by a process of repeating and emphasizing time after time the points they wish to stress. They do it with usage of words and variations of argument. Behind all there is that tap, tap, tap, tap—tapping—the subconscious—making the jurors believe.

If you will keep this idea of repetition in mind you will understand why members of a certain race of people are so successful in business. When families are gathered together, the subject of conversation is business, business. They talk their problems over—they keep before them constantly the idea of making money and making progress and never for a moment are they permitted to forget. And they stick together.

The idea there was born of necessity, just like a machine or an article is born of necessity. We are all familiar with the old adage, "Necessity is the mother of invention"—and it is true of all human impulses and endeavors. A drowning man grabs at a straw. A starving man at a crust of bread. The impulses come when you get up against it. You who have been there know what you had to rely on in times of acute pressure, and whether or not you heard a little voice from within.

There can be no gainsaying that once you have made up your mind to do a thing it will be done, but the trouble with most of us is that we sidestep, vacillate, and seldom make up our minds to what we want or determine clearly the road on which we wish to travel. All daydreams and wishes would become realities if we kept them constantly before us—put fear behind—shoved away all reservations, ifs, ands and buts. Again, a lot of us think we know what we want when, as a matter of fact, we don't. This sounds paradoxical but, if each of us knew what he wanted, he would get it, provided he had the will-power, the stamina, the dynamic force, the fight to go after it.

Where Are You Going?

Therefore, the first thing to do is get that spirit of determination. That may be obtained by constantly saying to yourself—*"I will," "I will," "I will" and "I will"* and BELIEVE it. Then before you know it you will have developed a will-power which, coupled with these other things I am about to explain, will change your whole scheme of things and get YOU on the road to success. If you haven't the desire to improve your own individual position in life, then you had better stop reading right now and burn this. However, should you have the desire, you are on your way to make progress.

No matter whether you be a salesman, an executive, a mechanic, a writer or what, or whether you are after money, love, improvement in social position, in the legal profession or medical profession, it makes absolutely no difference. You can utilize this POWER and acquire every single thing you want—whether it be a pair of shoes or a mansion.

What Do You Want?

Now if you have the desire, the foundation is laid. Get a perfect detailed picture of the exact thing, or things, you wish. If it is increased sales, fix the exact amounts; if it's something you want the other fellow to do for you, the love of a woman or the love of a man, a new suit of clothes or a new automobile—anything and everything. No matter what you are after under this system you can have it, provided the object of desire is morally right, and the picture definite and positive.

Tap No. 2

"He who knows how to plant, shall not have his plant uprooted; He who knows how to hold a thing, shall not have it taken away."

LAO TZU, THE CHINESE MYSTIC, 600 B.C.

When you have the picture firmly in mind begin using the tap, tap system as I have outlined. It is going to be the repetition, the reiteration of that picture upon the subconscious mind that will cause the little voice from within to speak and point out to you accurately and scientifically how you are to proceed to get what you want. And when it has spoken swing into action immediately. Then as you move all obstacles will dissolve into thin air.

Adopt This Tap System

The idea is to keep the picture or pictures before you constantly. As an aid in the visualization of the things you want and to keep them uppermost in your thoughts, write a word picture of them on several small cards. (Business card size is convenient.) Keep them always in your possession and look at them as frequently as possible—bearing in mind the more often you glance at them and visualize the pictures the firmer become the impressions upon your consciousness. As a suggestion, pin one card above the mirror to be looked at in the morning when you shave. Permit the details of your wishes outlined on the card to increase as you continue to develop the mental pictures. Have another card convenient to look at while you eat your lunch—your dinner. Use the cards again just before you go to sleep. Keep it up. Tap, tap, tap. However, there's no point to writing down your wishes until you have determined that every single detail of what you want is to be photographed permanently in your thoughts—to stay there until they become realities.

Use Small Cards

Remember that repetition of the same thought, the same suggestion, makes the picture positive. When you thoroughly comprehend this you will understand why thought always correlates with its object. Reflect for a moment. Where did the steamboat, the locomotive, the automobile, the electric light, the sewing machine, the radio, the typewriter and a million more objects and conveniences come from? All were thoughts or mental pictures in the minds of men before they became realities. Everything on this earth, except that which nature creates or has provided, is the result of sustained thought.

Powerful Thoughts Attract

Thought, contacting "THAT SOMETHING," brings every thing, with nature's exceptions, into manifestation

A single thought not to be followed up—a flash to be dismissed or lost—is like a bobbing cork, aimless and without purpose. However, the same thought, the picture of the thing you want kept constant, always attracts it object, just as a magnet attracts. The larger and more powerful the magnet, the greater its drawing force and so it is with sustained thought—the more powerful it becomes the more it attracts. Just as a huge magnifying glass drawing the sun's rays and kept focused on a certain spot will burn a hole so will powerful sustained thought (the vivid mental picture) directed to or on its object correlate. However you must mentally see the picture of your object or ideal as a reality—see every detail of the picture as being in existence just as you want the object or ideal to actually be—then as if by magic the chain will link itself together. Now go back and reread this again until it is permanently impressed upon you.

As an additional means of concentration augment the foregoing formula with the use of a mirror. Daily and as frequently as possible study yourself in the glass. Search deeply into your eyes until you can see the fire of enthusiasm mount and cold, steely determination take the place of doubt and indecision. Get to know yourself thoroughly and keep telling yourself where you are going and what you want. Sooner or later you will see, mentally, at least, the reflection of your inner most desires in the mirror and your day dreams will begin to take shape. (As you grasp the science behind this theme you will understand why many powerful characters have used this mirror idea with great effectiveness.) Once the pictures are clearly defined do not for an instant permit them to escape. Hold them with bands of steel.

Use Your Mirror

"So use all that is called Fortune. Most men gamble with her, and gain all, and lose all, as her wheels roll. But do thou leave as unlawful these winnings and deal with Cause and Effect, the chancellor of God. In the Will work and acquire, and thou hast chained, the wheels of Chance, and shall sit hereafter out of fear of her rotations."

EMERSON'S SELF RELIANCE

Constant practice of writing down your wishes and using a mirror will work wonders. Shortly you can form the pictures at will—without the use of either cards or mirrors—and you will find yourself tapping the subconscious mind almost automatically. Practice, practice—always keep tapping.

Don't be afraid of over-doing, or becoming extravagant with your wishes and desires because, as I said before, you can have every single thing you wish, but you must become adept at doing exactly as I tell you.

Start Wishing and Doing

When you visualize and keep the pictures constant, action follows because action after all is nothing more than energized thought. Never lose your vision (your mental pictures)—for it is as King Solomon said nearly 3000 years ago:

"Where there is no vision, the people perish."

Bear in mind this whole theme is as old as man. The only thing I do is to give you the message in words of today and outline a simple system of mechanics which may be used by anyone.

As we all know, "the proof of the pudding is in the eating," and it you have any doubts as to whether or not I am giving you an exact science, try it. The automobile will begin to take shape, you will get the new shoes and the bricks of the mansion will fall into place as though a magical hand has touched them.

I know it, I believe it and it's so.

You know something of the efficacy of prayer. What is prayer but the expression of a heartfelt, earnest, sincere want or desire? The Great Master said:

> *"What things soever ye desire, when ye pray BELIEVE that ye receive them, and ye shall have them."*

And it's true. All of us know the effect of our own desires on ourselves and how events are influenced by great desires. Every economic change down through the centuries has been due to the desire of man to benefit himself. However, we must BELIEVE—have FAITH—otherwise our innermost desires (prayers) become simply bursting bubbles.

The Great Master also said:

> *"If thou canst BELIEVE, all things are possible to him that BELIEVETH."*

I have pointed out the way that BELIEF—FAITH is engendered and kept constant—through repetition, reiteration of the same thought. It's now up to you to do the rest. Keep in mind always, as I said before you are appealing to the subconscious—"THAT SOMETHING" way down deep in all of us—universal thought—to the powerful force behind—that omnipotent power—a supreme intelligence—or whatever you wish to call it.

It is easier to go with the current than fight against it, but you must harmonize with others, with everything around you.

"No longer let thy breathing only act in concert with the air which surrounds thee, but let thy intelligence also now be in harmony with the intelligence which embraces all things."

THE WORDS OF A GREAT PHILOSOPHER

The Ancients Tapped

It shouldn't be necessary for me to explain that I am suggesting that you put yourself in tune with the very stream of life itself. You who understand will appreciate that nature provides ways and means for all things to grow rightly. Meditate for a moment and you'll realize I am giving truths which many may have forgotten. There's the great fundamental law of compensation which makes all things right.

There's no set rule for doing anything because some of us perform one way and some another, just as two people go across the river—one goes by one bridge and one another—but they both ultimately get to their destination. In other words, after all is said and done, it's results that count, and, if you will make up your mind to exactly what you want and follow the simple rules which are given herein, everything you are after will be yours.

I know it, I believe it and it's so.

After you get a grip on the POWER do not let the results of its usage surprise you.

Miracles will be performed.

You will do what previously you thought impossible.

As certain as night follows day, results will follow in a most astounding manner. Things will come to you from the most unexpected sources. Ideas for accomplishment will pop here and they'll pop there—then follow through. Others may say that as things happen for you, they are mere coincidences, that you are lucky, etc. Care not what they say. They are the scoffers, the non-believers, the ignorant. Remain steadfast in your BELIEF that they are the result of your own works coupled with "THAT SOMETHING."

In using this POWER you are setting up powerful vibrations among the unseen forces, therefore it is not well that you should tell anyone—not even your most intimate friends or relatives—of your inner most wishes or desires—your deep rooted ambitions. Keep them to yourself, for should some person learn what you are after they may, consciously or unconsciously, due to enviousness, or something else, set up counter vibrations, place obstacles in your way and otherwise attempt to hinder you. Should barriers accidentally fall or be placed in your path, climb over or go around them. Go whistling blithely by.

Tell No One

Now remember it is entirely up to you as to the kind of pictures you create and hold constant and subsequently bring into realities. Analyze this: YOU are today exactly where your thoughts have brought you and you will be tomorrow where your thoughts take you. YOU are the absolute boss. Therefore, bear in mind always, the only limit is the limit you fix for yourself and remember you start with your thoughts. It may take longer to get some of the things you are after than others. But never get discouraged Rome was not built in a day. Just maintain your FAITH—your BELIEF—and keep tapping away. Many things will be added unto you and your dreams (the positive pictures) will come true.

Remember nothing can stop you but yourself.

I know it, I believe it and it's so.

I also am one of those who believes that all things are relative. To my way of thinking if a man can earn one dollar he can as easily earn ten. If he has two suits of clothes—he can have ten. The only difference is the amount of energy he is willing to expend and this goes for acquiring $100 to $1000 and from then on it is a matter of only adding ciphers. There is no limit as to what a person may do or secure provided he makes up his mind and steadfastly and determinedly moves towards his goal.

"Look within. Within is the fountain of good, and it will ever bubble up, if thou wilt ever dig."

AN ANCIENT SAYING

As I said under Detonating Caps be careful how you use the POWER which is to be yours. It will act as a boomerang and destroy you and everything you hold dear if you use it for evil. Therefore, only use it for doing you and others the most **Good** and bringing **Happiness** for yourself and those around you. Do not talk or boast about what you may have done for others or of your good deeds. They will speak for themselves. Just continue to give thanks for the fact that you are on your way—that's enough.

— Tap — Tap — Tap —

Use It Only For Good

What is personality? What is it, when you get in the presence of another person who has personality, that grips you? What is it that causes you to feel his very presence—that overshadows you? It's nothing more than a dynamic force coupled with will power which is drawing from that huge reservoir of the subconscious. There are millions of people who have this personality—some say it's natural with them—perhaps it is—but they are unconsciously using this POWER. In other words, it's sort of been thrust upon them and when that thing called personality is backed up with will power, things move.

Have You Got "It?"

To my way of thinking selling bonds, books, clothes, insurance, electric service, washing machines, is no different than selling any other commodity—selling yourself or selling ideas. I have found that trying to put over an idea, firstly I have had to believe in the idea—dream it, eat with it, sleep with it—I had to have it with me every minute of the day until it became part of me—the old idea of repetition again—and I know it works in selling commodities. You have got to know what you are talking about and only hard, personal, persistent, intelligent study will enable you to do this.

One more thing, and that is keep informed as to what is going on in the world about you. You never know what a prospect may be interested in and it's sometimes necessary to get his attention or your "break" entirely through irrelevant subjects—that's why I repeat, read the newspapers, current periodicals, and read them thoroughly. I don't mean read every detail of some murder or suicide, but get a digest of the day's news.

Awaken, know what is going on about you. Get understanding.

Keep step with the world's affairs. The better informed a person, the better he is equipped to get what he wants.

Tap No. 3
Don't forget that Knowledge is Power—all of you should know that by this time.

> *"He who knows others is clever, but he who knows himself is enlightened."*
> From the Sayings of a Wise Oriental

Increase your knowledge and the scope of your activities will be enlarged and the desire for greater things—larger things, will come automatically and, as they do, the things which you previously thought you wanted will become to your mind trivial and will be disregarded, which is another way of saying that you ultimately will hitch your wagon to a star and, when you do, you'll move with lightning-like speed.

Study, learn and work. Develop a keenness of observation. Step on the gas. Become alive for yourself and you'll pass it on to the other fellow. Get confidence, enthusiasm and you'll set up like vibrations all around you and that's the theory of all life—as old as the world itself. Like begets like—a laugh brings a laugh— a good deed calls for a good deed—riches beget riches, love, love—and so on.

The old law of attraction stated in Ampere's theory of electrical magnetism is: *"Parallel currents in the same direc-*

tion attract one another"—and when you are out of tune and antagonistic you put others out of tune and make them antagonistic because: "Parallel currents in opposite directions repel one another."

However, don't get the thought that I have given you an over-size wishbone which will enable you to sit down and, by talking to yourself, through the idea of repetition, get what you want, because it will never work. You have got to have the wishbone backed up with a backbone and that isn't all—the wishbone and the backbone must be coordinated and synchronized to a point where they are running in perfect harmony, and when they are in tune, you will find personality developing. Then put action, energy into your scheme and everything will move before you.

Wishbones Need Backbones

I take it that all of us have admired that intense type of person. I mean by that, one whose shoulders are back, whose chest is out, whose head is up and whose eyes are alert. It is easy to pick out in any organization those whose feet lag, whose shoulders droop, whose chins sag and whose eyes are a blank. Drifters, loafers, quitters. First measure yourself. Then study those with whom you are associated and you can tell at almost a glance those who will make progress and those doomed to failure.

Every physical movement tells a story—each marks your personality. Your body and your mind are in reciprocal relationship—each acts and reacts upon the other. Your bodily movements—your facial expressions indicate the way you think. Now study yourself—your eyes—in the mirror again. The person you see in the mirror is the one the other person sees. What kind of an impression do you wish to make on him? That, too, is up to you. You know whether or not you have personality. If absent or undeveloped make up your mind to get it—you can and you will when you make up your mind, and do as suggested herein.

If you will develop that intensity of purpose, determination to get ahead, shortly that determination will show in your eyes. You have heard people say that a certain person has a penetrating gaze—that he looks right through one. What is it? Nothing more than that fire from within—intensity—or whatever you wish to call it, which means that the person who has that gaze usually gets what he wants. Remember the eyes are the windows of the soul. Look at the photographs of successful men—study their eyes and you will find that every one of them has that intensity; therefore, I say, let it be reflected in the way you walk, in the way you carry yourself and it will not be long before people will feel your presence when you walk through a crowd—and an individual prospect will feel that personality when you talk with him.

The Eyes Have "It"

All of this is to explain that it takes an affirmative type to make progress and the things I have pointed out may be utilized to develop you into an affirmative type. The negative type is sunk before he starts. Nature takes care of these situations through the old law of the survival of the fittest. We know what happened in the day of Sparta when children were put on their own at a baby age and only those who survived were given further chance. A negative type is a quitter, or, another way, a quitter is a negative type and, while there is no point to going around hitting everybody on the nose just to start something, always remember it's poor business to let yourself be put on the defensive as that is a negative sign. The person who won't be licked, can't be licked. If you are taken unawares and suddenly put on the defensive, snap out of it. Take the offensive because, if you remain on the defensive, you are beaten.

Of course, to bring about this intensity of being, it's necessary to be in good health. I do not claim that the power of will is a cure-all to mend broken legs and all that sort of thing, but I do know that constant application of the theory herein advanced will aid a person in ill health. All of you have heard of Dr. Emil Coue, the Frenchman, who was in this country a few years ago, telling people they could cure themselves if they would adopt his plan. His idea was that you should say to yourself—"Every day, in every way, I am getting better and better." Just ponder over that for a minute.

Every Day—in Every Way

There was nothing new in that idea, any more than there is in the ideas which I put forth. Simply another way of expressing the whole scheme—reiteration, repetition— keeping upper most in your mind all the time what you want and which positive thoughts, in turn, are passed on to the subconscious mind—the wonder thing. **Think health, wealth and happiness and they will all be yours.** It cannot be otherwise.

We all know of people who are continually talking about backaches, headaches or some other kind of aches. They harp on them and the first thing they know, with that reiteration, the aches become realities. If you have such an ache or pain there is no point to talking about it; neither is there any point to talking about your worries, your troubles. Do not talk about them. Do not think about them. Then they will not be in your mind. It is the repetition that keeps them there. Shift your gears—reverse the process. Get away from the negative side and become an affirmative type—think affirmatively and the first thing you know your aches, worries and troubles will disappear.

> *"If thou art pained by any external thing, it is not this thing which disturbs thee, but thy own judgment about it. And it is in thy power to wipe out this judgment now. But if anything in thy own disposition gives thee pain, who hinders thee from correcting thy opinion?"*
>
> Philosophy of the Ages

When a train roars across the track in front of you, you put on the brakes of your automobile, throw the gears into neutral and idle your engine—you are on your way again just as soon as the train passes but you certainly do not throw your gears into reverse and go backwards.

Are You in Reverse?

Compare yourself to the gears of your automobile. In reverse place all fears, worries, troubles, aches and pains. And when things go wrong simply put on the brakes, idle your engine until you can clearly see the road ahead. In high is everything you desire: health, wealth, happiness—success. No power in the world except your hand can put the gears of your automobile in reverse. If your own gears get in reverse remember you alone put them there. And you put them there with your own thoughts because:

> *"There is nothing either good or bad, but thinking makes it so."*
>
> Hamlet—Act ii, Sc. 2

Therefore, as you think, you move either forward or backward—in high gear or in reverse. When you place yourself in reverse, worry, stew and fret you are using the tap, tap idea to bring into existence the things you would most avoid.

Some 3500 years ago Job said:

"For the thing which I greatly feared is come upon me, and that which I too was afraid of is come unto me."

Certainly they came upon him because he, in his fears pictured them—he used the immutable law to attract them. Just as you bring the good things which you want into reality by holding the positive thoughts constant so do you bring the bad things— those which you fear—by holding the worry, the negative thoughts constant.

If you have read this far then you must realize that when you look after your thoughts—then your thoughts will look after you. Therefore, which will it be—grief, trouble, ill health, worry, failure or health, wealth, happiness— success? It's entirely up to you—no power on this earth but you can direct your thoughts—and the way you use your WILL to keep your thoughts positive is a matter solely under your control. Therefore, lose no time in erecting a steel wall on the right side of the reverse gear, close the door of yesterday—keep it closed always—then shift from low gear into high and stay there.

Which Will It Be?

Those of you with your own business, increase your business—or if you're a salesman, your sales—as a result of your own thinking. When others tell you that business is bad, things are tough, going to the bow-wows, etc., and you accept their thoughts and make them your own, your business will go to the bow-wows. Have no doubt about that. Then as you talk to others, with your chin on your chest, your feet dragging and the front of a professional mourner, then you tap them down and the more you circulate and the more you talk (tap, tap, tapping with the same story) especially, if you think and talk with an air of conviction, the more damage you do. You are setting up "thought"—in reality **FEAR**—vibrations which are far reaching. Fear thoughts are terrifically contagious and spread like wild fire. Conversely as you direct your thoughts (visualizing) towards increasing your business, your sales, your profits, etc., have no misgivings of your own (keeping your mind closed to the downward tapping thoughts of others) and put enthusiasm, energy and action into your program, your business, your sales automatically will increase. You must keep in mind always that the intense fire of enthusiasm from within becomes a conflagration which affects all on your wave length as long as you radiate it. The vibrations you set up with your powerful rays of enthusiasm inspire others, raise them up, build and attract business—just as FEAR vibrations tap others down, repel and destroy.

Close Your Eyes

It is an indisputable fact, irrespective of the times, that there is always business somewhere for the man who BE-LIEVES it exists and goes after it but none for the person who is positive that none exists and makes no endeavor to move.

Accept This!

Experiment, And Be Convinced.

Any downward or upward trend in our world wide economic scheme is due entirely to the way we think. When the great world leaders—the statesmen, the financiers, editors, publishers, economists—those who direct and influence the thoughts of millions in every part of the globe permit depressed thoughts to enter into their scheme, then depressed thoughts and FEAR vibrations enter into the scheme of those same millions and business comes to a near standstill. When the world's leaders change their way of thinking—toss out FEAR and move forward instead of backwards, then the thoughts of millions change for the better and as they think constructively business improves.

Thought Moves the World

Stop and meditate over this for a few moments. You will realize that "*thought*" operating in reverse was the great underlying factor which brought on the so-called economic depression. Human beings are human beings the world over—whether in Prague or Timbuctoo—all subject to the same emotions, the same influences, the same vibrations; and what is a community, a city, a nation but merely a collection of individual humans?

"As a man thinketh in his heart—so is he."

As members of a community think—so they are; as a city thinks—so is it, and as a nation thinks—so is it.

There is no other conclusion.

"We are living in a great crisis in human history. There is unlimited need for boldness and courage, but there is no occasion for dismay. On the one hand there is the way to such achievements, to such wealth and happiness as mankind has never before known . . . life, even as we know it

now, tastes very good at times. We spoil it a lot for ourselves and each other by fear, follies, hate, bickering, suspicion and anger. There is no need for us to go on spoiling it. We have not the health we might have. We have not a tithe of the happiness we might have. But it is within the power of the human will to change all that."

H. G. WELLS ENGLAND'S GREAT MAN OF LETTERS

— Tap — Tap — Tap —

This power—this vital energy—or whatever it is, is inexhaustible, and it is so easy to use it if you only have the key. I am fully appreciative of the fact that psychologists maintain that few persons really think. It is my hope that this message will cause **You** to **Think**. If you dismiss it as so much balderdash, then I shall know that you have never understood or appreciated how the great characters of history whom I have previously mentioned and many others with whom you yourself should be familiar made names for themselves or gained niches in the hall of fame.

Change Gears Now

Real people—successful people, are those who made themselves and not what others made them. After all, there are only two ways to move, forward and backward—why not forward? Watch the down-and-outer on the street. His whole trouble is lack of positive ideas. If he thinks he is down and out—he is. If he will change his ideas, he will be up and coming. All of us know that. You can shift your gears if you only realize it. You have been told how to keep out of reverse and it is simply a mechanical process for yourself. Understand and you will always keep your gears in high and move forward.

— Tap — Tap — Tap —

A sale is effected by getting a prospect to think as you do and, unless you believe that the thing you are selling is good then, obviously, you can't make the other fellow believe it.

Believe in Your Goods

That is just plain common sense—so, for those of you who may be selling, keep in mind what I have previously said about knowing your article and selling yourself—that is 99% of the success of selling—the other 1% is leg work contacting the prospect.

You should realize that the bending other people to your will or getting them to do as you wish is simply having them think as you think and that is very easy.

Charles M. Schwab said: *"Many of us think of salesmen as people traveling around with sample kits. Instead, are all salesmen, every day of our lives. We are selling our ideas, our plans, our energies, our enthusiasm to those with whom we come in contact."* So it is with every endeavor, and especially true of selling commodities because you must contact people.

Sell Yourself

And when I say contact, I mean contacting them face to face. The day of order taking is gone and it is only the persons who have got it in them who are to succeed now—all the others will sink. You cannot beat a fundamental law—*"the survival of the fittest."* Therefore, forget about order taking and keep in mind the only way you can close a sale is to make the prospect think as you think—the best way is in face to face contact—you have got to be in his presence—you have got to see his reactions—*"the old law of cause and effect"*—and you have got to adapt yourself to the conditions as they confront you with that individual prospect.

If you are intent on making a sale—and you must be if you are going to succeed—keep in mind my theme. The subconscious mind will be giving you ideas, hunches, inspirations, a perfect flood of them, which will guide you correctly. They will point out the way to get into a busy man's presence—into the privacy of his very self and, when you get there, stand on both feet.

Follow Your Hunches

Be alert. Make him feel your personality. Know what you are talking about. Be enthusiastic. Don't quail.

You are just as good as he is and, besides, you may have something which he hasn't and that is utmost confidence, utmost faith in the article you are selling. On the other hand, if he is a success he also has personality—therefore, be sure to put the contact on a fifty-fifty basis. Do not belittle him—do not let him belittle you. Meet on common ground. Make him like you and when he likes you and you him, success is on its way. Remember you are going to sell him.

There is strength in team work. The esprit de corps pounded into those of us who were in the army made the American forces what they were—and it's the esprit de corps, team work, determination to move forward which will shove us along. If this is accepted in the spirit in which it is given; put into execution, you will be unbeatable. And by getting in tune and getting others on the track, the world is yours.

"When Fear rules the will, nothing can be done, but when a man casts Fear out of his mind the world becomes his oyster. To lose a bit of money is nothing, but to lose hope—to lose nerve and ambition—that is what makes men cripples."

HERBERT N. CASSON

Ascertain exactly what you want and use the mechanics given and you will discover more gates open for you than you ever dreamed existed. I am not interested in any prophetic explanations—I am interested in results. A light will dawn upon you and you will see clearly ahead how to achieve what you are after. The same principles, the same methods can be successfully applied to any line.

The ability to accomplish anything in a convincing fashion depends entirely upon the degree of expert knowledge which you possess coupled with that intensity of purpose. Read and study, practice, practice, tap, tap, tap.

Before closing I should tell you that the conscious mind must be placed in a receptive condition to get the ideas from the subjective or subconscious. Of course, we all know it is the conscious mind which reasons, which weighs, which calculates—the subconscious mind does not do any of these things—it simply passes on ideas to the conscious mind.

Open the Door

You have heard a lot of people say: *"play your hunches"*—what are those hunches? Where do they come from? They come from the workings of the subconscious mind. Psychologists tell us—you will soon understand the reason—that to put the human mind in a receptive condition you must relax. If you have ever laid on the massage table and been told by the masseur to relax then you know what I mean. Let the body go limp. If you have trouble at first, try it with your arm—both arms—both legs, until the whole body is relaxed and the mind automatically will relax. When that is accomplished concentrate on what you want—then hunches come. Grab them, execute them as the little voice tells you. Do not reason or argue, but do as you are told and do it immediately.

Relax and Tap

You will understand what psychologists, mystics and students mean when they tell you to stop, relax—Think of nothing—when you wish to draw on the subconscious and have the little inner voice speak. As you further progress you will also begin to realize what the seers of the East had in mind when they said: *"Become at ease, meditate, go into the great silence, continue to meditate and your problems will fade into nothingness."*

The road ahead will become illuminated and your burdens will fall away one by one. Is there anything clearer than "Pilgrim's Progress"? My message is no different than that which was conveyed there—only, as I said before—I put it to you in perhaps different words.

The late Thomas A. Edison explaining his success of inventing said: *"I begin by using my accumulated knowledge but most of my inventions are completed with Ideas which flash into my mind out of thin air."* Fred Ott and Charles Dally, associated with Mr. Edison for more than 50 years, solved the secret of making synthetic rubber.

The Mysterious Nothingness

I quote from a newspaper story dated October 21, 1931: *"On Monday, he (Mr. Edison), started to sink into a stupor.*

But Dally and Ott were still pounding doggedly (determinedly, concentrating, tap, tap, tap) at their experiments. And on Tuesday night the solution flashed out of the mysterious nothingness."

The little voice spoke—just like it always does when you make up your mind what you want and when you go after it. If your own little inner voice suggests that you ask for something, do not be backward about asking. You have nothing to fear. The other person will never help unless he knows your wishes so you must ask.

Accept the theory advanced herein and practice intelligently and the voice will speak just like it did for Edison, Ott, Dally and thousands of others, and you will get results—all will be yours.

In Julius Caesar, Cassius, he of the lean and hungry look, talking to Brutus, of the Roman Emperor's power, said:

> *"The fault, dear Brutus, is not in our stars, But in Ourselves that we are underlings."*

As you know, William Shakespeare wrote that, and he himself arose above the commonplace by using this POWER.

If you are timid, backward, in a rut and an underling, it is because of yourself. Blame not the stars. Blame not society. Blame not the world. Blame **Yourself**. Again I say, change gears. Put them in **High** and **Begin** to **Move**.

Who Is to Blame?

Some people not thoroughly understanding may say that you are conceited, self-centered, or selfish but care not what they say. Those are the scoffers—those who would put rocks in your road and otherwise impede your progress. Those who

understand will be helpful—they will be eager to serve y
The intelligent ones will begin to study you to determin
what you have that they haven't and try to learn your secret.

I have given you a grip on it; hold it to you tightly and
start moving forward.

George Jean Nathan, one of America's foremost critics, in a compilation of *"Living Philosophies"* declares he has
never known a man who succeeded in life in a material way
who did not think of himself first, last and all the time.
Naturally I don't know just how Nathan meant that but
I am sure he did not mean that a successful man is selfish
to the point where he isn't helpful to others because if you
follow the theme as I have outlined it and get on the road
to success you will not be led to act ruthlessly.

Service Pays Dividends

As a matter of fact, the exact opposite is true because you
will find that you will wish to do charitable things, good
things for other people, performing services involving the
throwing out of crumbs as it were, and your willingness to
do something Grip Tightly for the other fellow will bring
about a willingness on his part to do something for you.
There is nothing selfish about this—it's just a matter of
cause and effect.

Remember Ampere's laws of attraction. *Like begets like.*
When you perform a service you will be paid huge dividends. There is no mystery about it, it's just so.

— Tap — Tap — Tap —

"I am the master of my fate,"
I am the captain of my soul."

HENLEY

— Tap — Tap — Tap —

As a man thinketh in his heart—so is he.

— Tap — Tap — Tap —

I know it, I believe it and it's so.

— Tap — Tap — Tap —

T.N.T.—It rocks the earth!

This little book will do everything for you that is claimed but you must reread it and reread it until every sentence, every word is thoroughly understood and then you must apply the principles and mechanics with your whole heart and soul. Make them a part of your daily life and when you put into practice the ideas offered you will find that they will work just as they've always worked and always will. If you are in deadly earnest with yourself you will find the whole scheme very simple.

Practice Tap, Tap, Tap.

After you have studied the book and have reflected upon the ideas set forth you will appreciate the tremendous force which lies in the science of thought repetition and positive action. You can, by repetition of the same thought, "tap" yourself upward or downward—dependent on whether you have depressed or constructive thoughts and as you build yourself powerfully you will find that you can influence others by your thoughts. Therefore, let me again admonish you to exercise great care that you do not misuse your POWER. Keep your mind filled with good, constructive thoughts and then act with all the energy you possess as

the ideas come to you. Remember: *Every thought, kept eve.
constant, leads to action and results follow.* So keep this book
and reread it, study it and reread and study it as frequently
as possible. Practice Tap, Tap, Tap.

Reread It. Reread It. Reread It.

*In the beginning all things were good. Man, himself, made them
bad. You do evil and evil will be done you. You do good and you
Practice Tap, Tap, Tap will receive good in return. You can be
what you wish and have everything you want, provided, you
are willing to pay the price in time, thought, effort and energy.
You now have the key—may you make it work.*

T.N.T.—IT ROCKS THE EARTH !

The theme of this book was broadcast daily for a month
to many thousands by the author over K. G. W. (well
known Pacific Coast radio station—affiliated N. B. C.).
Excerpts have been read and the book referred to over the
air frequently by many speakers.

STUDY GUIDE

T.N.T.: It Rocks the Earth

1. Claude Bristol ends the book encouraging FAITH. *"FAITH in your belief; FAITH in Yourself; FAITH in the persons with whom you are associated; FAITH in a Power; FAITH in "THAT SOMETHING" which controls the destines of everyone."* Write a statement of declaration of FAITH for each of the areas in your life that he listed:
   * FAITH in my belief:
   * FAITH in Myself:
   * FAITH in the persons with whom I am associated:
   * FAITH in a Power:
   * FAITH in "THAT SOMETHING" which controls the destines of everyone:

2. Start each day and end each night making a statement with conviction, faith and dedication. Create your own empowering pledge or use the following: *"I have faith that negativity is dissipating in my life, and I trust that I am surrounded by love, magic and protection. With each powerful thought I think, I manifest great peace, joy and abundance."*

3. Under the title of *T.N.T It Rocks the Earth,* is written *"A philosophy for today, tomorrow and thereafter with some practical suggestions as to how to get what you want in life."* It was completed and copyrighted in 1933. Once you complete this booklet, review the contents and observe how much it applies to your current life. Do you believe the information shared is timeless? Why or why not?

4. The *foreword* starts with a list of excuses many make when they allow the negatives to creep in. With each of the excuses, write out a dialogue with your negative self.

First state all of the negative thoughts you've been feeling or avoiding, then write the positive shifting thoughts that you will speak and think to replace them. For example,

Excuse: *"It can't be done"* . . . because I am not good enough, someone else is probably doing it, I don't have the time, I'll be ridiculed. Response: It can be done because I am a wonderful, passionate, creative being. No one can do it as I do it, because there is only one "me" in the world. I can commit to focusing on this for 30 minute each day. As I do, I trust that time will open up for me, so that I can see this manifest in all of its glory. I will be honored and celebrated for successfully completing this. I feel deep gratitude and joy, as I experience abundance, connection and financial support as I manifest this into my life and into the lives of others. I know that this and more are coming to me here and now. And so it is! Excuse: *"I'm afraid"* . . . Response: Excuse: *"What will happen if I do it?"* . . . Response: Excuse: *"People won't understand"* . . . Response: Excuse: *"It isn't worth it."* . . . Response: Excuse: *"I haven't the time"* . . . Response: Other Excuses: Responses: **The Voice Speaks—Tap No. 1**

5. Do you believe that faith is something you can cultivate through perseverance and intention? Please explain.

6. Envy is a natural human feeling. It can be our guide and teacher. Write a list of those whom you envy in your life.

7. Then write what it is that you envy about each of them.

8. Why do you believe you envy them? Do you believe that you are incapable of achieving what they have? Please explain.

9. With each of the individuals that you envy, look at the traits or achievements they each have that you envy.

See yourself manifesting those same traits and experiences easily and effortlessly in your own life. Remember to experience them in the here and now, as if they are already manifest.

10. For each of the traits and achievements you experienced in the previous question, express joy and gratitude to the person you envied, and to the universe for taking you one step closer to manifesting your desires. Then continue to trust in yourself and the magic of your beliefs.

11. Mahatma Gandhi arrived in England stating, *"I'm doing this because a voice within me speaks."* Take a couple of minutes to meditate. Then ask the voice of your higher self to share its wisdom with you. Ask it *"What message(s) do you have for me. What do I need to hear?"* Write down the responses you receive. If you don't initially receive anything, be patient and trust that you will receive wise guidance.

12. Write a list of the "divine messages" that you have received in your life, and then fill your heart with gratitude for those messages you have received, and for those that you are eventually going to receive.

Reaffirmation and Repetition—
The Science of Suggestion

13. Reaffirmation and repetition are the additional ingredients that makes suggestion that more powerful. They are used in advertising and many other forms of influential messaging. Do you believe you have been repeating positive messages to yourself as much as you have the negative ones?

14. Track the messages that your mind sends you for a day. On a piece of paper, create two columns—one for positive messages and the other for negative. Then each time you note messages that are going on in your head, put a mark in the column that corresponds to the tone of the message. At the end of the day, count how many posi-

tive messages you noted and how many negative. Wh— messages did you most feed yourself?

15. The first thing you need to do is to build your spirit of determination. This may be obtained by constantly repeating to yourself, *"I will, I will, I will . . ."* and BELIEVE it. For the next 30 days, focus on one thing that you want to manifest in your life. Believe in it with all of your passion and will. Constantly repeat to yourself, *"I will . . . I will . . ."* Journal about your experiences and findings as you focus on this exercise.

16. The second thing you need is desire. According to the writer, if you have a strong desire, the foundation is laid. Are there any childhood desires that you remember having and have since given up hope and repressed? Meditate on this and list them. Could you resurrect these desires back into your life? If you can, do so. If you don't believe you can, why not? Please explain.

17. For your desires to be manifest, the requirements are that: 1) the object of desire is morally right, 2 & 3) the picture is definite and positive. Reflect on your deepest desires. Are they all morally right? Is the picture you have of them definite and positive?

18. The Chinese mystic, Lao Tsu stated, *"He who knows how to plant, shall not have his plant uprooted; He who knows how to hold a thing, shall not have it taken away."* Do you believe you are grounded and that your desires are firmly planted? Do you believe that you also have a strong hold on that which you desire?

Adopt This Tap System—Use Small Cards
19. To feed your subconscious and your conscious mind, you should *"keep the picture or pictures before you constantly . . . write a word picture of them on several small cards (Business card size is convenient.)"* Do not wait. Complete this exercise right now.

. It is suggested that you place a card above your bathroom mirror. Allow the details you place on the card to increase as you further develop the mental picture of what you want to manifest. If you haven't already done so, place a card on your bathroom mirror. Be sure to update it as needed.

21. Place another card in the kitchen, and view it while you eat your meals. Have a card ready to view when you wake up in the morning and when you go to bed. Perhaps you should also place a card in your car, your wallet or any other areas in which you often frequent.

22. It is suggested that you keep writing every detail on your card until it is permanently photographed in your thoughts and eventually becomes your reality. Review your cards to ensure that what you have written is detailed so that the vision of your success is firmly planted in your mind. Write about how you felt after creating and placing your cards.

23. You are encouraged to read and re-read the following segment of the Foreword: "*the same thought, the picture of the thing you want kept constant, always attracts it object, just as a magnet attracts. The larger and more powerful the magnet, the greater its drawing force and so it is with sustained thought—the more powerful it becomes the more it attracts. Just as a huge magnifying glass drawing the sun's rays and kept focused on a certain spot will burn a hole so will powerful sustained thought (the vivid mental picture) directed to or on its object correlate. However, you must mentally see the picture of your object or ideal as a reality—see every detail of the picture as being in existence just as you want the object or ideal to actually be—then as if by magic the chain will link itself together. Now go back and reread this again until it is permanently impressed upon you.*" Read this segment again at least three times, and then re-write what you read in your own words.

Powerful Thoughts Attract—Use Your Mirror

24. You are also encouraged to frequently gaze at yourself in the mirror: *"Search deeply into your eyes until you can see the fire of enthusiasm mount and cold, steely determination take the place of doubt and indecision. Get to know yourself thoroughly and keep telling yourself where you are going and what you want. Sooner or later you will see, mentally, at least, the reflection of your innermost desires in the mirror and your daydreams will begin to take shape."* Practice this at least three times a day for at least a month or more. Write about how this exercise affected you.

25. Eventually you will form the pictures without the need of the mirror or cards. You will find yourself tapping the subconscious mind automatically. Then follow with action. The author writes, *"Action . . . is nothing more than energized thought."* When you hear this definition of action, what thoughts enter your head? Write them down.

26. The author likens these practices to prayer, for he states, *"What is prayer but the expression of a heartfelt, earnest, sincere want or desire."* Do you pray? If so, perhaps each time you take the outlined steps, offer your commitment as a prayer to your divine. Don't forget to show gratitude for your prayers being answered, and see them as if they are.

27. *"The Great Master said: 'What things soever ye desire, when ye pray BELIEVE that ye receive them, and ye shall have them'"* Do you believe that Christ was referencing the power of your mind? Please explain.

28. The author asserts, *"Nature provides ways and means for all things to grow rightly."* If you consider this statement, when a seed is planted, no matter what the obstacles may be, it finds its way out of the earth and into the sunlight. Can you imagine and trust that the seeds you plant are naturally meant to bloom; that they will do the same? Write about your thoughts and feelings on this subject.

29. According to the author, *"results will follow a most astounding manner."* Often our desires are manifested in ways that we do not anticipate. Write about things that have manifested in your life in ways that you did not anticipate. Also, as the desires you are currently focusing on are manifest, keep a journal of the magical and magnificent way in which they did so.

Tell No One

30. Because you are *"setting up powerful vibrations among the unseen forces"* you are discouraged from sharing your desires with others as they could set up countervibrations. Have you shared your desires with others? Write a list of those with whom you have shared them. Then state an intention of protection. See your desires safe and unaffected. Then make a point of keeping them to yourself from hereon in.

31. You are encouraged not to get discouraged if some things take longer to manifest than others. Remember that nothing can stop you but you, yourself. Reviewing what you have learned, what action steps can you take so that you are continuously faithful?

32. The author makes a powerful and thought-provoking point when he states, *"To my way of thinking if a man can earn one dollar he can as easily earn ten. If he has two suits of clothes—he can have ten. The only difference is the amount of energy he is willing to expend and this goes for acquiring $100 to $1000 and from then on it is a matter of only adding ciphers. There is no limit as to what a person may do or secure provided he makes up his mind and steadfastly and determinedly moves towards his goal."* Write about the thoughts and feelings that arise as you ponder this statement.

Use It Only For Good

33. This power can *"act as a boomerang and destroy you and everything you hold dear if you use it for evil."* Be sure to

only use it for the highest good. In fact, when you set your intention, you can state, *"This or more, for the highest good of all."* Practice using this phrase. How does doing so make you feel?

34. The author asserts, *"Do not talk or boast about what you may have done for others or of your good deeds.' They will speak for themselves. Just continue to give thanks for the fact that you are on your way—that's enough."* Do you find yourself boasting at times? Often when we do this, deep down inside we question our worthiness. Why do you believe you boast, if you do?

35. On selling yourself or your ideas, the writer states, *"I have found that trying to put over an idea, firstly I have had to believe in the idea—dream it, eat with it, sleep with it—I had to have it with me every minute of the day until it became part of me—the old idea of repetition again—and I know it works in selling commodities. You have got to know what you are talking about and only hard, personal, persistent, intelligent study will enable you to do this."* Have you ever had to sell anything? If so, did you practice this technique? Were you effective in sales? Could you be? Why or why not?

36. You are also encouraged to keep informed about what is going on in the world around you. Thoroughly read the newspapers and current periodicals. You do not have to read the details of negative media; in fact, you are discouraged from doing so. Are you informed of the world's events? If not, why not?

37. There are two perspectives on keeping up with current news. There is so much negative news and fear-mongering; many wise teachers suggest that you stay away from it. This is contrary to what you are instructed in this book. Meditate and go within. What does your wisest self believe is best for you? Follow that wisdom and trust in it.

38. *"He who knows others is clever, but he who knows himself is enlightened."* Do you believe you are clever, enlightened or neither? Why?

Tap No. 3

39. Sitting down and talking to yourself about what you want will not work. According to the author *"you have to have wishbone backed up with a backbone and that isn't all— the wishbone and the backbone must be coordinated and synchronized to a point where they are running in perfect harmony, and when they are in tune, you will find personality developing."* You will grow more magnetic as your desires grow to fruition. On a scale from one to ten (one being "very little" and ten being "a great deal"), rate how much magnetism or charisma you believe you currently have:

1——2——3——4——5——6——7——8——9——10

40. The author encourages you to first measure yourself and then study those with whom you associate. He asserts that every physical movement tells a story. Do you have a strong, self-assured posture? On a scale from one to ten (one being "very weak" and ten being "extremely strong"), rate how much self-assured your posture is:

1——2——3——4——5——6——7——8——9——10

41. Study yourself in the mirror. Look deeply into your eyes. What kind of impression do you believe you make on others? Write about it.

42. What kind of impression do you want to make on others? How far are you from making that impression?

The Eyes Have "It"

43. Write a list of the successful men and women that you most admire. Now take some time to look at photographs of them. Note their expression, especially their eyes. Do

they have intensity in their eyes? Is there fire lit within them? Write a list of what you see as you observe each of their photos.

44. Go through the list of traits that you just created. Do you possess each of them yourself?

45. The author states, *"It's poor business to let yourself be put on the defensive as that is a negative sign."* Study your life. Write a list of when and with whom you feel on the defensive. Is there a way you can turn your defensiveness around? If you find you are never on the defensive, then what does that say about you?

46. It is important that you remain in good health. Dr. Emil Coue told people that they could cure themselves by saying to themselves, *"Every day, in every way, I am getting better and better."* Try frequently repeating this phrase to yourself. How does it make you feel? Do you believe you can remain healthy by believing you are healthy? Write down your beliefs about your health.

47. You are discouraged from talking about your worries, aches and pains. Write a list of the negative things that you talk about. Then make a commitment to no longer give voice to them. Finally, burn the list, and make a commitment to no longer focus on them.

48. It is stated in Philosophy of the Ages, *"If thou art pained by any external thing, it is not this thing which disturbs thee, but thy own judgment about it. And it is in thy power to wipe out this judgment now. But if anything in thy own disposition gives thee pain, who hinders thee from correcting thy opinion?"* Thus you are most upset by your own critical mind. Do you believe this to be true? Why or why not?

Every Day—in Every Way

49. Similar to the previous exercise, write a list of all your fears. Be sure to include everything that you fear could

happen in your life. Then burn the list, making a commitment to put them behind you, and focus on the future.

50. The author states, *"When you look after your thoughts, then your thoughts will look after you."* He encourages you to *"close the door of yesterday."* Take a few minutes and visualize that door closing. See yourself saying goodbye to the past and moving confidently and passionately forward. Then write about what you felt as you did this exercise.

51. *"Fear thoughts are terrifically contagious and spread like wildfire. Conversely as you direct your thoughts (visualizing) towards increasing your business, your sales, your profits, etc. have no misgivings of your own (keeping your mind closed to the downward tapping thoughts of others) and put enthusiasm, energy, and action into your program your business, your sales automatically will increase."* How do you plan on responding to the fear-based thoughts of those around you? Is there a way you can protect yourself from their thoughts and feelings? Explain.

Thought Moves the World

52. *"When the world's leaders change their way of thinking— toss out FEAR and move forward instead of backwards, then the thoughts of millions change for the better and as they think constructively business improves. Stop and meditate over this for a few moments. You will realize that "thought" operating in reverse was the great underlying factor which brought on the so-called economic depression."* Do you believe this statement to be true? Why or why not?

53. What is the current political climate in the world? Do you believe it reflects the innermost thoughts and convictions of the world's political leaders? How? Give examples.

54. The author states, *"As a man thinketh in his heart—so he is. As members of a community thinketh—so they are; as*

a city thinketh so it is, and as a nation thinketh—so it is." What is the current climate of your community? Your city? Your nation? How do you contribute to this climate?

55. In England's Great Man of Letters, H.G. Well wrote, *"We spoil a lot for ourselves and each other by fear, follies, hate, bickering, suspicion and anger."* Do an honest inner inventory of yourself. Then write a list of the ways in which you perpetuate fear, follies, hate, bickering suspicion and anger in your life. Then contemplate each of the ways you listed, and commit to perpetuating the behavior any longer. Finally, imagine yourself behaving the way you wish to behave, seeing the situation energetically shifting to a more positive one.

Change Gears Now—Believe in Your Goods

56. According to the author, knowing your article and selling yourself is 99% of the success of selling. Do you have 100% faith in yourself and what you are manifesting? What can you do to strengthen your faith to sell yourself?

57. The best way to close a sale is to make the prospect think the way that you think. According to the author *"the subconscious mind will be giving you ideas, hunches, inspirations, a perfect flood of them, which will guide you correctly . . . they will point the way."* As you think about making prospects think the way that you do in relation to your success, what ideas, hunches or inspirations come to mind? Write them down, and then be sure to follow through on them.

58. You are encouraged not to belittle your prospect and to meet him on common ground. You are encouraged to make him like you, and for you to like him. Relating this to manifesting your desire, how would you do so?

59. Teamwork is also key to success. How can you instill strong team commitment among those with whom you spend your time, whether work or recreation?

60. *"When Fear rules the will, nothing can be done, but when a man casts Fear out of his mind the world becomes his oyster. To lose a bit of money is nothing, but to lose hope—to lose nerve and ambition—that is what makes men cripples."* Herbert N. Casson. Have you ever lost money? Were you devastated? What were your feelings at the time? Did your feelings eventually shift? If so, how?

61. *"The ability to accomplish anything in a convincing fashion depends entirely upon the degree of expert knowledge which you possess coupled with that intensity of purpose."* Do you believe you have all of the necessary expertise about the area(s) in which you wish to manifest your desires? Is there additional knowledge that you can build? If so, be sure to do so.

62. The author emphasizes that *"the conscious mind must be placed in a receptive condition to get the ideas from the subjective or subconscious."* You must, therefore, act upon your hunches. In order to hear them, however, you must relax. On a scale from one to ten (one being "very little" and ten being "a great deal"), rate how relaxed and receptive you believe yourself to be:

1——2——3——4——5——6——7——8——9——10

63. Write a list of three things you can incorporate into your day that will assist you in further relaxing (meditating, taking an afternoon stroll or nap, listening to music that you love, spending time in nature, etc.). Integrate at least one of them into your daily routine and note how it has shifted your life. Eventually add the other two and note any changes.

64. Do the exercise that the author outlined. Lie down and focus on each part of your body. As you do, allow it to go limp. Then concentrate on what you want, allowing any hunches to arise. Write them down and be sure to execute them immediately.

Open the Door, Relax and Tap

65. Meditation silences the mind and allows the insights and wisdom of your subconscious to arise. There are many benefits that you can achieve through the daily practice of meditation. If you do not already do so, try meditating each day. You may only have the patience for one minute each day. If so, that is fine. Commit to one minute each day for a week. Then next week, commit to two minutes. After each meditation, ask your subconscious mind for any messages about manifesting your desires. Continue growing your commitment and concentration and note your progress.

66. According to the author, when you meditate, *the road ahead will become illuminated and your burdens will fall away one by one."* Imagine yourself living a life that is burden-free. Take some time to feel all of your burdens lifting. Stay with that feeling for a while and once you have, write about how you felt, and what you saw in your mind's eye. Go to that good feeling place often. It is a powerful place to be!

67. *"The late Thomas A. Edison explaining his success of inventing said: "I begin by using my accumulated knowledge but most of my inventions are completed with Ideas which flash into my mind out of thin air."* Be open to receiving even more creative ideas, and insights from your subconscious. If you haven't already done so, be sure to purchase a notepad and always keep it nearby to record those "flashes" when they arise. Then don't hesitate to follow through on them.

68. The author encourages, *"If your own little inner voice suggests that you ask for something, do not be backward about asking. You have nothing to fear. The other person will never help unless he knows your wishes, so you must ask."* Do you have difficulty asking others for help? On a scale from one to ten (one being "very little" and ten being "a great deal"), rate how much you ask others for help when you are in need:

1——2——3——4——5——6——7——8——9——10

69. Some of us feel that we are burdening others when we ask for help. If you feel this at times, why do you believe this? Where did this feeling of being a "burden" come from?

70. Do you complain that others are a burden when they ask for help? If so, could you shift your perception and welcome helping others? Do you believe that your feelings of being a burden can shift if you shift your beliefs that others are a burden to you?

71. Have you ever considered that perhaps when you don't ask for help, you are preventing others from their opportunity to do a good deed? Does seeing "asking for help" in this light, shift your perception in any way? If so, how?

72. What additional steps can you take to get over those feelings of being burdensome or intrusive? List them and then take action on them.

73. The author asserts that when you follow these guidelines *"the voice will speak just like it did for Edison, Otto Dally and thousands of others, and you will get results—all will be yours."* How does knowing that you have access to that same voice that the famous geniuses in history accessed, make you feel?

The Mysterious Nothingness

74. William Shakespeare wrote in Julius Caesar, *"The fault, dear Brutus, is not in our stars, But in ourselves that we are underlings."* What do you think he meant by that? Please explain.

75. Be truly honest with yourself, and write a list of those you have blamed for the shortcomings you have had in your life (your parents, siblings, friends, co-workers, politicians, banks, etc.).

76. Write a declaration and say it aloud to each of those you blamed. If you feel you have to forgive them, state some-

thing to the effect of, "_____, I forgive you." You may want to add, "I am fully responsible for the choices that I make in my life. I hold no one to blame. I release all whom I have blamed in the past, and move forward enthusiastic, passionate and committed to living, breathing and experiencing my highest good . . . and so it is." After completing this exercise with everyone you have listed, meditate for a few minutes and note your feelings. Then write about your new found freedom from past grudges, and how this exercise made you feel.

77. The author warns that some people, who don't understand, may say that you are self-centered, conceited or selfish. He encourages you not to care about what they say. This can be difficult to do. One of the things you can do is to keep positive, affirming and supportive statements that others have made to you nearby, so that you can read them when you need a boost. What other steps can you take towards shifting away from caring what they say?

78. Like you have done with other successful individuals, as you become successful, intelligent people will study you and how you have achieved your goals. Take some time to envision yourself achieving your goals. Seeing others noting the fire in your eyes. See them reading your biography of success. Imagine them trying to contact you so that you can mentor them. See this transpiring in the here and now, and in full color. Enjoy this vision. When you are through, write about what you experienced.

79. The author references one of America's foremost critics, George Jean Nathan when he states that he has never known a man who succeeded in life in a material way who did not think of himself first, last and all the time. Perhaps humankind is selfish by nature. Do you believe you are selfish? If so, do you judge your selfishness?

80. Reframe the term, "I am selfish" to "I am self-full." Be comfortable with the fact that you are fulfilling your life and that doing so raises the vibratory frequency of the world. Your success encourages others and breeds further success in the world. This is true, is it not? Write about your thoughts and feelings as you re-frame yourself as being "self-full."

81. Do you believe that as you amass success, you will look forward to mentoring others to do the same?

82. Do you believe that as you gain financial abundance, you will want to share it with others, providing workers with wonderful salaries, donating to charities that you believe in? Explain how you feel and what your "giving" plans are as your desires come to fruition.

83. According to the author, the law of cause and effect asserts that as you perform a service you will reap great dividends. Do you believe this to be true? How have you experienced it in the past? How do you plan on experiencing it in the future?

84. You are encouraged to read and re-read *The Magic of Believing* until every word is thoroughly understood. Then you must apply the principles with your whole heart and soul, making them a part of your everyday life. He states *"if you are in deadly earnest with yourself, you will find the whole scheme very simple."* You have to have the courage to be totally honest with yourself. Take a final inner inventory of yourself. Where are you not in integrity in your life? Where are you hard on yourself and others? When and where have you been dishonest or manipulative? Write down a list, then forgive yourself, put these actions behind you and look forward to moving ahead toward manifesting the life of your dreams!

Read This Digest Comment
of Thousands

———

"Your series of T.N.T. broadcasts are still coming back to this station. While you were on the air, I, personally, received calls every day from house wives and business men. Their general comment hinged on the fact that you had hit an optimistic note which could be practically applied. I write this letter because it takes more than the old sunshine in your voice to convince a hardboiled listening public that you know what you are talking about."

The Oregonian—K.G.W. by Cliff R. Engle

"The more you spread your message the greater will become the service you are rendering to your fellow men."

Paul R. Kelty, Editor, The Oregonian, Portland, Oregon.

Many others believing that great good must follow, urged me to get my message circulated and this little book is the result. The whole theme came to be when I "thought" I was licked and knew not which way to turn. However, I was seeking and when "ye seek, ye shall find."

This book is published with the sincere desire that it will help everyone. Already it has helped thousands and it will help you. When you catch the "secret" of the book, tell others about it, for then you, too, will be rendering a service to your fellow men and it will pay you dividends. You, perhaps, have friends and acquaintances who are depressed; are in ill health; are worried over financial affairs; whose worlds are topsy-turvy; dissatisfied with their lot in life— lost in the wilderness. You may have a son or a daughter, a relative or know a boy or girl whom you would like to see make a place in the world. Place copies of this book into the hands of those you wish to help and admonish them to study it—rereading it as frequently as possible. Should you be unable to get copies from your local book dealer or the distributor from whom this copy came, write direct to the publishers.

    — C.M.B.

ALL WHO USE IT—PROFIT ! !

Excerpts from a few of the letters from firms where executives and employees have copies:

OLDS, WORTMAN & KING (One of the oldest department stores on the Pacific Coast) bought 400 copies. D. D. JOHNSON, General Superintendent, wrote: "Inasmuch as our executives, buyers and department heads are enthused over results from usage of '*T.N.T.: It Rocks the Earth*', we are purchasing 400 more copies for distribution among our employees. Positive the book will do as claimed. If adopted generally there will be an immediate improvement in all lines of business."

INDEPENDENCE FUND OF NORTH AMERICA, INC., One Cedar Street, New York City, purchased 100 copies for salesmen. DOUGLAS LAIRD, vice-president, wrote: "Ship us immediately 100 copies. It will have a great effect on anyone who reads it carefully and keeps following the thoughts contained in it."

SAM'L G. SUPPLEE & CO., 17-19 Union Square, New York City, bought 12 copies. MR. SUPPLEE wrote: "It is a pleasure to review the book from time to time and I expect to make good use of it through our executive force."

ARTHUR L. FIELDS, Chairman of the Board of Directors, PORTLAND CHAMBER OF COMMERCE, 1933 and head of FIELDS MOTOR CAR CO., bought 11 copies. He says: "I purchased 10 additional copies the first week in March and our business has shown a marked upturn since. March, April and May of this year will show a favorable profit instead of a decided loss for the same period last year."

MATTHEW LAHTI of MATTHEW LAHTI & CO., Boston, Mass., bought 5 copies and followed it with an order for 7 more, writing: "Very interesting. It is the connecting link between the intangible and the tangible."

FRANK L. HAMON, Division Cable Manager, POSTAL TELEGRAPHCABLE CO., wrote: "Bought 20 copies for employes of the Portland office. Our business has increased a large percentage since the theme was introduced. Will make any firm or set of individuals more successful."

D. KORK, Portland Manager LYBRAND, ROSS BROTHERS & MONTGOMERY, bought 50 copies.

He said: "The fact that I bought 50 copies for distribution in our organization indicates what I think of '*T.N.T.: It Rocks the Earth*.' It will get results wherever used."

THE WASHINGTON STATE FARM BUREAU of the STATE FARM INSURANCE COMPANIES of Bloomington, Ill., bought 30 copies saying: "You have our permission to state the number of books purchased by our organization. Your good title book is still being used by members of this organization to the mutual benefit of all concerned."

FRED. E. GULICK, D.M.D., President of the ITECO LABORATORIES, Portland, Ore., with a world wide sales organization, bought 45 copies. He wrote: "I want 20 more copies. Words will not express the good the books already placed in my organization have done for my people and my business. Sales have increased steadily since we found the 'Secret' in 'T.N.T.' Every sales organization, every business concern, in fact all firms should have copies for their executives and employees and when they understand what is in the book and use it, they will give you their everlasting thanks just as you have mine."

A. GREEN, President of the DOERNBECHER MANUFACTURING CO., the largest furniture factory under one roof in the world, said: "A wonderful piece of work. It is making the rounds of our entire organization."

MEIER & FRANK CO. (largest department store in the West) requested its employees to read the book. VIVIAN P. COOLEY, Manager, book department, wrote: "Consis-

tently continues to be one of our best sellers. We continu
to get orders from all parts of the country. You know, o₁
course, that our many employees were asked to read the
book and I believe those who have applied the principles
have been helped tremendously."

THE FIRST NATIONAL BANK, Portland, Ore.,
bought 10 copies for its branch managers. C. C. COLT,
senior vice-president wrote: "After I read it several times
I was impressed with the thought that it was a splendid
thing for anyone to use. As a starter I have purchased 10
copies for managers of our various branches." FRANKLIN
T. GRIFFITH, President of THE PORTLAND ELEC-
TRIC POWER CO., THE PORTLAND GENERAL
ELECTRIC CO., wrote: "I'm going to use 10 copies as
trial seed. You have set forth the vital principles of success . . . Faith In Oneself."

THOMAS (TOMMY) LUKE, formerly President FLO-
RISTS' TELEGRAPH DELIVERY ASSOCIATION:
"I have had my employees read every edition a number of
times. It is just what the name implies. It is exactly "THAT
SOMETHING" you and I need most in our problems of
today and tomorrow."

RICHARD G. MONTGOMERY, Assistant Manager,
THE J. GILL CO., (largest book dealers on the Pacific
Coast) said: "Just to let you know your book is still eagerly
sought after. I do not know how many times we have repeated our orders for additional copies but I do know your
book has headed the list of our best sellers since it was first
published. Literally, it sells itself." ZELL BROS., well

nown northwest Jewelers, bought copies for all major employees. J. S. ZELL wrote: "Can't say too much for it. Biggest, little volume I've ever read. I have procured copies for all my major employees."

The late CHARLES F. BERG, after 20 copies were put to use in his organization, CHARLES F. BERG, INC., wrote: "Wish everybody could have a copy. I especially recommend it to heads of firms where employees come in contact with the public."

What Others Say
WALTER P. CHRYSLER, Chairman of Board and President of CHRYSLER CORP.—"It is a very stimulating document and one that would be decidedly helpful to anyone who is interested in making his own place in the world."

MARIE DRESSLER, Famous Screen and Stage Actress—"What a book if used rightly!!" (She purchased 20 copies for friends).

GENE TUNNEY, 230 Park Avenue, New York City: "It is a fine story, as old as man himself, told in a new way at a most opportune time. May I congratulate you."

ALFRED E. SMITH, former Governor of the State of New York—"Most interesting."

FRANK KNOX, Publisher of CHICAGO DAILY NEWS: "Your booklet 'T.N.T.' makes interesting reading, contains many inspirational messages and should be most helpful."

THEODORE ROOSEVELT, formerly Governor-General, PHILIPPINE ISLANDS: "I read '*T.N.T.*' with interest and liked it. It is full of good sound philosophy."

LEWIS E. LAWES, Warden, SING SING PRISON, author "20,000 Years in Sing Sing," wrote: "It is of practical value to anyone who will follow its suggestions."

REV. S. PARKES CADMAN, D.D., Pastor, CENTRAL CONGREGATIONAL CHURCH, Brooklyn: "I have read your booklet with keen interest . . . I am glad that you are devoting your splendid energies in an effort to elucidate the problems which have hitherto challenged the best efforts of our finest thinkers."

JOHN E. EDGERTON, Chairman of the Board, 1933, NATIONAL ASSOCIATION OF MANUFACTURERS of the UNITED STATES of AMERICA,—"The most fundamental truths of life . . . Possesses peculiar value. I both congratulate and commend you upon the excellent contribution which you have thus made to the Most Essential Processes of Recovery . . . Almost envy you . . . the great good which your work is accomplishing for others."

ROGER W. BABSON, Economist and Statistician—"I think it is fine. Keep up the good work."

EDWARD G. SEUBERT, President, STANDARD OIL CO., of Indiana: "It is a dynamic presentation of the merits of a positive and confident approach to the problems of life."

COL. FREDERICK PALMER, Noted War Correspondent—"Have read your booklet, which was so dynamic that it emitted electric sparks as I turned the pages. It's a knockout."

RALPH BUDD, President, BURLINGTON LINES: "I congratulate you on this work, and I believe the suggestions contained therein are very useful and helpful."

PENNEY, Chairman of Board, J. C. PENNEY COMPANY, INC.: "I read it thoroughly and enjoyed it. I consider its philosophy so good that I am passing it around among my friends."

AMOS PARRISH, of AMOS PARRISH AND COMPANY, New York City: "You are to be congratulated on a fine piece of work. We found it most interesting."

GEN. W. W. ATTERBURY, President, PENNSYLVANIA RAILROAD COMPANY: "Most interesting and worth while." JOHN B. KENNEDY, Associate Editor, COLLIER'S: "I enjoyed reading the booklet, and believe it should have a great effect on the public."

WALTER A. STAUB, Partner, LYBRAND, ROSS BROS. & MONTGOMERY, New York City: "I have read it with interest and am particularly impressed with its timeliness. If we could set off enough charges of your T.N.T. of faith, courage and determined 'tap, tap, tap,' it would break up the present jam of fear, pessimism and feeling of impotence. We certainly need it."

BAKER, of COLLEGE OF NEW YORK; Secretary of DIVISION OF CHEMICAL EDUCATION of the AMERICAN CHEMICAL SOCIETY: "The point of view which you present in your booklet is a powerful one. I can readily see how it would enable many people to achieve an independence of thought and philosophy which would enable them to rise above their immediate difficulties."

CHARLES T. SIDLO, of SIDLO, SIMONS, DAY & CO., Denver, Colorado;—"Have read it through several times and am very much impressed with the message which it contains."

ALFRED J. DIESCHER, Consulting Engineer, Winfield, Kansas: "Can aid anyone who reads it thoughtfully and observes its tenets faithfully."

E. TRAYLOR, President, AMERICAN TRUSTEE SHARE CORP., New York: "I think you have a very interesting way of presenting a number of truths that cannot be brought to our attention too often. I am sure your book will be helpful to anyone who reads it in a receptive frame of mind."

REV. DANIEL A. POLING, President, CHRISTIAN HERALD ASSOCIATION, New York City: "I like it immensely."

A. GLADDING, Vice-President, E. C. ATKINS & COMPANY, INC., Indianapolis, Ind.: "Makes it a mighty valuable companion for one to carry around in his portfolio for frequent reference."

HENRY L. STEVENS, JR., formerly National Commander, AMERICAN LEGION: "Am convinced of its worth-whileness and shall get out of it all there is in it for me."

EARL D. WISE, Vice-President and General Manager, THE PACIFIC TELEPHONE & TELEGRAPH COMPANY: "*'T.N.T.: It Rocks the Earth'* beats out all of its competitors for attention, I read it immediately and think it excellent. It pulls one along so irresistibly that there is no stopping in its reading. It registers from first paragraph to last."

CARL S. KELTY, LOS ANGELES EVENING HERALD-EXPRESS, Los Angeles, Cal.: "You have caught from the ether something that has a mystical quality—a something that explains the magic of coincidence, the mystery of what makes some men 'lucky'."

MERLE THORPE, Editor, NATION'S BUSINESS: "I agree with you that what we need today is to regain that elusive thing called confidence. Whatever can be done to bring this about is a public service at this time."

ORRA E. MONNETTE, Vice-Chairman of Board, BANK OF AMERICA, NATIONAL TRUST & SAVINGS ASSN., Los Angeles, Cal.: "Should be helpful to individuals and organizations."

JOHN D. CURTIS, CURTIS, STEPHENSON & CO., Boston, Mass.—"Every one of normal intelligence has the desire to accomplish great things but does not force the stored ability locked up within himself to assert its f[...] power. Your booklet surely is a master key to the lock an[...] should inspire its readers to a realization of such desires."

PAUL R. KELTY, Editor, THE OREGONIAN, Portland, Ore.: "Could the basic truth of your booklet but be fully apprehended and understood and held by all of us, life's problems would vanish into nothingness. Your presentation is very compelling. The more you spread it the greater will become the service you are rendering to your fellow men."

F. IRVINE, Editor, THE JOURNAL, Portland, Ore.: "'*T.N.T.: It Rocks the Earth*' carries a theme which will help all who will accept it. Mr. Bristol has a grip on 'THAT SOMETHING' which many seek but few find. I, too, know it, believe it and it's so."

P. GUILD, Business Manager, LOS ANGELES EXAMINER, Los Angeles, Cal.: "Well worth while. You have put it over with a big punch. I defy anyone to read it without getting a real message. It is the truth and can be made to work out successfully in every day life."

C. SAMMONS, Vice-President, IRON FIREMAN MANUFACTURING COMPANY: "It's a knockout. Your message is so forceful I am sure it will receive a great welcome everywhere."

TOM BURNS of Burnside, Independent Thinker and Philosopher, Portland, Ore.: "'T.N.T.' Touches the Spot because that reflex action of the nervous system called the and can be pepped up by injections of the self confidence which is the essence of T.N.T. Besides sales people of the collapsed tissue type (and they are about nine out of ten) can be 'Born Again' through the injections of T.N.T. which, when digested, is the Ne Plus Ultra of Self-confidence."

George Olsen, of George Olsen and His Music, nationally known orchestra leader and well known to radio listeners, said: "Your book has become an invaluable stimulant to me. I keep it right near my bed and open it at random and read a paragraph or two at least once a day, and I know you will be happy to know that it has revived in me a lot of dormant energy and a desire to keep forging ahead."

— Tap — Tap — Tap —

Do not loan or give this book away but keep it to read a paragraph or two a day. It is the tap, tap, tap which gets results and which will give you everything you want.

Tell others about this book that they likewise may get copies and be helped.

IF YOU BELIEVE IT >>

It is so!

About the Author

A native of Portland, Oregon, Claude M. Bristol (1891-1951) worked for nearly forty years as a newspaper reporter and editor, during which time he also studied law, became an investment banker, and travelled extensively. After serving in World War One, Bristol became an advocate for the rights of veterans, whom he believed could attain success in civilian life by harnessing the powers of the mind. Bristol spent most of his adult life researching and tracking discoveries in psychical abilities and ESP, which he believed held the key to greater human potential, a theme explored in his two classic guides, *The Magic of Believing* (1948) and *T.N.T.* (1932), both collected in this volume.

Printed in the USA
CPSIA information can be obtained
at www.ICGtesting.com
JSHW012018140824
68134JS00033B/2757